DELETED

Praise for *No Country for Jewish Liberals*

"An insightful, eloquent, intimate book about the liberal Jewish dilemma: How to love a country whose policies you hate."

—Peter Beinart
author, *The Crisis of Zionism*

"*No Country for Jewish Liberals* is a masterful personal analysis of the deterioration of Israel's relations with its Palestinian neighbors and its deleterious impact on the country's democratic ethos. Larry Derfner's political awakening is a bittersweet story of love of Israel and disillusion with its trajectory, of alienation from its policies and complete involvement with its people and their future. Any liberal will recognize the evolution of feelings and insights that he conveys so skillfully in this accessible and poignant political memoir. This is truly a must read for those who care deeply about Israel and worry about where it's going."

—Naomi Chazan
former Deputy Speaker of the Knesset,
Professor (emerita) of political science at the
Hebrew University of Jerusalem

"I've read Larry Derfner's impassioned but also factual columns with considerable interest over the years. He's insightful, clever and even manages to be funny. The publication of this book is a welcome capstone to his career."

—Norman G. Finkelstein
writer and lecturer

"Larry Derfner has written a street-talking, brash, incredibly readable and thoughtful memoir about his 30-plus years in Israel, and the battle between his ideals and his affection for the country. It's a useful antidote for the usual shouting points of debate about Israel. No matter what view of Israel you have when you begin reading, you'll have a more complicated and conflicted view when you finish."

—Gershom Gorenberg
author, *The Unmaking of Israel*

"Derfner—who does not cease to be a field reporter even after being fired for his non-kosher views—offers much more than a memoir. An insider and an outsider in his adopted country, his personal journey is a description of a society's contradictions, and his own contemplative zigzags—a tale about Israel's drift into an abyss."

—Amira Hass
Haaretz's correspondent for the Occupied Territories,
author, *Drinking the Sea at Gaza.*

"Larry Derfner has written a fascinating memoir of growing up in Los Angeles and moving to Israel and finding happiness in his everyday life there, but being beset by a growing realization that he is living in a morally failed state, and can do little to change it. It is a riveting account of Israel's history told through the lens of Derfner's life. I had trouble putting it down."

—John B. Judis
author, *Genesis: Truman, American Jews, and the Origins of the Arab/Israeli Conflict*

"This is a coming of age book—a very personal story by an Israeli journalist, not about learning the hard truths of the world that bring an end to adolescence, but about the intellectual, emotional, and political turmoil of trading feel-good enthusiasm for real empathy and clear-eyed application of liberal principles. It is a compellingly readable account of an immigrant who became an insider; and about his jagged journey from naiveté to carefully managed limits to knowledge, to a strained search for excuses, and, finally, to a searing acceptance of the near impossibility of a liberal democratic Israel.

"The book will teach most readers a great deal about what Israel is and how it differs from what they thought it was. Derfner declares that his hope is not lost. That he does so, even while admitting that he encourages his sons to emigrate, reflects a rare and unsettling combination of acute analysis and emotional honesty."

—Ian S. Lustick
Bess W. Heyman Professor in the
Political Science Dept., University of Pennsylvania

NO COUNTRY FOR JEWISH LIBERALS

Just World Books
Timely Books for Changing Times

Just World Books exists to expand the discourse in the United States and worldwide on issues of vital international concern. We are committed to building a more just, equitable, and peaceable world. We uphold the equality of all human persons. We aim for our books to contribute to increasing understanding across national, religious, ethnic, and racial lines; to share more broadly the reflections, analyses, and policy prescriptions of pathbreaking activists for peace; and to help to prevent war.

To learn about our existing and upcoming titles or to buy our books, visit our website:

www.JustWorldBooks.com

Also, follow us on Facebook and Twitter!

Our recent titles include:

- *Condition Critical: Life and Death in Israel/Palestine*, by Alice Rothchild
- *The Gaza Kitchen: A Palestinian Culinary Journey*, by Laila El-Haddad and Maggie Schmitt
- *Lens on Syria: A Photographic Tour of its Ancient and Modern Culture*, by Daniel Demeter
- *Never Can I Write of Damascus: When Syria Became Our Home*, by Theresa Kubasak and Gabe Huck
- *America's Continuing Misadventures in the Middle East*, by Chas W. Freeman, Jr.
- *Arabia Incognita: Dispatches from Yemen and the Gulf*, edited by Sheila Carapico
- *War Is a Lie*, by David Swanson
- *The People Make the Peace: Lessons from the Vietnam Antiwar Movement*, edited by Karín Aguilar-San Juan and Frank Joyce

NO COUNTRY FOR JEWISH LIBERALS

LARRY DERFNER

Just World Books
Charlottesville, Virginia

Just World Books is an imprint of Just World Publishing, LLC

Cover design by The Book Designers
Typesetting by PerfecType, Nashville, TN
Project management and proofreading by Marissa Wold Uhrina

Publisher's Cataloging-In-Publication Data
(Prepared by The Donohue Group, Inc.)

Names: Derfner, Larry.
Title: No country for Jewish liberals / Larry Derfner.
Description: Charlottesville, Virginia : Just World Books, an imprint of Just World Publishing, LLC, [2017] | Includes bibliographical references.
Identifiers: LCCN 2016954451 | ISBN 978-1-68257-064-7 | ISBN 978-1-68257-068-5 (ePub) | ISBN 978-1-68257-069-2 (mobi) | ISBN 978-1-68257-070-8 (PDF)
Subjects: LCSH: Derfner, Larry. | Jews, American--Israel. | Liberals--Israel. | Israel--Politics and government--20th century. | Israel--Politics and government--21st century. | Israel--Social conditions--20th century. | Israel--Social conditions--21st century. | Arab-Israeli conflict. | Values--Israel.
Classification: LCC DS113.8.A4 D47 2017 (print) | LCC DS113.8.A4 (ebook) | DDC 956.94004924073--dc23

This book is dedicated to my late parents, Emanuel and Sylvia Derfner, lifelong book-lovers, who gave me more than I can ever put into words;

To my wife Philippa, my *besheert,* who always told me that I could write this book but also that if it turned out I couldn't, she'd still believe in me;

And to my sons, Alon and Gilad, in the hope that they will be proud of me, because they make me so damn proud of them.

CONTENTS

CITY
OF THE
FUTURE

This is a political and personal story about Israel, about how over the years it went one way and I went the other. I'm going to start where I live, literally—in the city (actually the sprawling suburban bedroom community) of Modi'in, which is truly a showcase Israeli community. It's kind of embarrassing to remember the dreams I had for this place when my pregnant wife, Philippa, and I bought an apartment off the blueprints in 1995. And when I think of the dreams the Rabin government of the time had for it, I can hardly believe they, or the rest of us, were really living in Israel, seeing how this country has long since stopped dreaming.

I was writing for the *Jerusalem Post* and had done stories about the startup of Modi'in, and how the government, then in the midst of the Oslo peace process, saw it as the embodiment of its vision for the country: a cornerstone of the "New Middle East." They had a map showing Modi'in, which was still not much more than a mass of empty, rocky hills, as an Israeli stop on a future highway between Damascus to the north and Amman to the east. They were building this mammoth project right smack against Israel's pre-occupation border with the West Bank to make a political statement, to show that while the previous Likud government had put its energy into building West Bank settlements, the Rabin government would forget about settlements and build on the Israeli side of the old pre-1967 Six-Day War border. (The Rabin government might have forgotten about building settlements, but the settlers, their friends in the bureaucracy, and the real estate companies didn't.)

This was going to be a model city, unlike any place built in Israel before—with vast parks bounded by wide boulevards in the valleys and streets winding up and around the hills. Israel's great international architect, Moshe Safdie, designed the master plan, taking his inspiration from Byzantine Jerusalem—it would be a place swirling with movement where people naturally met up with one another. On the practical side, Modi'in was centrally located, midway between Jerusalem and Tel Aviv and commuter distance from both, and the apartments would be big by Israeli standards and relatively cheap, much cheaper than in metropolitan Tel Aviv, the better to lure the target population of young, middle-class families. The city, said its political patron, housing minister Binyamin Ben-Eliezer, would be a grand illustration of the new Israeli ethos, in which "the citizen no longer exists to serve the state, the state exists to serve the citizen." Its founders gave Modi'in the official motto "City of the Future."

Heady stuff. We bought our apartment mainly because it was big and affordable and because it was exciting to be moving into a promising new place—but for me, it was also all the New Middle East jazz, plus my now-embarrassing, nostalgic, socialist idea that Modi'in would be the modern-day Israeli version of my Aunt Rose's apartment complex in the Bronx that we used to visit in the '50s: a humble community where Jewish working people gather in the evenings on the benches on the big lawn to kibitz. A down-to-earth, decent, human place to live. The funny thing is that more than 20 years later, Modi'in (pop. 85,000) actually is a down-to-earth, decent, human place to live—like probably any non-rich, non-destitute place in this country. The "architecture" is sterile—block after block of nearly identical beige stucco apartment buildings, mercifully broken up by lots of greenery. Still, the social vibe is very warm. People really do sit on benches in the parks and talk while their kids are playing. It's hard to go shopping on a Friday and not run into someone you know. Our building has three other families besides us who've been here since it was built, and we go to each other's kids' bar mitzvahs and parents' shivas. (At times we also fight like neighbors; one of the veteran families chased one of our favorite neighbors out with a lawsuit over noise, and we fell out with them—but we made up at the shiva for the husband's mother.) My younger son, Gilad, is close friends with one boy from upstairs and another from downstairs. So in this way, Modi'in is a very homey place, like my Aunt Rose's old complex in the Bronx.

But otherwise, this is not the Bronx, Toto. The Jews who live here are nothing like my socialist, garment-worker aunt and her Yiddish neighbors. Modi'in is the gleaming city on the hill that looks down on the Palestinians living in the West Bank, on the other side of the pre-occupation border a few hundred yards away, past the army checkpoint on Route 443, the Modi'in-Jerusalem highway. This highway runs through the West Bank but is off-limits to Palestinians. It is often referred to, imprecisely but fairly enough, as one of our occupation's many "apartheid roads." When the Supreme Court decided in 2010 that it was unjust to keep Palestinian drivers off the 443—the travel ban had disrupted their lives and, after all, the highway had been built on private, Palestinian-owned land—Modi'in's mayor, Haim Bibas, fumed at the "judges in their ivory towers," and promised that "we're not going to take this lying down." Prime Minister Binyamin Netanyahu reportedly "reacted furiously" to the Supreme Court's decision. In the end, it was never implemented. When driving past the Arab villages on the West Bank hillsides overlooking the highway, you still don't see any green Palestinian license plates, only yellow Israeli ones.

Like my neighbors, and despite my political views, I drive the 443 whenever I go to Jerusalem. It's much quicker than taking Route 1, the "old road" that runs strictly within pre-occupation "Israel proper." On the 443 we travel along the separation wall that lines the highway and protects the all-Israeli cars from potential Palestinian stone-throwers, and that was actually painted in sections with blue skies and grass—an amazing illustration of Israeli denial but which you stop noticing after a few trips. To us in Modi'in, the West Bank and the Palestinians are invisible. They're only a few hundred yards away, but may as well be living in another hemisphere. Some of them come into the city early in the morning to work on the construction sites, where many of them sleep over, and sometimes the cops arrest the ones who don't have work permits. In the second intifada in the early 2000s, I used to see them, sometimes dozens of them, sitting quietly in the fenced yard of the police station on my morning walks. After a while, the police covered the fence with green fabric (but no painted trees and blue skies) so no one could see them anymore. Once, in those fretful years, I walked up to the Titora, the scenic hill in the center of town, and saw a young Palestinian shepherd minding his flock. We were the only people up there, out of earshot of anyone down below, and I got a little scared. When I got close enough to see his face, I saw that he was scared of me.

That was then. The second intifada, whose early days saw a few drive-by killings of Israelis on the 443, as well as a female suicide bomber blowing herself up at the army checkpoint on the highway just out-side town, is more than a decade past. With the exception of late 2015 through early 2016, when a wave of Palestinian knifings and car-rammings broke out, lethal terror is a rarity in Israel now; a few hundred yards from the West Bank, teenagers in Modi'in hang out in the parks until the middle of the night, with parental approval, and the only danger they may face is not from Palestinian infiltra-tors, but from packs of drunken Jewish kids looking for a fight.

Politically, the city is somewhat more liberal than Israel at large; over the years, local voters have given pluralities to centrist parties—Ariel Sharon and Ehud Olmert's Kadima, Yair Lapid's Yesh Atid, and Isaac Herzog's Zionist Union—ahead of Netanyahu's Likud. This is in line with the residents' high educational level and general middle-class prosperity as well as their secular bent. But liberal is a relative term; based on the parties and politicians they vote for and the news media they absorb, the people of Modi'in sit very comfortably within the Israeli "security hawk" consensus: unhappy with the "isolated, ideological" West Bank settlements, but untroubled by the expansion of the large "settlement blocs" closer to Israel proper, not to mention the Jewish neighborhoods in occupied East Jerusalem. The majority of Modi'in residents are theoretically in favor of the two-state solution, but suspicious, at best, of even the most moderate Palestinians and resentful of foreign pressure on any Israeli government. And they are fully behind every Israeli war against Gaza, Lebanon, or any-place else as a war "for our home," a war "of no choice."

But the truth is that I'm largely inferring these views from the parties and politicians that my fellow townspeople vote for and the news media they consume, because I've hardly ever discussed politics with anyone here, except when I've done man-on-the-street interviews with them for stories. As for the neighbors in my building whom I've known for 20 years, right after the last election, in March 2015, one of the husbands mentioned to me that he'd voted for Herzog; otherwise, I don't know any of their political opinions because the subject never comes up. Same with my native Israeli relatives in other parts of the country—we don't talk politics. Some of my friends will start a political discussion when I'm around to humor me, or maybe to preempt me, but with those exceptions, it has been many years since I've gotten into a conversation about politics that I didn't initiate with Israelis.

People overseas don't know this about Israeli life. They think Israelis are obsessed with politics, but this is a terribly outdated image. When I came here in 1985, and for years afterward, it was still accurate. For instance, while American comic impressionists' repertoire of politicians was limited to the president, or at most the two contenders in an election year, Israel's national mimic, Tuvia Tzafir, would draw from a gallery of at least two dozen local politicians in his TV appearances. The clichés of heated political debate around the Friday night dinner table, and of bus drivers turning up the radio for the hourly news headlines so the passengers can hear—I was at those dinners and rode on those buses, that's really the way it was.

But that's been finished for a long time—15, even 20 years. Today, except for people whose work is connected to politics, and those on the far right and far left—who altogether make up a small minority in this country—Israelis have stopped thinking or talking about politics. "I don't know anything about it, Larry," a friend of mine, whose son is an Air Force pilot, said during the last election campaign when I started saying how Netanyahu was smearing Herzog's Zionist Union as a party of traitors. "I pay no attention to it. They're all liars. All they care about is themselves; they don't give a shit about anybody else," my friend said, articulating the popular Israeli view. Occupation, shmockupation, it's all "politics," all bullshit, something people watch on TV if there's nothing better on; it's another reality show. The press plays it as a reality show, too, or a wrestling match. During election campaigns, one is expected in polite company to groan in passing about the candidates, but not to say much more. During wartime the danger, the worry, the sadness over Israeli casualties, the security measures one is taking—these are the first topic of conversation. But to discuss the war as an issue, to talk about whether it's right or wrong, except if you want to say, "We should just bomb the hell out of them"—what is there to talk about?

There used to be discussion about politics. The outbreak of the second intifada killed it all. In the space of one riotous, bloody weekend at the end of September 2000, the Palestinians, and with them the Arab citizens of Israel, turned into scorpions in the eyes of the Israeli Jewish public. The best description of the national mentality in the 21st century was given by *Haaretz* columnist Gideon Levy. "It used to be," he said, "that if you asked two Jews a question, you'd get three opinions. Now you only get one."

At a wedding in the late '90s, after Netanyahu had taken over and everybody I knew supported the Oslo Accord and couldn't stand Bibi, I was dancing with an old friend, and she told me, with real urgency in her voice, "I can't believe it. Bibi is killing the peace process, and nobody's doing anything. There should be demonstrations, something." Then in 2001 or 2002, when the second intifada was on and Israelis and Palestinians were killing each other full tilt, she and I found ourselves dancing at another wedding, and, thinking she would agree with me, I made some disparaging remark about Israel's policy of going for a military victory instead of trying to calm things down. She just shook her head. "I don't care what happens to the Palestinians anymore. I just want the army to stop the terrorism, whatever it takes." By January 2009, when Israel was bombing Gaza to hell in "Operation Cast Lead," killing 1,400 Palestinians while losing 13 Israeli lives, she told me over the phone, "Larry, I heard you're against the war. I can't believe it—why?" And my friend is no right-winger, either; she voted for Herzog in the last election. For that matter, Herzog, the most recent candidate of "change," also supported Operation Cast Lead, and every other little war Israel has gotten itself into.

And when the wars are on—the Second Lebanon War in 2006, Operation Cast Lead (Gaza) in 2009, Operation Pillar of Defense (Gaza) in 2012, Operation Protective Edge (Gaza) in 2014—polls find that 90 percent to upward of 95 percent of Israeli Jews support them, too.

One might think this has turned Israelis into terrible people, terrible on a personal level—callous even with each other, with non-Arabs. But what I've seen is actually the opposite. As Israeli Jews have grown more and more dismissive of Palestinians and Arabs in general, more blithely uninterested in the way we kick them around, Israeli Jews have become pretty nice people. They didn't used to

be, not when I got here and, from what I heard from veteran immigrants at the time, not before then, either. They were abrasive, they
smacked you around verbally when you opened your mouth, standing in line with them was a nightmare. Around the middle to late
'90s, I began to notice a difference. A few years ago, I was talking
with a South African relative who's been visiting regularly since the
'70s, and she said, "It used to be such an ordeal going to a restaurant or getting on a bus. Now it's a pleasure. Israelis have changed."
I asked a 35-year veteran Jerusalem bus driver if Israeli passengers'
behavior had changed. "It's better, definitely," he said. "Now they're
nicer. They talk nicer." Do they still push? "Nah, are you kidding?
Now you don't get that street behavior; now it's civilized."

I put this down to the advent of prosperity, consumerism,
careerism, foreign travel, even air conditioning. Life in Israel isn't
so pinched like it was before the mid-'90s; now people can breathe.
Also, the old-timers for whom gruffness and abrasiveness were a
point of national pride, who weren't about to act like the soft, silly
Jews in the fleshpots of the West—most of those Israelis, with all due
respect to their sacrifices and decency of character, have passed on.
Their children, and certainly their grandchildren and great-grand-
children, are not such boors. They're okay, they're friendly, you can
get through a day in this country now without feeling pummeled.

But in a way, I suppose there is a unity between the new Israeli
civility and the new political complacency: People here aren't bothered enough anymore by the Arabs, morally or militarily, to let
them get in the way of their middle-class fun, to ruin their cheer-
ful, shopping-mall mood. "What's important to me is the economy.
I'm a man of the middle class," a Modi'in resident told me after the
2013 election campaign, explaining why he'd voted for Yair Lapid's
party. "I didn't care that Lapid didn't talk about the Palestinians
and the conflict. It's not important to me." In the last decade, a key
component of Israelis' good humor is the near-absence of Arab violence, except during the wars, which are measured in weeks, and
the low-level, "lone-wolf" intifada, whose six months of stabbings
and car-rammings largely petered out in spring 2016. Maybe Israelis

becoming nicer personally and coarser politically isn't such an anomaly; taken together, they're a portrait of a smug society.

In Modi'in, there isn't a single Arab resident, certainly no Arab homeowner, unless one or two are "passing." It's not illegal for Arabs to rent or buy apartments here (or anyplace else in the country), but for a Jew in Modi'in to rent or, especially, sell his apartment to an Arab would be taken as an act of betrayal—political, social, and economic—by far too many neighbors for it to be a likely option in this neighborly city.

Another side of Modi'in that belies its liberal reputation is the small acts of right-wing sabotage that crop up during a national "battle for the street." Before the last election, there was a huge Likud sign on the exterior of one of the ground-floor apartments in the building next to ours, and an equally huge Zionist Union sign on the exterior of the other ground-floor flat. A couple of days before the March election, the Zionist Union sign disappeared. The tenant who put it up confirmed, as if it was necessary, that he didn't take it down himself. Then on Election Day, my mother-in-law went to her neighborhood precinct to vote for Zionist Union, but when she entered the booth she found there were no Zionist Union slips to put in the ballot box. The precinct supervisor inspected and found that somebody had hidden them.

This sort of thing is not new around here. In 2005, ahead of the pull-out from Gaza, supporters of the "disengagement" were flying blue ribbons from their car antennas all over the country, and opponents were flying orange ones. After a while, the blue ribbons disappeared, as did the pro-disengagement signs from the streets and highways. I myself had a blue ribbon torn off my antenna, then another. The signs at the highway intersection at the entrance to Modi'in, a mile or so from a string of West Bank settlements, turned steadily from orange and blue to solid orange.

But ultimately, the politics of Modi'in, no matter for whom the residents vote, is embedded in the facts on the ground here—in the 443 "apartheid road," for instance, and in the total absence of Arabs. It's also there in the local rituals, especially those connected to school and the inculcation of "Zionist values" in the young, which has succeeded spectacularly: Year after year, Modi'in ranks number one among the country's municipalities for percentage of army recruits signing up for combat units. The city puts on a pool party for each cohort of 18-year-old inductees. The chief rabbi of Modi'in addresses high school students going on the de rigeur trip to Poland and the concentration camps. There's a three-day hike and a "citizenship" assembly for the 16-year-olds getting their Israeli ID cards. On Independence Day, half the town turns out for the fireworks and concert in the main park, and the air is rich with the smell of meat on the barbeque. During Operation Protective Edge, signs went up reading, "Modi'in salutes the IDF." Nationalism, patriotism, military service—Israelis imbibe this, as the saying goes, with their mother's milk, and in all but a few cases drink it eagerly. The mindset here is very much like that in red-state America. I think of Israel as a small, Hebrew-speaking Texas, with Tel Aviv the country's answer to Austin. Like Israel, Texas used to be split between its liberal and hardass wings, but in recent decades the hardasses have taken over completely there, too.

So it is here in Little Texas. Elections are no longer fought over how to solve the conflict with the Palestinians; they're fought over security and economics, because the politicians on the so-called left know that the Israeli public does not want to hear any more about solving the conflict with the Palestinians. Let me rephrase that: The Israeli public is sick to death from hearing the same boring, monotonous shit year after year, decade after decade, about solving the goddamn conflict with the goddamn fucking Palestinians. Israelis don't believe in a solution; they think that trying to solve things will only make them worse, like it did before, and get a lot of them killed. The army has the Palestinians under control—why tamper with the way things are? And why do these idiots overseas keep talking to us about it? It's a dead letter, the deadest of dead Israeli political issues.

And under the circumstances, there is no defending or excusing or "understanding" Israelis for taking this view, and for consistently electing leaders who put it into practice with a vengeance. I could understand Israelis turning away from the possibility of peace, from the idea of making a deal with the Palestinians, if buses were still blowing up in the streets. But they're not. And possibly the most important reason they're not is that Palestinian troops have been working alongside, or more accurately under, the Israeli army and Shin Bet every day since 2004—when Yasser Arafat died and Mahmoud Abbas (Abu Mazen) took over the Palestinian Authority (PA)—to put down Palestinian terrorism in the West Bank. It's PA troops, not Israeli ones, who are deployed in the Palestinian cities, villages, and refugee camps. True, Israeli forces raid those places when they want, Israeli soldiers guard the highways and border crossings, and ultimately it's Israel, not the PA, who's in charge of protecting Israelis from Palestinian attacks. But Palestinian troops are the ones on the front line 24/7, who maintain control over the Palestinians where they live, and the result of this—as well as of the separation barrier and the millions of things the Israeli army and Shin Bet do—is that the West Bank, except for during the lone-wolf intifada, has been largely quiet since 2004.

Israelis don't know this. We've got it so good. But the luxury we enjoy doesn't register in the Israeli mind because Israelis are by now incapable of giving Arabs any credit for anything. Abu Mazen is hated here; not as much as Arafat, not as much as Hamas, but enough—despite having done more for Israeli security than most Israel Defense Forces (IDF) generals. A few years back, I asked Ehud Ya'ari, dean of the country's Arab affairs journalists, a security hawk and a political analyst of great intellectual pride, what if anything had surprised him about the peace process. "That somebody like Abu Mazen can take such a consistent, public position against violence was a surprise to me," he said. "Not that I thought he was in favor of violence, he hasn't been in favor of violence since Oslo, but that he would take such a public line and order his security chiefs so explicitly to prohibit violence—this is a surprise."

I used to think that if the Palestinians gave up terror, the occupation was finished, it wouldn't have a leg to stand on anymore in the eyes of the world. Well, the Palestinian Authority has not only given up terror for more than a decade, it's been fighting terror in conjunction with the IDF and Shin Bet—yet the occupation isn't finished, it's getting stronger every day, and the world is watching this happen. Israel's mouthpieces liked to say once upon a time that if the Palestinians recognized Israel and gave up terror, they would be amazed at how generous we would be. Well, the PLO recognized Israel in 1988, and since then hundreds of thousands of Israelis have moved into West Bank settlements, and meanwhile Abu Mazen's men are still protecting us, so Israeli generosity turned out to be somewhat less amazing than advertised. Remember the old formula for solving the conflict—"land for peace," meaning Israel gives the Palestinians land in return for the Palestinians giving Israel peace? Which side has kept their part of the bargain, and which side has broken theirs?

Fear and aggression, this has become the Israeli way—not only toward Palestinians, but toward tens of thousands of desperate African refugees, whom the government and media refer to as "infiltrators," and whom the immigration police hound on the streets and in their apartments, locking up as many of them as possible in a "detention facility" in the desert, the declared goal being to drive them all out of the country. Fear and aggression is also the policy toward the country's nearly two million Arab citizens, whose children not only can't dream of growing up to become president, they can't dream of growing up to become a high official in any Israeli civilian company, public or private, that's even indirectly "security-related," which is a whole lot of companies. Before an Israeli Arab family can get on a plane for a vacation overseas, they must endure lengthy, humiliating interrogations and searches at Ben-Gurion Airport, while Israeli Jewish families answer a few routine questions and are waved through. In countless ways, Arab citizens in this country are separate and unequal.

The same belligerent paranoia toward Arabs and Muslims guides Israel's military policy beyond its borders. We bomb Hezbollah and Syria every few months to keep Hezbollah from getting Syria's fancier weapons (this is one of the important ways we maintain our "qualitative edge" on the battlefield), and when Hezbollah hits back or tries to, that just proves we were right to bomb them in the first place, and sets the stage for us to bomb them again "at a time of our choosing." We kill Iranian nuclear scientists because only Israel is allowed to have nuclear bombs, and if Bibi and his then-defense minister, Ehud Barak, had had their way and not been overruled by the comparatively sober military-intelligence establishment, they would have bombed Iran in the early 2010s. Fear and aggression—that is the modern Israeli political mentality. It's always been a part of it, a big part, but never in the 32 years I've been here was it such a dominant feature as it is now.

In these years, again, Israel and I have gone in opposite directions. And in terms of political morality—how Israel treats other people, and above all how it treats Palestinians—my view is that Israel has gone beyond the pale. The occupation is not just a flaw, but a morally fatal flaw. It is different from apartheid, different from Jim Crow, but the same in one overriding way: It is a species of tyranny, a system of government in which the strong trample the weak. The system Israel runs on the three million people of the West Bank is military dictatorship. It used to run the same thing on the now nearly two million people of Gaza, before scaling back a dozen years ago from military dictatorship to a suffocating, often-lethal military blockade—a lesser species of tyranny.

And in the face of that, Palestinian terrorism, for all its hellishness and its innocent victims, amounts to self-defense. America doesn't understand—much of the West doesn't understand—but the Israeli-Palestinian conflict is not a two-sided affair in which both sides are partly at fault. Since Israel conquered the West Bank and Gaza in the 1967 Six-Day War, it has been a one-sided affair in which Israel is all but completely at fault and the Palestinians are basically blameless. To describe things in the plainest terms, Israel is a nation of free people that denies another nation its freedom at gunpoint, and has been doing so for half a century. Believe me, this was not my view of things when I came here from Los Angeles in 1985.

Why do I stay? For one thing, I'm too old now to start over, and I've got a wife and two sons who are happy here. And here's the strange, or maybe not so strange, thing: I'm happy here, too. I have a great life; I've had a great 32 years. Aside from being able to earn my living as a journalist in one of the world's most interesting "conflict zones," I've been able to criticize the Israeli government and society as harshly as I please and go on living my comfortable middle-class life in this nice suburb. One thing I wrote cost me my job at the *Jerusalem Post,* an episode that made waves publicly as well as in my own psyche, but I found freelance work immediately as well as a writing perch at a widely read, left-wing website, and soon enough I got hired at my present job as a copyeditor at *Haaretz,* which is every bit as lucrative a sinecure as the one I held at the *Post.* As far as danger goes, it's more dangerous in L.A., where good parents do not let their kids roam the streets all night like they do here. My older son, Alon, recently completed his army service in a combat unit and now faces annual reserve duty, which of course worries me, but so far so good, and he hasn't been stationed in the West Bank or on the Gazan border, and I have to say that the army has been very good for his personal growth. My younger son, Gilad, will be going into the army soon, and I have every reason to believe that his blessed asthma, together with his computer skills, will land him an interesting desk job. Alon hasn't faced any moral dilemmas yet, and I hope it stays that way; meanwhile I'm extremely proud of him, and we'll see what, if any, dilemmas his younger brother faces. As a parent here you have to push a lot out of your mind, but one of the things I still like about Israel, especially compared to the United States, is that everybody—rich, poor, and middle class—serves in the army.

In case it isn't clear by now, I don't hate this country. I hate what it does to Arabs and African refugees. I can't bear Israelis' political mentality, but I don't hate Israelis, even with all their callousness toward the country's victims. I don't think Israelis are more racist or brutal toward their enemies than Americans or Europeans are when they're at war. Moreover, Israelis, by and large, have good hearts. Very few have any inclination toward brutality against a random

Arab. Very few are sadists in that way; the problem is that the general atmosphere inevitably produces acts of sadism. Also, the cliché about Israelis being there for you in times of trouble is true, from what I've found. Once, on reserve duty in around 1990, an unusually introspective Israeli and I were bitching about local behavior (which in those days still seemed generally obnoxious), but then he told me a story that put things in some perspective. He and his wife were eating lunch once in a large, crowded restaurant in Bern, Switzerland, when one of the diners suddenly collapsed and was lying on the floor. "We rushed over there to help him, but he was unconscious, he wasn't breathing. We shouted for someone to call an ambulance. But no one moved. We were the only ones in this whole big place who moved a muscle. Finally we made such a noise that the manager or someone called an ambulance. This was in Bern, the 'height of civilization,'" he said.

For all the bullshit, the blaring popular media, the non-stop hucksterism and consumerism, the conformism, the lowest-common-denominator popular culture, even the segregation and redneck politics, I feel very comfortable here. Often I notice something and say, "This could be a great country if it wasn't for the politics, for the thing with the Arabs." For instance, my wife's relations with her co-workers. They're social workers who deal with old people in a poor neighborhood of Tel Aviv, she's been together with some of them for 20 years, they know each other's idiosyncrasies and sorrows, they gossip constantly, they message each other while they're on vacation, they go to each other's catered affairs, they fight and make up, they know each other's husbands—they're true friends, they're devoted to each other. I'm not saying Israel is the only country where this sort of thing happens, but it seems to me a signature national characteristic—the closeness between the people.

Do I love Israel? I don't know, but I know I feel much more attached to it than I ever did to America. (Not surprisingly, the one time I felt something akin to love for America was after 9/11.) During Operation Protective Edge in summer 2014, there was a collection box at my neighborhood grocery store for personal hygiene items and other things customers could buy for the soldiers stuck in the field. Another box was for food we could buy for the shiva being held by the economically strapped family of a local soldier who'd been killed in the fighting. Did I love Israel then, even while I hated that war? I loved the Israeli parents who were suffering, and I loved the soldiers who were getting killed, that's for sure. And I felt at one with the society that was mourning them.

One other thing I noticed: When an Israeli does something truly great, I'm proud in a way I never was in the United States about an American achiever. I was driving into Jerusalem in 2009 when I heard on the radio that Ada Yonath of the Weizmann Institute of Science had been named the winner of the Nobel Prize for Chemistry—and I began jumping up and down in the driver's seat, something I guarantee I never did back in Los Angeles when I heard that an American won a Nobel. This is the Israel that I root for: the little guy, the underdog, this pisher that goes and produces a Nobel Prize winner. That's the Israel that makes me proud. That's my idea of a Jewish country.

But that, in the main, is not this Jewish country. In the decisive ways, in the way it treats others, in matters of war and peace, Israel is not the little guy, not the underdog; it's the bully. And I doubt that's going to change. It may, I haven't entirely given up hope, but I know the odds are strongly against it. This is my country, and I love it as much as I'm capable of loving a country, but it has done awesome damage to the Jewish soul and Jewish conscience by subjugating the Palestinians, which has led it into an ongoing series of wars and which goes hand in hand with its abusive treatment of its Arab citizens and African refugees. Israel, which has given my family and me a great life, has turned into what I would call a morally failed state. It didn't used to be that, not by any means, but that's what it's become.

How did it get to this point? How did my opinions about it get to this point? To try to explain, first, where I'm coming from, I'll answer that hoariest of conversation-starters among new immigrants: Why did you move to Israel?

CHAPTER ONE

ON HOLOCAUST SURVIVORS LANE

Until a month before I boarded a plane in L.A. on January 15, 1985, for Ben-Gurion Airport, a month in which I boned up on Israel, I couldn't have said which countries lay on its borders. I'd heard of Abraham, but except for his being a Jew in the Bible, I didn't know who he was. Eleven years earlier, when I was a politically aware 22-year-old, the Yom Kippur War was fought, and I paid no attention to it whatsoever. The only time in my life as a "Diaspora Jew" that I ever had any interest in Israel, any feeling about it, was during the run-up to the Six-Day War, when it somehow trickled down to me that Israel was facing the possibility of destruction (a grossly exaggerated fear, I've since learned, but that was the common belief). Otherwise, I just never took an interest in this place—the whole issue seemed too grave, too humorless, and Israel too hot, sandy, and barren. I was a city boy, the son of secular, Yiddish-speaking Polish immigrants to America, and my Jewish interests were Lenny Bruce, Philip Roth, and immigrant Jewish New York, the "world of our fathers." In other words, American Jewish rebellion and American Jewish nostalgia.

I wasn't anti-Israel, or even critical of it, by any means. The friends I grew up with were all the sons and daughters of Holocaust survivors, and for them, as for their parents, Israel was fighting for us and Jews everywhere against the homicidally anti-Semitic Arabs. I thought of Israelis as being on the front lines for me—they had to fight to live as Jews; I didn't. My mental picture of the country was of old but vital Polish Jewish men firing rifles and ducking bullets in a trench in the desert. Who was I to criticize them? (Not that I was inclined to, or knew enough to.)

My father, Emanuel Derfner, didn't agree with this view; he thought Israel was wrong all the time, just like he thought America was wrong all the time, and while I agreed with him about America, I didn't know what he was talking about with Israel. I put it down to his old boyhood communism and to his hard times in Palestine, where his family moved from their Polish *shtetl* in the 1920s. He was 12 at the time, and followed them by boat two weeks afterward, having stayed behind to get his eye treated, and the first thing they told him when he got off the boat was that his father had been killed accidentally by the blast from a demolition crew in Haifa. A couple of years later he became a communist, ran with both Jews and Arabs in the Galilee, got thrown in prison for a year or two by the British when he was 16 or 17, and then deported back to Poland, after which he didn't see his family for nearly 50 years. So I figured he had this deep grudge against the country because that's where he lost his father and was separated from his mother and all his brothers and sisters. But he didn't talk much about Israel except for the occasional outburst, and the plain fact is his views on that subject didn't influence mine, which is fairly ironic because I've gradually come around to a set of views that isn't far from what he believed as an adolescent nearly a century ago.

Instead, growing up in L.A., I was influenced by my friends, by my sense of being Jewish, and by the general atmosphere in America, which treated Israel as the good guy and the Arabs as the bad ones. The Vietnam War may have been a controversial issue on the Johnny Carson and Merv Griffin shows, but the Six-Day War wasn't. Everybody was cheering. Vanessa Redgrave, with her bit about "Zionist hoodlums" at the Oscar ceremony, was branded a Jew-hater. That's what everyone thought, and that's what I thought too. Later, after the massacre at Sabra and Chatilla in 1982, there was so much bad press about Israel, I didn't know what to think. But then I heard the prime minister, Menachem Begin, say, "Christians kill Muslims and they blame the Jews," which I thought was such a great line, and for me, that settled it. Israel was still the good guy.

In the '60s and '70s, unlike today, Israel was not an issue for young, mainstream leftists, at least not Jewish ones like in my crowd. We saw no contradiction between, on the one hand, hating the Vietnam War and supporting the Black Power movement, and, on the other, siding with Israel automatically against the Arabs. If there were strains of anti-Israel rhetoric or anti-Semitism coming out of black militants, we wrote it off as fringe lunacy. (Although I remember a friend of mine, a very adamant leftist and hater of white racism but also a very feisty Jew from Brooklyn, saying, "If the Black Panthers are against Israel, I hope they get eaten by lions," and feeling a little uncomfortable at hearing such political incorrectness.)

My decision later to move to Israel grew out of my being a Jew and a liberal, a pair of identities that meshed very smoothly, of course. And the kind of Jew and liberal I would become was heavily influenced by my childhood in Los Angeles, which took place in a magical setting dominated by Jews and black people, one that's long gone and whose like will not be seen again.

If Rodeo Lane, the street in L.A. where I grew up in the early '60s, could be transposed as it was then to the present day, it would be famous. Holocaust Survivors Lane, it might be called. Back then there was no such term as "Holocaust survivors," or even "Holocaust." Then, the people who would later be called Holocaust survivors didn't have a name; the ones on our street spoke of themselves just as having been "in the camps."

There were about 20 such families on Rodeo Lane, a two-block-long street in the middle of an all-white, lower-middle-class complex of pastel-painted apartment buildings with nice lawns in the Crenshaw Area, surrounded by neighborhoods of blacks mixed in with Japanese and Chinese. There were blood ties and Polish *shtetl* ties and concentration camp ties among most of the families; my parents knew one of them from Davenport, Iowa, in the early '50s, when my father had worked at their uncle's dress factory. My parents had not been in the camps, though; they'd moved to Paris and escaped in 1940 on the famous last train out of the city before the Nazis moved in, then made it to Portugal and, vouched for by my father's rich, Polish-immigrant uncle in New York, came to America.

The popular image now of Holocaust survivors is of haunted, distraught, teary-eyed people overwhelmed by their memories. That was not how my friends' parents behaved back then. Most were in their early 40s and were full of life, talking and laughing loudly, taking vacations in Las Vegas and Palm Springs, playing cards, working hard, full of ambition, despite the numbers tattooed on their forearms. They weren't happy-go-lucky, of course. They were driven, insecure, and vulnerable; they carried the Holocaust with them. The mother of one of my friends told me once that when they would throw a party, "We like to have a drink or two, because you know what we went through." But the soundtrack of their lives wasn't a dark cello, or anyway it wasn't only that; it was more like a klezmer band, with music for a whole range of moods.

I've known a lot of Polish Jewish immigrants of that generation—some who went through the camps, some who didn't—and I can't think of anything that distinguishes the survivors' behavior from that of the others; I don't know of any telltale sign of a Holocaust survivor. But then I don't know what they were thinking or feeling inside, and I don't know how they behaved when they were alone. My mother, Sylvia Derfner, wasn't a Holocaust survivor; she lost her family after she'd already gone off to Paris and America. She almost never talked about Poland; sometimes she would begin telling about a brother or someone else in the family, and her voice would get quieter and quieter, until it became an indistinct whisper, and then she'd say, "Well, it's finished," slap her hands on her lap, get up, and do some housework. I always considered my parents lucky, compared to my friends' parents, that the Nazis hadn't gotten them: They had missed the concentration camps; they'd escaped the Holocaust. Later, when I was living in Israel and my mother came for a few years, the siren sounded on the morning of Yom Hashoah, Holocaust Remembrance Day, when everyone stands silent for a minute. Just after the siren ended, my phone rang, and I picked it up and said hello. On the other end was silence. "Ma?" I said, and after a couple of seconds, the phone at the other end was replaced on the receiver.

Except for our parents' background, Jewish life for my friends and me was pretty much out of Philip Roth or Mordecai Richler. We were street kids but far from wild; in the back of our minds, we knew we didn't want to do anything that could screw up our future. Being Jewish was something we didn't think about. We went to Hebrew school at Bnei Israel Synagogue on Santa Barbara Avenue (later to become Bethany Baptist Church on Martin Luther King Jr. Boulevard). It was a Conservative synagogue, but it seemed very old-fashioned Jewish to me with all the Yiddish-accented men mumbling their prayers. We went to High Holiday services at the Baldwin Theater, which was where we went to the movies—except on Saturday night, "blood night," when it was unofficially reserved for the "bloods," or blacks.

The girls didn't have bat mitzvahs, and our bar mitzvahs featured something a bit less in the way of spectacle than bar mitzvahs do now. You could either have it at the Savoy or the Highland, and for entertainment you could have either Manny Glass or Bill Roberts

("What a day this has been / What a rare mood I'm in / It's Jack's bar mitzvah tonight!"), for dinner either brisket or chicken, and for hors d'oeuvres either little meatballs or cocktail wieners. For my friends and me, a good bar mitzvah was one with cocktail wieners.

There's a tribal Jewish myth that American Jews in the early to mid-'60s walked around brimming with pride that Sandy Koufax was Jewish. The idea is that in those days we still felt insecure in goyish America and so we reveled in American Jewish heroes, especially one who could conquer such an American thing as baseball. On Rodeo Lane, that simply was not true, and I'm talking about not just American Jews, but the sons of Holocaust survivors who were fanatics for the Los Angeles Dodgers. (I rooted for the San Francisco Giants out of loyalty to my family, who had been New York Giants fans; it was invaluable training for being a leftist in Israel.) They idolized Koufax because he was the greatest pitcher; that he was Jewish never, ever came up. Dodger pitcher Larry Sherry and his brother, catcher Norm, were also Jewish, but nobody ever mentioned that, either. And in 1962, when Maury Wills broke Ty Cobb's stolen bases record, the main topic of conversation among my Jewish, Dodger-lunatic friends was not Jewish Sandy Koufax but gentile Maury Wills. Tribal Jewish myths are made up by *alteh cockers* (old farts), and that was not where young American Jews were at in the early '60s, at least not on my block.

My family and I were a little different from the others on Rodeo Lane, aside from my parents having missed the concentration camps. My folks were a little older, had lived in New York, had been in America a little longer; privately, we referred to the other immigrants as the *greeneh*. Also, my father was an inactive but still believing communist, even though, being a practical man, he now voted Democrat, and, like the others, was a small businessman. He'd bought a liquor store (actually a liquor/grocery store) for relatively little in L.A.'s black south side and was working his way up.

Lots of Jews owned stores in south L.A. in those days, before blacks themselves and Korean immigrants started buying them. Another American Jewish myth I can dispel is that Jewish shopkeepers in the area faced anti-Semitism from blacks and that the 1965 Watts Riots were accompanied by anti-Jewish feeling. I worked at a succession of my father's liquor stores in basically all-black neighborhoods in the '60s through the early '70s, and I never once heard an anti-Semitic remark. Not once. I heard about eight million anti-white remarks, but never anti-Jewish. Two of my closest friends worked at their fathers' liquor stores in South-Central, and we talked endlessly about our experiences, and they never mentioned anti-Semitism either.

In fact, between the stories my friends told me and what I saw myself, our Jewish fathers were out-and-out beloved by a great many of their black customers, including just about all of the regulars, even in the late '60s, the days of black militancy. My father, known to all as Manny, was this audacious, warm, jocular, take-no-crap, hefty 5'6" bull of man with a funny accent. The store was his stage and the customers, clerks, deliverymen, and I, too, when I was there, were the supporting players. From his boyhood he was legendary for his physical strength, and he was always challenging customers to arm wrestle right there on the counter, and he always won. In the late '60s, when he would shake hands with someone, and they gave him the Black Power handshake with the hooked thumbs, he would instinctively pin the guy's forearm down. They laughed, I laughed. He got away with this shit, an old Jewish liquor store owner in South-Central L.A. in the era of Huey Newton and H. Rap Brown.

We were open 365 days a year. Once, before I became an atheist, I asked him why he didn't close for Yom Kippur and Rosh Hashanah, and he said, "If I do that, I have to close for Christmas and Easter, too." Sure, Pop. Like I said, he got away with everything.

On paper, it seems like quite a stretch: being a believer in communism and owning a liquor store in a poor black area. In the late '60s, talk began about white businesses taking money out of the black community and the owners spending it in their white neighborhoods and putting it in white banks, and how this was fleecing blacks of their resources, and how the only answer was for them to own the businesses in the community. There was also talk about how prices in the ghetto stores were higher than those in white neighborhoods. That bothered me. Later on I found out the reason wasn't racism on the part of the often Jewish shopkeepers in the ghetto; the lower prices were at supermarkets, which could buy in bulk, and in those days there were no or virtually no supermarkets in south L.A. Later, my father began consolidating his grocery purchases with one wholesaler, which cut his costs considerably. He told me, "I'm going to pass some of the savings on to the customers." And he did. He could have kept prices as they'd been and people would have bought just as much as before, only he would have made a bigger profit. I thought that was a nice gesture, but nothing special. I didn't realize at the time what an extraordinary move it was for the owner of a hole-in-the-wall grocery store with a liquor license.

My father treated his poor and working-class black customers with respect. He cashed checks and gave credit. He hired almost only black clerks. My friends' fathers ran their stores the same way. Again, I didn't think this was special at the time, until Korean immigrants began buying stores in the ghetto—no check cashing, no credit, no hiring outside the family, and reportedly not a lot of laughs or arm wrestling. And when blacks started buying the liquor stores, prices somehow remained high, even though racism couldn't have been the reason.

It wasn't easy being a white boy, the boss's son, in the ghetto in the '60s and early '70s. I got eyeballed by customers at least once every day; I got tested all the time. Once my father told me, "If they ever get the idea they can take advantage of you, you might as well close the doors and go home." He was right. He taught me how to throw an obstreperous customer out the door: "You don't go from non-violence to violence gradually, you do it all at once. You ask the guy nicely to leave, then you ask again, and if he doesn't leave, you get behind him, grab him by the collar with one hand and the belt with the other, and give him the bum's rush." I never had to do this; luckily, I got by. This was in the '60s, which were bisected by the Watts Riots, through the early '70s. I often hitchhiked to work, and worked plenty of Saturday nights. There are no Jews there anymore—probably no whites, either. For awhile my father had two stores, Handy Liquor at

74th and Vermont, and Handy Liquor #2 at 83rd and Normandie, which were about a dozen blocks apart. At a spot halfway between the two is where the 1992 Los Angeles riots broke out.

As my parents were a little different from my friends' parents, I was a little different from my friends. They were a few years older, yet I was less cautious (or naïve and foolhardy, in their view), and less restrained by my parents, who weren't as conservative. I was the only one who went to the swimming pool in the park across the boulevard, which was used mainly by blacks, and the only one who played in the park's Little League, where I was the only white kid on my team. Between the neighborhood beyond Rodeo Lane, the school we went to and our fathers' stores, the social and increasingly political issue of our lives had nothing to do with being Jewish—it was about being white in a milieu that was filled with black people. The most important political opinion we had in the early '60s, if not the only important one, was how we felt about blacks, whom we called "colored" to be respectful, except for those of us who didn't.

Being the only white boy on my Little League team, and being athletic and surrounded by blacks at school, I was dazzled by black style and wanted to fit in, so at age 11 I started talking and later dressing like a black kid. Not on Rodeo Lane among my real friends, and damn sure not when I was hanging around the liquor store with the black clerks and customers. But when I was at school or playing ball with black kids, I acted black. I was also heavily into black music, but that wasn't a pose; everyone was. Half the white kids in America today are imitation black people; I was just exposed to them earlier than most, and I fell especially hard for their style. And though I didn't have any political ideas at the time, that experience—of identifying with people who happened to be society's most feared and hated outsiders—helped shape the ideas I would come up with later.

Soon enough the Jews of Rodeo Lane, including my father, began to make enough money to move to the Jewish west side. We bought a house in Beverlywood, a heavily upper-middle-class Jewish neighbor-hood, and suddenly the children of upper-middle-class American Jews were my friends, or anyway my companions. More than a few of them were snotty, spoiled, sheltered, and mean. We had a sim-ple house, not like the typically rich-looking ones of Beverlywood. I once overheard a couple of new friends who'd come over say, "I'm glad I don't have to live in a house like this." Once we went to a foot-ball game at the Coliseum, which is in the middle of a rough South-Central neighborhood, and one of them joked that this was where I'd grown up. For them the Crenshaw Area, not to mention the neighborhood further south where my father had his liquor store, was the dark continent.

Before moving to West L.A., I didn't know anything about the place or its people, didn't know that these were the L.A. Jews who counted and that we were the upstarts, the Polish immigrants who had to make their money ringing up a cash register in the ghetto. It was there in Beverlywood that I first came in contact with rich peo-ple, or relatively rich people, and where I developed an instinctive dislike for them. In retrospect, that's also where I learned the differ-ence between insecure East European Jewish immigrants and smug, established American Jews with their JAP children.

One afternoon when I was 14, I was skateboarding in our backyard when my first "serious" thought formed gradually in my mind: that I didn't believe in God. I felt guilty; I'd been saying *Shema Yisrael* every night before bed for years. My father was reading at the dining room table, and finally I went in to get it off my chest. I told him what I'd decided, and he replied, "I haven't believed in God since I was 12." I was shocked. Every year he led the family Passover seder, took me to High Holiday services, put me through Hebrew school, had me bar mitzvahed—and all this time he didn't believe in God. I began reading and thinking about things, and we had a whole new world of ideas to talk about.

We began discussing politics—mainly he talked and I listened—and I began to understand, which I hadn't before when the only times he talked politics to me was when I had a current events report to do at the last minute, and I'd ask him to tell me what to write. When I was in seventh grade, Ngo Dinh Diem, the president of South Vietnam, was assassinated, and my father explained to me about "American imperialism" and how America "invaded Vietnam" and "installed their puppet Diem," and I wrote it down in neat handwriting and turned it in to my social studies teacher. I have no idea how she reacted, nor was I aware that what I'd written was pretty incendiary for 1963 America. But a few years later I would know what my father was talking about when it came to Vietnam, and workers' rights, and black people's rights, and I agreed with him. About Israel, though, I wasn't interested enough to ask, and he didn't offer, except for a rare, incomprehensible explosion.

He subscribed to the *I.F. Stone Weekly* and to *Soviet Life,* a magazine that arrived in the mail at our Beverlywood home in a brown paper wrapper. After the Prague Spring of 1968, the crackdown on Dubcek and the Czechoslovakian dissidents, I asked what he thought of the Soviets now, and he said, with a tone of regret, "They still haven't learned . . ." and didn't finish the sentence. I kept pressing, trying to get him to admit that the Russians were wrong, and finally he exploded, "That country lost 20 million people to Hitler!" End of discussion.

He'd come of age as a communist in Kfar Hasidim, a *moshav,* or cooperative farm, outside Haifa where his family, who'd been Hasidic Jews back in their Polish shtetl, were among the first settlers. He was a shepherd, and though Arabs were among his comrades, the Arabs in the fields around Kfar Hasidim didn't know that, so they would throw stones at him and he would have to fight his way home. The communists believed in driving out the British and building a workers' state where Arabs and Jews would be equal, where their religion and ethnicity would be irrelevant. One of his proudest memories was of being a guard at a school where Martin Buber taught. He lost much of his extended family in the Holocaust;

he hated all Germans and would not allow a German product in our house or the store.

In March 1978, my father was 65 and semi-retired, with a lot of time to think, and Israel was one of the things he thought about. One afternoon he came home winded but elated. He had grass stains on his pants. He tossed a cardboard placard on the dining room table—I remember it said either "Israel = Nazi Germany" or "Begin = Hitler." That afternoon he'd stood alone in front of the Israeli consulate on Wilshire Boulevard and held up the placard. He was protesting the Litani Operation, in which Israel invaded south Lebanon and would kill 1,000 to 2,000 Palestinians and Lebanese, with 20 Israelis getting killed. This was in retaliation for the Coastal Road Massacre, in which an 18-year-old Palestinian girl led the hijacking of two buses, during which 38 Israeli passengers were killed, most of them during the shootout at the end. That massacre was preceded by years of cross-border fighting in which the Palestinians and Lebanese got much the worse of the exchange.

"They were shouting down at me, 'Why didn't Hitler get you instead?'" he told me. He was proud of himself, and I was proud of him. I didn't know at the time what his cause was, I didn't know whether he was right or wrong, or if the "Israel = Nazi Germany" was fair, but this was my father: standing up against the whole world for what he believed in. That demonstration was his last political act; less than a month later, he suffered a stroke that left him paralyzed and speechless until his death.

And now that I know what Israel was doing in Lebanon, I'm not only proud of the incredible guts he showed, I also think he was right. Not the words he wrote on the placard—even if, as I suspect, he didn't mean them literally but was just so morally outraged and in such a lather to shock the Jews awake, they were way, way over the top, an exercise in verbal overkill. Nonetheless, I'll take that over all the other Jews' silence in the face of the Litani Operation and all the other Israeli exercises in literal overkill that would follow. The political example I took from my father, finally, was not about examining my own beliefs, but about being zealous on their behalf, in the face of any opposition.

And another example: to appreciate decent people regardless of their politics. He was an old-guard communist egalitarian and thus an anti-Zionist. What sort of Jew was he? In America he wrote a remembrance of his shtetl, Ryki, for the *yizkorbuch*, or book of memory, that was published by those who left the village before the Nazis came. A few years ago, my sister Suzie got it translated from Yiddish into English. There was one thing my atheist-at-age-12 father wrote that surprised me: "Was there anything more beautiful than studying the Torah aloud!" Otherwise, I wasn't surprised. "Every day of my life," he wrote, "the eyes, the eyes of my loved ones and dear friends stare at me, eyes that were closed shut so early when they died horrible deaths. . . . Deep within me I feel a duty to connect with them in my thoughts, to walk with them through the deserted streets of our shtetl; to look through the empty windows, from where our mothers' Sabbath candles would shine on Friday nights. . . ." That's the sort of Jew he was.

When I started thinking and reading and became outraged over the Vietnam War and white racism, I found myself well to the left of my peers in high school, few of whom had begun thinking yet. By the time we were in college, many of them, and certainly the cutting-edge members of my generation, had left me behind, excuse the pun. I didn't support revolution, or even socialism. I had my doubts about a couple of points in the Black Panthers' 10-Point-Program. I didn't hero-worship Huey Newton for killing a cop in Oakland. And all these white kids who were imitating black militants, they were doing such a bad job of it, brooding and acting sullen and venting their anger at whomever they pleased.

A few images from that time: An editorial in the *Daily Cal*, the student newspaper at UC Berkeley, derided some proposal or other as "jive liberal bullshit" (virtually guaranteed to have been written by a white student). At San Fernando Valley State College, a Jewish girl I knew with a thick New York accent was walking among the students (99 percent white) sitting on the lawn, holding a collection box and calling out, "Collecting for the Soledad Brothers"—the radical black convicts, led by author-idol George Jackson, who was charged with killing a Soledad Prison guard. (Not long afterward Jackson was killed in a prison break, during which he and other black inmates butchered six guards and white prisoners.) Along the way, Jackson's 17-year-old brother Jonathan tried to free the Soledad Brothers by leading the kidnapping of a judge and other hostages from a Northern California courthouse; in the shootout, the 65-year-old judge was killed along with Jonathan and his accomplices, and another hostage, a deputy DA, was paralyzed for life. A few days later, I went to hear Roberta Flack and saxophonist Cannonball Adderley at UC Berkeley, and at the start of the concert Flack asked the audience (overwhelmingly white) to stand for a minute of silence for Jonathan Jackson, and of course everyone stood. I had my doubts about what Jonathan Jackson had done, but I wasn't ready to be the only one in an audience of thousands not to stand, so I stood up, too.

Still, I was 100 percent against the Vietnam War, as fervently as anyone, and when I turned 18 it seemed by happy coincidence that my political principles and my self-interest—staying the hell out of the army—went hand in hand. And since I didn't feel any responsibility to go to prison for years, or become a medic, or serve in a hospital (what right does Nixon and his war-crazed army have to fuck up my life?), I went out to beat the draft, which I never had any doubt I could do. The Selective Service Law was full of holes, there were free draft counselors to help you, and while some of my more self-dramatizing friends felt mortally threatened, I never worried for a moment. I was so confident about getting out that I let my college deferment slip out of sheer laziness. The draft board called me for a physical, I weighed in a few pounds over the limit, and a sympathetic clerk told me that if I came in overweight again at the next physical, I'd get an exemption and be out for good. So I made damn sure to do just that. I'd joke to my friends that it was my revolutionary duty to hit the pizza parlor, and in the end I got my exemption. Very '60s: beating the system in a purely hedonistic way.

In the '70s, with left-wing politics having gotten so far out, with liberal politics having failed, with the draft gone and the army now all-volunteer, with the Vietnam War being fought more and more from the air so American casualties diminished and became easier to ignore (whatever was happening to the Vietnamese), my generation "turned inward." I decided to become an actor, and was acting and later directing in L.A. "little theater," making no money, getting nowhere in my so-called career while running my father's latest and last liquor store, in a poor-to-working-class, largely Mexican neighborhood of Hollywood. Then, in my late 20s, the big fear hit: If I don't change my life, I'm going to piss it away as a wannabe actor working in my father's liquor store. I'd written some freelance articles and taken a lot of journalism courses, so I decided to go back one last time to college, write for the college newspaper, get my degree and find a job as a reporter. And in a complete reversal of character—prompted by an acute awareness that this was my last chance to make something of myself—that's what I did. Purely by luck, or maybe psychological necessity, I found that I loved reporting and writing.

And in that last year of college (1980–81), among ethnically mixed students from average economic backgrounds at a campus on the invisible eastside of L.A., I began to question the political and social assumptions I'd developed and just sort of worn like a uniform. That was the year of the Vietnam veteran. America had "healed" from the trauma of Vietnam, and the 20-year-old elite college students who had maligned the soldiers were now, as 30-year-old yuppies, feeling bad about the poor losers with their PTSD and their broken lives. Tom Hayden, who'd gone from SDS to the California State Senate, was standing up in Sacramento for the vets. Bruce Springsteen, whose audiences used to whoop when he'd tell the story of how he'd failed his army physical, was giving benefit concerts for them. I did a story for the Cal State L.A. student newspaper about a Vietnam vet on campus who'd been through hell, and by then I realized that what I'd done when I was 18 was shameful. I should have gone to jail, or been a medic, or done something to pay

my dues to the country I lived in, and to prove that I really was acting on principle, instead of skipping off to find myself, or whatever
it was I'd been doing.

Everybody I knew, without exception, had beaten the draft
legally, either by college deferment or lottery number. All my friends
were middle-class liberal/leftist Jews, while all my acquaintances
were either that or middle-class liberal/leftist gentiles. We were the
'60s generation, or those who counted, anyway—the rebels, now
grown out of our rebellion and claiming our places that, son of a
gun, were always waiting for us near the front of American society's
line. And it occurred to me how many of the most popular, most
likely to succeed kids in high school had become radical leaders in
college. And how the most revolutionary campuses also happened to
have been the most prestigious—Harvard, Yale, Columbia, Berkeley.
And I realized that a lot of what we thought, said, and did hadn't
reflected our enlightened ideals, as we naturally assumed, but our
middle-class, college-educated, urban/suburban sense of entitle-
ment. The Middle Americans who grew up believing that the war
was right backed up their beliefs by fighting in Vietnam. We par-
agons of the '60s generation who grew up believing that the war
was wrong backed up our beliefs by going to peace marches, where
we got loaded, hit on chicks, and listened to Crosby, Stills & Nash.
In the end, the Middle Americans, blacks, and Mexican Americans
who went to Vietnam got fucked, while we revolutionaries, who'd
had the time of our lives, cashed in. Oh, definitely, ours had been a
noble cause.

It was my first job in journalism, at a local wire service called City
News Service, that led me to Israel. I covered everything worth cov-
ering in L.A., culminating with the 1984 Olympics, and when the
Games were over, I felt I'd topped out as an urban beat reporter in
America, which was all I could imagine wanting to be. City News,
however, paid dreck. It was anonymous—I couldn't stay there forever,

but any job I was likely to get at a newspaper, while paying more and publishing my byline in print, wouldn't be a fraction as interesting as the one I had. So I was in a bind. Then a good friend of mine, a TV news editor who'd recently gone to live in Israel, wrote me that he'd just gotten a job in Jerusalem in TV—and I said to myself, "If he can get a job in journalism in Israel, so can I." I was 33, unattached, figuring that within a couple of years I was going to get serious about getting married, I'd never lived further away from L.A. than San Francisco and Berkeley, I saw that this was probably my last chance to go off and have an adventure before I settled down, and being a journalist in Israel and writing about the Middle East for a year or two seemed like a hell of a lot better professional option than I had at home. Plus, the absorption center in Jerusalem where my friend had stayed gave Jewish immigrants five months' room, board, and intensive Hebrew instruction for $500, and Israel paid for your flight, so that was it. I went to Israel's aliyah (Jewish immigration) emissaries in Los Angeles, told them I wanted to make aliyah (even though I was only planning on staying a year or two before returning), and started filling out forms.

It had nothing whatsoever to do with Zionism, or my Jewish identity, or, certainly, anti-Semitism in America. I could count on one hand the number of times I'd heard anti-Semitic remarks, and I'd never let them pass, I'd always shut the offender up (except once around 1970, when I was hitchhiking in the middle of the night in Bakersfield, and the twangy-accented guy standing with my friend and me didn't know we were Jewish, and he said something about the Jews, and I let it go, telling myself, "Forget it, Jake; it's Bakersfield.").

Just about everybody thought my going to Israel was a great idea. Even my widowed mother was for it. "Go out and see the world," she said. "Have an adventure." Israel sounded just right—not totally alien, not like living in the mountains of Chile or something, but definitely far away and brand new. A perceptive editor of mine said, "Israel might be good for you—it's a country with a purpose." For the first time, I began reading about the place, starting with the brochures I got from the aliyah office at the turn of 1985.

One of them was sort of a fact sheet about the Israeli-Palestinian conflict, and one of the things it said was that Israel controlled the West Bank and Gaza, where the population included about 30,000 Jews who were Israeli citizens, and about 1.5 million Palestinians who were not. That didn't sound like a fair arrangement to me. It might be necessary temporarily for whatever reasons Israel had, but it wasn't a permanent solution. You can't keep permanent military control over 1.5 million people and not let them vote, not let them be citizens. This was the first time I had ever begun to grasp what was going on between Israel and the Palestinians; this was the first real thinking I'd ever done about it. Yet while I figured there was something out of place here, I was not ready, even in the privacy of my mind, to criticize what Israel was doing. They must have good reasons. Maybe they have to control the Arabs, because otherwise the Arabs will kill them; maybe they can't let them vote, at least not now. I was stuck. (It's interesting where I got the idea of Arabs as killing machines, because it definitely didn't come from home.) And then I read in that brochure that the Likud, led by Yitzhak Shamir, wanted to hold onto the territories, while the Labor Party, led by Shimon Peres, wanted to trade land for peace—and I said, "That's my side: Labor and Peres." So it was only when I understood (for the first time!) that lots of Israelis thought the situation should change that I allowed myself to think so, too.

Still, I was in no way prepared to imagine that Israel, or Shamir and the Likud, were doing anything wrong—no, they were doing the best they could; they just saw things differently than Peres and Labor did. This was not a moral issue; the Palestinians had no kick coming—it was because they were such mindless killers that Israel had set this whole operation up in the West Bank and Gaza. The only question was what was best for Israel, and on that question, on the eve of my sojourn in the country, I could honestly (if mistakenly) say that I was a liberal.

Two weeks after I arrived in Jerusalem, I suspended my plans for returning after a year or two, and decided to try to make a permanent go of it. All the other people at the absorption center were making aliyah, and they just seemed intoxicated with the idea. I wanted to be intoxicated too. I wanted to cut the rope and set out on a whole new life, one a little more adventurous than what seemed on offer in L.A. or some other American town, a little bit more like the one my father had lived, a little more in keeping with the '60s spirit I'd been touched with. And here was the opportunity—in a country that was welcoming me in. That new life was mine for the taking. I was Jewish and happy to be so. I cared about Israel, in my ignorant way. I couldn't ask for a better place to be a journalist. But I wouldn't be just a journalist writing about things from a distance—I'd be writing about the country that had also become my cause. And I wouldn't be a liberal in safe, middle-class America, but in the Middle East, where my principles would be tested, where politics would have real, possibly life-or-death consequences for me personally.

I set three goals that I had to fulfill before I'd allow myself to consider going back home, otherwise I'd always wonder if I'd just quit. One was becoming functional in Hebrew, two was getting a job in journalism, and three was doing the army, which would draft me in another three years—at my age, not for a stretch of a few years, thankfully, but of a few months. It was a way of at least partially paying some dues I owed. All in all, I was signing on for a very, very belated rite of passage. As for my mother and the rest of my family, I thought it wouldn't hurt to put some distance between them and myself for a while; I just wish it hadn't been so much distance for so long.

One of the things that struck me about Jerusalem right away was the sky: It was more intensely blue than any I'd ever seen. It looked lower, too, closer to the earth.

CHAPTER TWO

LAND OF UNCOMPLICATED JEWS

My first impression of Israel in January 1985 was that it was okay, materially, but it wasn't America; it looked more like my idea of 1961 Hungary. The apartment buildings, except in Jerusalem, with its stone-tile exteriors, were these squat blocks of corroded beige stucco tenements with lines of laundry hanging out of the windows, water heaters sticking up out of the roofs, and aluminum shutters enclosing the balconies, which made a residential street look like a row of old air conditioners. Because the economy was heavily protectionist, all the products available were Made in Israel and there wasn't much to choose from, so everybody's apartment looked pretty much the same: the same dark brown furniture, same white or brown appliances, lots of plants, and 10,000 paintings and tchotchkes on the walls. Everybody dressed the same, too: one brand of winter coat, one or two styles of biblical sandals in summer, two or three kinds of shoes, and one kind of boots and slippers. The men still wore the collars of their white or light blue shirts flattened and splayed out, Ben-Gurion-style, the single ugliest adult fashion style I've ever seen in my life.

But except for the corroded stucco and the collars, I liked what I saw: a non-materialistic society, a semi-socialist country. A bus ride cost less than a dime, and middle-class people rode them. The simplicity of the kibbutzim, with their little boxy houses and communal dining rooms and murals, seemed noble. The TV news announcers and reporters weren't glamorous or even good-looking, they didn't chat and laugh; they intoned, like on CBS in the '50s, and there was only one, state-run channel, with no commercials but lots of talk shows and concerts, like PBS. The prime minister of the country, Shimon Peres, described himself proudly as a socialist.

But there was a less attractive side to this austere, purposeful culture that I would discover soon enough. The work ethic was shocking; Israel seemed like a nation of listless clerks. When something didn't work, when somebody didn't do his job, which was all the time, the expression I kept hearing was *mah la'asot?*—what can you do? Once I went to see a movie that was advertised in the paper, and when I got to the ticket counter it wasn't playing. "But the paper said it was playing," I insisted to the gray-haired, sullen clerk. "You believe everything you read in the papers?" he shot back, unblinking.

Getting a job required *protekzia*, connections, and my cousins were always trying to help me, calling somebody they knew who might know somebody who knew somebody. That's how people found jobs. Nobody I met had a college degree, which was strange in a place called a Jewish state. People were looking to land some steady, reasonably paying job, to manage not to get fired for 30 days, and then they had *kviyut*, tenure. "Then you're set. They can't touch you," as an older cousin put it. This was unionism at its paralyzing worst: You didn't get fired for doing a lousy job, and you didn't get promoted for doing a good job, only for seniority and kissing the right asses—so why not do a lousy job? The results were right there on the surface—not just in the irritated droopiness of the clerks, but in the appalling shoddiness of the built environment, not only the buildings but even the sidewalks. I don't know that the building trades have improved much since; when they were putting up our apartment in Modi'in, I had to point out to the plasterers that in the hallway, there wasn't one angle anywhere close to 90 degrees. I met some young British building tradesmen traveling through Israel and working short-term jobs to pay their way, guys who'd trained and apprenticed for years before they were allowed to lay a floor tile in England, and one of them described what it was like working for Israeli contractors: "They don't give a fuck about the quality. They just want it done as soon as possible. All you hear from them is *'chick chock, yalla yalla'*—'hurry up, come on.'" I'd heard, and would see for myself, that the doctors, lawyers, professors, and others in the prestigious professions were very good, and those at the top of those fields were world-class—but below those levels, Israelis tended to be mediocre or worse at their jobs. (The exception, I consistently found, was teachers, where Israelis' down-to-earth, sociable personality make them naturals. My Hebrew teachers were great, most of my kids' teachers have been great, the guy who lectured us for four hours in traffic school even made that interesting.) The common explanation for this huge gap in quality between "academic" work and "non-academic" work was that socialism or not, Jews were Jews, they didn't respect *shleppers*, and there may be something to that.

Neither did Israelis respect employees who were willing to do any crappy job that had to be done: In America that showed commitment; in Israel it showed you were the sorriest of creatures, a *freier*, a sucker—that you didn't respect your own worth. After I quit my first job at a left-wing magazine in Tel Aviv, a co-worker, a German Jewish immigrant, asked me what my plans were, and I said I was thinking about radio, which I'd never worked in. "Maybe I'll go to Voice of Israel and offer to come in and work part-time for free, just to learn the ropes, and see if anything comes of it," I said. She told me, "If you offer to work for free, they'll have you making coffee and running errands and nothing more, because in this country a person who works for free is a freier, and a freier is not someone to be respected."

Israel in 1985 wasn't a Third World country by any means, but it wasn't a First World country, either. People's ambition was to have an adventure in the army, then find a job through someone they knew, get kviyut, then stay there until they were pensioned off, then take their big trip to Disneyland, Universal Studios, the Grand Canyon, and Niagara Falls, and that was basically it. That's what young Israelis wanted, too, only with more traveling. That was the limit of their dreams, at least the Israelis I was coming into contact with, who weren't the doctors, lawyers, and professors. It was dispiriting; the country was 37 years old when I got here, yet it seemed old, much older than America—and much older than it seems now. The inefficiency was maddening; if you didn't have a home phone number, you would spend literally years on a waiting list before you got one, and it would cost you two weeks' salary. Though I was relieved at the absence of American-style money-madness, hucksterism, and competitiveness (all of which would come later), after a few months I decided, for the first time in my heretofore American life, that capitalism, with all its horrible faults, was better than socialism.

There was another problem I came up against before long: the Israeli personality. Though the abrasiveness has since eased off considerably, in those days it was hard to take. It seemed to be embedded in the language. I noticed that when Israelis talked to me in (usually broken) English, they would be very nice, but when they switched to Hebrew they often reverted to routine, casual aggression. Later on, in my army reserve unit there was a veteran South African immigrant, a kibbutznik who, in the company of other English-speakers, was perfectly polite, but one time when he, an Israeli, and I were talking with each other in Hebrew, and I asked, "Does the bus go straight to Jerusalem, or does it stop along the way?" the South African turned to me and said, "Why are you talking nonsense? Of course it goes straight to Jerusalem." *Why are you talking nonsense, what are you talking about? Have you gone crazy? Did you fall and crack your head?* These were the kinds of responses you often got from Israelis to the simplest question or remark; this was the way they talked to each other in those days, and it was very, very rough on Western ears. "For the first five years I couldn't talk to these people at all," a British woman who'd immigrated in the '50s and married an Israeli told me by way of encouragement. There were therapy groups for mixed Western-Israeli marriages, which came down to solving the problem of the Israeli husband walking all over his surprised, unprepared Western wife.

You could see, though, that they weren't bad people. They really did help you when you needed it, and they were always offering. There wasn't that coldness and distance you find in big-city America, not in Jerusalem, Tel Aviv, or any other part of the country. They were down-to-earth, they weren't stuck-up, and what you saw was what you got—they weren't phonies. The kids were unusually affectionate and unguarded. The fathers doted on their children in a way that American fathers, on the whole, didn't, at least not when I was growing up. And while people yelled and got angry a lot, they weren't violent (with each other). Several times I'd object to some fellow cutting in line or making too much noise, he'd lay into me verbally, and I'd get ready to fight, because in America when somebody gets in your face like that, the next step is to square off—but not in Israel. Israelis didn't kill each other on the streets or in their homes like Americans did. The people were hard on my nerves, but I also felt surrounded by a warmth I'd never felt in big-city California, to say the least. I sensed I wouldn't be allowed to hit the skids in Israel like I would in the United States. Much of this had to do with my extended family, my uncles and cousins, who took me into their hearts.

One of the weird things I discovered about Israelis was their relationship to money. Between seller and buyer, when negotiations were involved and a lot of money was at stake, I learned to be scared to death; these people were sharks. And when Israelis have the money to pay what they owe you, they will, but when they don't, well, why shouldn't you suffer along with them? What makes you special? I know three Western immigrants whose businesses went under back then because clients didn't pay. In Tel Aviv my wife and I had a plumber who would come to us right away, anytime we had a problem, and when we told him this was rare for an Israeli plumber, he explained,

"You Americans [my wife is South African] are the only customers I've got who pay me on the spot, who I don't have to chase."

But there was another side to this issue. When there was no scarcity and no tug of war for the money, Israelis were incredibly trusting and generous. You'd walk into a shop and there would be no one behind the counter; the owner or clerk knew that no one would go into his cash register. On the bus, people would pass the fare from passenger to passenger until it reached the driver, who would pass the change back the same way. Strangers weren't strangers like they were in America. Once I needed change for the parking meter and asked a couple of men standing on the sidewalk, and they didn't have change for my bill, but one of them insisted on giving me a 10-shekel coin—about $2.50—to put in the meter. Another incident showed me how for Israelis, it really isn't the money, it really is the principle of the thing: In Jerusalem I saw a cab driver, a big guy of Mizrahi (Middle Eastern) Jewish heritage, shlepping the suitcases and boxes of a newly arrived Russian immigrant, a small, older man, up three flights of stairs to the man's apartment. At the end, the Russian, who didn't speak or understand more than a few words of Hebrew, paid the cabbie the flat rate for the fare, without any tip for hauling his belongings up all those stairs. The cab driver started protesting, the Russian stood his ground, and soon the cab driver was enraged, shouting, leaning into the little man with his fists balled behind his back; he was restraining himself from killing the guy. I'd been watching this in the parking lot, and I went over and asked what was going on, they told me, and I told the Russian immigrant, who spoke a little English, that he had to give the cabbie a tip. The Russian asked how much, and I told him 20 shekels. He took out a 20-shekel bill and handed it to the cab driver—but the cab driver pushed it away, shaking his head. He refused to take it. After all that rage and near-bloodshed, it wasn't about money for him, it was about being treated fairly.

They have good hearts, Israelis. They're good people. Amos Oz said in a speech a few years ago, "If I am fated to fall in the street one day, I want to fall on a street in Israel. Not in London, not in Paris, not in Berlin, and not in New York. Here, people will pick me up." That's absolutely true, and it was readily apparent to me when I arrived. But there were other, disconcerting things about Israelis I also saw right off. The eyes. So many Israelis had a hardness in their eyes, often an anger, that was off-putting. Often a blankness, too. These were not what I thought of as Jewish eyes. There seemed to be no irony there, no doubt, no thoughtfulness, either—just practicality and toughness. And it wasn't my imagination; Israelis, it turned out, were not like the Jews I'd known. Arthur Koestler, a genuine Israelophile, wrote something amazingly prescient about the Israeli personality in November 1948 in the *Manchester Guardian,* titled "The Native Generation":

> In his mental make-up the average young sabra is fearless to the point of recklessness, bold, extroverted, and little inclined towards, if not openly contemptuous of, intellectual pursuits. The children are particularly good-looking; after puberty, however, their features and voices coarsen and seem never quite to reach the balance of maturity. The typical sabra's face has something unfinished about it: the still undetermined character of a race in transition. The sabra's outlook on the world is rather provincial and hyper-chauvinistic. This could hardly be otherwise in a small and exposed pioneer community which had to defend its physical existence and its State against almost impossible odds. One cannot create a nation without nationalism. . . . (O)ne thing seems fairly certain: within a generation or two Israel will have become an entirely "un-Jewish" country.[1]

I don't know about the "unfinished" part, but Israeli facial features are certainly tough, though I wouldn't say coarse, and I would say their voices do tend to grow hoarse, or at least they used to, from all that yelling. In all, I think Koestler saw it clearly: The native Israeli, in his essence, down to the cast of his face, was fundamentally

---

1. Arthur Koestler, "The Native Generation," *Manchester Guardian,* November 19, 1948.

different from the Diaspora Jew. In her autobiography, *My Life*, the American-bred Golda Meir made a similar observation (though in altogether glowing terms) about the sabras, or native-born. Quoting from a speech she gave to a conference of Diaspora Zionists in 1946, she told how native-born Israeli youths had risked their lives without a second thought to carry Holocaust survivors ashore from their illegal immigration ships. "They are strangers to casuistry and abstract precepts," she said. "They are plain and pure as the sun of Palestine. For them, matters are simple, clear and uncomplicated."

Simple, clear, and uncomplicated: How much more un-Jewish could you get? This was a real virtue to the old Zionists—not to be like the Diaspora Jews, with their neuroses. Amos Oz told the *New Yorker*'s David Remnick in 2004 that this was the way members of the kibbutz he joined as a teenager indoctrinated newcomers: "[T]he idea was always transmitted to me that you will have to be completely different. You will have to be simple, uncomplicated tractor drivers and soldiers."[2]

I suppose I tried briefly to find the virtue in this way of being. But after 33 years as a complicated, neurotic son of Polish Jewish immigrants, I stopped trying pretty soon and admitted to myself that these were just not my kind of people. They were like what I thought of as Middle Americans, goyim, only non-violent (again, with each other) and much more verbose. As Arthur Miller described heartland Americans, Israelis were "the unalienated." The majority in their own country. Insiders. There were other things about the native personality I didn't like: The people didn't listen; they didn't let you finish a sentence. In conversation, they just seemed to be waiting to make their ever-ready set of points, and whatever you might say didn't cause them to modify those points, or become particularly curious about yours. "Israelis have no inner life. They just have opinions, and their opinions never change," as an American relative described the older generation some years ago. On top of that,

---

2. David Remnick, "Amos Oz Writes the Story of Israel," *New Yorker*, November 8, 2004.

their use of language, while copious, was impoverished and loaded down with clichés. They were also very straight, in the '60s meaning of the term—they wrote off unusual ideas or behavior as *shtuyot*, nonsense, they never allowed themselves to be vulnerable, to make light of themselves, they didn't let themselves go; the Ashkenazi males danced like they were wearing backpacks. My favorite celebrity in those days was Ariel Zilber, a raw-voiced singer-songwriter who would go wild onstage, dancing around on his prosthetic leg; he didn't care what anyone thought of him. Very un-Israeli. (Zilber has since gotten religion and become an Arab-hating fascist; I'm not sure what the moral is there.) Another thing about Israelis: Their moods hardly seemed to vary; they either felt sunny or pissed off. They were outgoing, warm, and talkative but didn't seem to have much depth or reserve; when you met an Israeli the fourth time, it wasn't much different from meeting him the first time. An American online commenter, a Judeophile but not an Israelophile, remarked that while the Diaspora Jews she knew tended to have all sorts of subtlety, the Israelis she'd met were "binary" types. It was an amazing contradiction: Israel was such an interesting country, and Israelis, just by being here, lived such eventful lives, yet in person I often found them to be fairly predictable and boring, I'm sorry to say.

Today I don't have the same problems with the people that I had before, except for their noisiness and inconsideration in public, which is still beyond the pale. Otherwise, I find that on balance, they're okay. Some of the change in my attitude has to do with my becoming comfortable in Hebrew, and thus able to appreciate Israeli humor, which new immigrants don't and which can be damn funny in its blunt or offbeat way. (The offbeat arrived in Israel in the '90s.) And maybe I've changed, assimilated, though I don't notice it, nor do my old friends and family—but at the very least the culture shock has long worn off me. Still, I'm convinced that the main reason I'm more at ease with Israelis is that *they've* changed. A few months after I got here a close friend came to visit, and he was questioning my decision to stay. "Larry," he said as we waded into the Tel Aviv surf, "these people are nuts." I couldn't disagree. They were shouting and arguing all the time; they were hearty, earthy, and unreasonable, like drunken peasants except that they didn't drink; how could I live in such a backward country? That was then. But come around 2000, that perceptive American relative of mine who'd commented on older Israelis' absence of inner lives offered another observation: "Israelis under 50 are sane." By 2000 I couldn't disagree with that either. Now, 17 years later, this would mean that Israelis under 67 are sane. So much sane behavior in this country, it's going to plotz from sanity. The people aren't peasants anymore, their children and grandchildren go to college, they travel abroad, they're hooked in to global culture. They've even become nice. If Israel wasn't a First World country in 1985, if it wasn't like America then, it is today. So I think the main reason I get along much better with Israelis now is not because I've become more like them; it's because they've become more like me.

But however rough a time I had with the people here before, it was never enough to make me seriously consider going back to America. It was so exciting being an immigrant. I loved walking the streets of Jerusalem. My family here was a real anchor. My friends were Western immigrants like me; we were on a great adventure together. I was in one of the world's most interesting places, where one of the world's most compelling stories was playing out—and one day, I would be writing about it. Also, I knew the folks back home thought I'd done something pretty special, and I definitely felt the same way. If anyone asked me how I liked Israel during my first couple of years here, I would have said: as a symbol, as a cause, great; as a day-to-day society, trying; as the setting for my life, heaven.

The Zionist indoctrination I received at the Jerusalem absorption center, Ulpan Etzion, required no hard sell. Like nearly all my 100 or so fellow immigrant boarders, I believed in the justice of Israel's fight against its enemies; if I didn't, why would I be there? This Labor-Likud thing, the debate over the settlements—this was a tactical argument among allies; when it came to Israel versus the Palestinians, or versus any Arab entity, or versus Israel's biased critics abroad like Dan Rather and Tom Brokaw (even "moderates" told me they were anti-Israel, and I believed it) then there was no argument. We indoctrinated one another.

In Hebrew class we learned, among other things, Israeli history, which meant Israeli heroism—Hannah Senesh, who parachuted behind Nazi lines and was tortured to death; the "Lamed Heh," the Haganah fighters killed trying to rescue Gush Etzion in the War of Independence; the "silver platter," poet Natan Alterman's poignant metaphor for the youth killed fighting in that war. We had a brilliant teacher in my class, Simcha, who kept her right-wing politics in check except for once describing then-Knesset member and ex-terrorist Geula Cohen as a great woman. Once, when a student made a critical remark about the settlements, Simcha said, with a gleam in her eye, "I'm not allowed to present my political views in class, but if I could, I would demolish what you just said." She taught us to write down in Hebrew: "When I lived in [country of origin] I had my family, my friends, and a nice life, but in Israel I have my own country, where I am at home."

We learned about the holidays, and on Yom Hashoah we had the lesson sitting in a circle outside on the lawn; we sang "Eli, Eli," and then stood together when the siren sounded. Everything just seemed heightened; the grass and the building stones seemed imbued with history, everything that surrounded me had been built under pressure, under threat of annihilation, and with the highest purpose. In the two minutes we stood silent, our heads bowed, I tried my best, as I would for many years, to call up images of my mother, of photos of my lost relatives, of random images of Jewish refugees' faces—to immerse myself in Holocaust grief, on cue.

I watched the televised ceremonies for Yom Hashoah and Memorial Day with my relatives, and what struck me was the heavy melodrama, the motionless undertaker's expression on the faces of all the speakers and announcers, the unchanging somberness and sorrowfulness in their voices. This was not how people look and sound when they're aggrieved; it's how they look and sound when they're trying to give an impression of grief. It was the oratorical equivalent of cantorial singing: stylized grief. This should have been obvious to everyone; politicians, emcees, and anchormen who do these ceremonies year after year, who are professionals at it, who are taking cues from technicians, are putting on a show for the folks sitting in the audience and watching at home. That's not to say they have no feelings about the victims of the Holocaust or Israel's wars; I'm sure they do, and I'm sure that when they do, it doesn't look or sound like their performances at these ceremonies. They really schmaltzed things up. Yet everybody kept a straight face. And everybody watched; me too. And believe me, I didn't make these sorts of observations to anybody I was watching with; I didn't like even thinking these sorts of thoughts and kept trying to push them out of my mind.

Another, much lighter nationalistic ritual in those days involved rooting for the Israeli performer in the annual Eurovision Song Contest; another was cheering for Israel's European Cup contender, the Maccabi Tel Aviv basketball team. But this wasn't an Israeli thing so much as it was a feature of living in a small country; Slovenians and Cameroonians go crazy, too, for their hometown entries in any foreign competition. Yet in Israel, the smallness of the country, in comparison to the size of the neighboring, enemy countries, is linked to the country's nationalism, militarism, paranoia, and social cohesion, which is not found—not to this degree, anyway—in other small countries. In short, Israelis rooting for Israel at Eurovision was a much more politically charged act than, say, the Maltese rooting for Malta.

Politically, it was an optimistic time. In July 1985, after inflation had reached an annual rate of 1,000 percent, the government agreed to a "package deal," a combination of radical devaluation of the shekel, steep cuts in government spending, and wage and price freezes, and it worked astoundingly well. Almost overnight, inflation was cut to 30 percent and soon to 20 percent, lower than it had been in many years; the economy had been saved. Together with the Free Trade Agreement signed with the United States earlier in the year, the package deal marked the beginning of the end of Israeli socialism. The price of a bus ride began multiplying. The kibbutzim and Histadrut began turning into shadows of themselves. Beyond that, Israel was on its way to what Peres much later would call "swinish capitalism." At about the same time, Israel pulled the army out of most of Lebanon, concentrating the thousands of remaining troops in a "security zone" in the south of the country, leading people into the delusion that the three-year Lebanon War was over. It would be 15 bloody years later when Israel actually ended the war by pulling its troops out of the "security zone" as well.

With the Palestinians, nothing was happening—no violence to speak of and no peace process, except for the mandatory blabber. Nobody was talking about a Palestinian state. Between the package deal and the "end" of the Lebanon War, Peres was very popular; he seemed a masterful leader. I loved him. A close cousin of mine was a translator in his office, so he was like family. I went to a symposium at Haifa University on Saul Bellow's writing, which was held in the presence of the novelist and the prime minister; Peres spent *six hours* of his day there, listening. How could you not love a prime minister who would do something like that? Peres got up to speak in praise of "Sa-ool Baa-low" and literature in general, saying "a book is like a ship, you sail aboard it to distant lands" or something. In the United States, they had Reagan. I felt so privileged, so lucky.

I also went to hear the dark alien of Israeli politics, Meir Kahane, then a Knesset member. Naturally, there were a lot of American immigrants in attendance. A big New Yorker in my ulpan class, Reuven, was Kahane's proud bodyguard. A guy I knew warned me, "His ideas are crazy, but boy is he charismatic." That's what everybody said about Kahane. Standing in the crowd inside the Jerusalem hall, I was shocked at how unimpressive, how transparently phony he was, declaiming his outrage at how his beloved nation had been debased by its leaders' iniquity. He was gesticulating, grimacing, gritting his teeth, muttering ancient curses under his breath. "Chaim Herzog, *yemach shemo* . . . Teddy Kollek, *yemach shemo*," he said, wishing the president of Israel and mayor of Jerusalem's names to be erased. The crowd, of course, loved him. I didn't get it.

In America, I'd believed, like all American Jews did, that Israeli racism was confined to the pro-Kahane fringe; otherwise Israelis fought and killed the Arabs only because they had to; they didn't hate them just because they were Arabs. Then a couple weeks after I arrived, I was standing outside Ulpan Etzion, and an elderly lady sitting on a bench started talking to me in broken English, asking why I came to Israel, congratulating me on my aliyah—and suddenly she got angry at a boy of about 12 standing nearby. "Get away from her," she snapped. The boy just smiled. "Look, he's talking to the Jewish girl," the woman said. The boy was Arab. I turned away and said— quietly, so she couldn't hear—"What is this, Alabama in 1911?" A couple of weeks later, I was visiting cousins in Haifa, and two of them from out of town, a middle-class couple in their 30s and their two young daughters, with whom I really hit it off, showed me around the north. We ended up in Nazareth, and the husband parked the car in an alley. I was sitting in the passenger seat, and in those younger days of mine I used to fling open car doors and sort of catapult myself out, so I flung open the door—and it caught an Arab man passing by in the ribs, full force. It sent him hurtling forward until he slumped over the hood of a car parked up ahead. I went to him and asked if he was okay, and he didn't move or say anything. I asked again, and finally he straightened up slowly, an unshaven Arab man of about 50, and gave me a pained smile, raised his hand as if to say it was all right, and shuffled away. I felt horrible, of course, and it must have shown on my face, because the wife, standing with her family outside their car, said with a big smile, "Why are you sad? We were laughing." The husband, smiling cynically, said, "You should have killed him." The two young daughters smiled along with their parents. I got into the car and didn't say anything, I'm ashamed to recall.

This was a kind of raw, wanton racism that I'd never seen in the United States; it was out of a movie set in the American '50s. And

I had no idea it existed in Israel. These were just two "isolated incidents," as they say. Very few Israelis would react like the old woman in Jerusalem and my cousins visiting Nazareth did. But that it could happen—that Israelis, normal, average Israelis, my cousins, could act that way in broad daylight, could get the idea that such behavior was permissible—said something about Israeli society as a whole that left me with a hollow feeling.

But it passed soon enough. I was a real Zionist in those days. I preferred to date sabra girls, I would only fly El Al, and I even planned on buying a Susita, the Israeli Edsel, of which there were still a few models sitting around somewhere. I adopted the belief that the only fit place for a Jew to live was Israel—not because of anti-Semitism abroad, which I knew was negligible, but because it was the only country where a Jew could give his full loyalty, where he was at home and not a foreign national of sorts, where the country was his, not somebody else's. Once I put the killer Zionist question to my older sister Suzie in L.A.: If Israel were at war with America, which side would you be on? "Don't be a fanatic," she said, understandably impatient. "Israel and America aren't going to war with each other." My old cousin Yankif, a National Religious Party man, would tell me how he often asked my older brother Armand, a prominent, veteran civil rights lawyer in the South and Washington, DC, why he devoted his life to helping other people instead of his own— and soon enough I agreed with Yankif. I came to believe that Jewish life in the Diaspora was inauthentic, no matter what you were doing, and that the only country in which a Jew could be his authentic self was the Jewish state. It's hard for me now to believe I could have actually swallowed such nonsense—and not for a month or two, but for a good couple of years.

Politically, I was quite the Labor hawk, ready to divide the territories with the Palestinians or Jordanians, but very tough on terror. The occupation was awkward, it had to be solved, but it was something that had been forced on Israel, as I saw it, by Palestinian and pan-Arab aggression, which certainly hadn't disappeared. The settlers and yahoos of the right left me cold; they were zealots, picking fights for no reason—but the army's presence in the West Bank and Gaza was unfortunately necessary because the Palestinians didn't recognize Israel and were always plotting terror attacks against us. We were on the defensive, I believed—and I loved being there. At long last. Shortly after I decided to stay in Israel, we were on an ulpan field trip to the Knesset, we were getting off the bus, there was snow on the ground, and the thought ran through my mind: *Thank God I don't have to be a liberal anymore. Over here, my side is the underdog.*

I was still in the throes of '60s revisionism—I didn't want to be a leftist, didn't want to always apologize, to always give in, to always be the guilty one, to always justify the other side's anger, hatred and violence against me and mine, whether it was the Vietnamese, the Salvadorans and Nicaraguans, or the blacks. I wanted to be a little staunch for once, a little proud, and firm, too. No compromise on Jerusalem, no slack toward terror. I told my friend visiting from California that America and Israel were the two best countries on earth. When I first heard of Peace Now, I didn't like them, identifying these leftists with those of my generation. Then when I found out that they all served in the army, usually in combat units, I fell in love with the Israeli peace movement. I saw myself as being on the right wing of Peace Now. Without knowing it, I was still extremely concerned with "positioning," with choosing a political stance at least partly because of the image it conferred on me, and because of the kind of allies and enemies it gave me—and the position I liked, my political comfort zone, was on the left, but on the "muscular" end of it.

I got a job as managing editor of *New Outlook,* a left-wing, English-language magazine that was read by a few hundred people, and survived on subsidies from the socialist, kibbutz-centered Mapam party and donations from aged East Coast veterans of the socialist Zionist movement Hashomer Hatzair. *New Outlook* was a sleepy operation that purported to publish 10 issues a year but usually published about seven. They had a big suite of offices near the beach in Tel Aviv and a full-time staff of nearly 10; such was Israeli socialism at the time. The ads were so funny—page after page of them for kibbutz-manufactured irrigation systems, pumps, and other farm equipment, pitched to an audience of retired East Coast Jewish intellectuals; the reason was that Mapam, in return for its subsidies to *New Outlook*, got free ad space. The magazine was known for advocacy of a Palestinian state and negotiations with the PLO. It wasn't a good publication; the articles tended to be dry and academic. The one important journalist who had worked there was former editor in chief Simha Flapan, a pioneer among Israeli "new historians." Still, it was good that *New Outlook* existed; it was way ahead of its time. When I was offered the job, I thought the magazine might be too left wing for me, but the charismatic editor in chief, Chaim Shur, a kibbutz wheel and former editor of the Mapam-backed newspaper, assured me that since I was in favor of territorial compromise, there wouldn't be a problem.

He turned out to be wrong. One of my colleagues soon dubbed me the in-house "voice of the right." I was happy to edit stories that bashed the settlers and the occupation, and I came to see nothing wrong about negotiating with the PLO toward a Palestinian state, once they cleaned up their act. But the people who ran the magazine were so eager to foster dialogue with the Palestinians—I tried to cut the use of the word "dialogue" to three or four times per article, which took some editing—that they never criticized the Palestinians. They treated them with kid gloves. I got into arguments over terminology; I wanted to use the word "terror," but the accepted term was "armed struggle." I began to feel I was doing wrong by my newly adopted country. Finally, the magazine's editorial board decided to run an exceptionally long article by Afif Safieh, then a Harvard academic and later a leading PLO diplomat, in which he slammed the Arab world for not fighting Israel hard enough and leaving the Palestinians alone in the field. In the same issue, they were going to run an ad for the *Journal of Palestinian Studies* that highlighted an article by ultra-terrorist George Habash. That was it. I told Chaim I was quitting due to political incompatibility and gave him a month's notice. He tried to talk me into staying, and when that didn't work, the business manager, an old gentleman named Baruch Fishman, who had yet more charisma and Eastern

European Yiddish charm than Chaim, took his shot. Every morning I'd go into Baruch's office and he'd pour the vodka and cut up the apple slices and we'd talk. I loved Baruch; again, I felt surrounded by warmth. But the magazine's editorial board had voted to publish Safieh's article; they couldn't go back on it now, I was told. So I left the magazine and spent the next six months unemployed. In retrospect, I did the right thing given my political beliefs at the time. Today, though, I would have no problem working at a magazine that published Safieh's article, while the terms "armed struggle" and "terror" have become interchangeable for me.

Finally, I got a job at the Technion-Israel Institute of Technology in Haifa, putting out their English-language fundraising material. For the first and last time, I would have an inside view of the "partnership"—a word that was to the Technion fundraising department what "dialogue" was to *New Outlook*—between rich Diaspora Jews, mainly Americans, and their Israeli recipients. What I saw was a black comedy. Another thing I saw while I was there: The 20 years of quiet that Israel had enjoyed from the Palestinians under its control would come to an end. There were lively times ahead for both sides. Also deadly times, but mainly for the other side.

CHAPTER THREE

HUMILIATIONS

The first apartment I rented in Haifa was right on the seam line between a Jewish neighborhood and an Arab one in the city's Kababir neighborhood, up on the ridge of the Carmel Mountains overlooking the Mediterranean Sea. Of the dozen or so families in our building, two were Arab—one Christian, one Muslim. I got to know the Christian family pretty well, especially their son, who naturally wanted to talk about American sports. As far as I knew, everyone in the building got along. I'd see one of the Jews gabbing with one of the Arabs, complaining about the upkeep of the building like neighbors will. On Saturday, when all the Jewish shops were closed, I'd go to the grocery store at the edge of the Arab neighborhood, near the mosque, a couple of hundred yards from my front door. After a year my landlord decided to sell the apartment, and I went to tell the Christian family and say goodbye. "Oh no," the father groaned. "First of all, I'm sorry to lose you as a neighbor. Second, I'm worried that Muslims are going to rent the apartment." I figured my living arrangement had been pretty exotic but didn't realize to what extent. In my time in Israel, I've lived in eight different apartments in five cities, and that year in Kababir was the only time I've lived with Arabs in my building or neighborhood—which was one time more than the overwhelming majority of Israeli Jews have ever experienced. The way I live now, in a city that's 100 percent Jewish, is the Israeli norm.

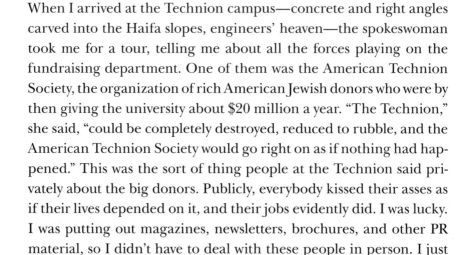

When I arrived at the Technion campus—concrete and right angles carved into the Haifa slopes, engineers' heaven—the spokeswoman took me for a tour, telling me about all the forces playing on the fundraising department. One of them was the American Technion Society, the organization of rich American Jewish donors who were by then giving the university about $20 million a year. "The Technion," she said, "could be completely destroyed, reduced to rubble, and the American Technion Society would go right on as if nothing had happened." This was the sort of thing people at the Technion said privately about the big donors. Publicly, everybody kissed their asses as if their lives depended on it, and their jobs evidently did. I was lucky. I was putting out magazines, newsletters, brochures, and other PR material, so I didn't have to deal with these people in person. I just had to kiss their asses in print. I took the job despite my reservations about working in PR, but figured it was just for a couple of years until I learned enough Hebrew to work as a reporter; meanwhile, the Technion did good work, I reasoned, so there was no shame in writing good things about it. That's what I figured fundraising for the Technion was about: telling donors how wonderful the Technion was. I would find out that fundraising for the Technion was almost solely about telling the donors how wonderful they were.

I didn't deal with them one-on-one, but I saw them in action plenty. Some of the heavy hitters were real terrors, and nobody ever dared make a peep to them. One of the biggest donors was David Azrieli, the Israeli Canadian who became Israel's shopping-mall king and whose trio of high-rise Azrieli Towers are the pride of the Tel Aviv skyline. I saw the annual newsletter of the Canadian Technion Society, of which Azrieli was president, and as I recall it was 12 pages long, with 13 photos of him. During some fundraising event on campus, a couple of men on the fundraising staff of the Canadian Technion Society's Montreal chapter, regular working stiffs, told me how abusive he was to them. "I got to the point where I wasn't sleeping at night," said one.

But the worst was a Sheldon Adelson type, someone whose contemptuousness and domineering personality was right there on his face, not to mention in his voice. After an American Technion Society event on campus, a colleague told me she'd asked him if he'd enjoyed the breakfast. "He said 'no.' Period. Just like that."

I saw him abuse one of my colleagues something awful at a Board of Governors meeting. This is the annual big event for the universities, when they give out the honorary doctorates and honorary fellowships to the major donors (and to some political or cultural figure to add star power, as well as to a couple of actual scientists), and the donors get to sit with administrators in so-called strategy sessions to plot the university's direction for the coming year. In fact these are charades the Technion puts on to make the donors feel important. ("I give them the mushroom treatment—keep them in the dark and feed them plenty of bullshit," said the Technion's president at the time, privately.) The strategy session on fundraising would produce weeks of high anxiety in my department; everyone was afraid the donors would zero in on the performance in their area of responsibility. The meeting was held in the auditorium of the Coler Visitor Center, a glorified gift shop that the Technion built because Mr. Coler was donating $3 million, and for whatever reason it was decided the money would go for a visitor center, which, of course, no technological institute can do without.

Walking into the auditorium, accompanied by his escort from the American Technion Society and greeted by the fundraising department's manager of the Coler Center, the donor in question looked at a map of the world displayed at the entrance, with its tiny light bulbs marking all the cities that had Technion Society chapters. "Why are some of these lights not on?" the donor asked. In all the frenzied polishing of plaques and campus-wide primping that takes place before the Board of Governors meeting, some of the tiny lights on the map in the Coler Center weren't working. The manager of the center apologized to the donor and said he would get it seen to ASAP. "When?" demanded the donor, and the manager apologized again and promised he would take care of it as soon as the meeting was over. "These are some of the most important donors in the world!" the donor cried. "Fix it," his American escort ordered the manager. And the manager, a former American rabbi who told me he'd quit that profession because he couldn't take the synagogue politics, ran off to find an electrician to fix the little lights in the map. Later, while the fundraising meeting was underway, he came into the auditorium and hustled his way down the aisle, probably to give the donor's escort a progress report. His face was glowing red with humiliation.

This bully and some of the other big donors gave the head of the fundraising department, Pini Pinchasi, a retired Israel Navy brigadier general, the treatment once. They didn't like him, they didn't think he was doing a good job, he wasn't smooth, his accent and English weren't good enough, he wasn't their type. And at one of these strategy sessions a few of them were up on the panel with Pini, grilling him, putting him on the defensive, and Pini accidentally touched the arm of the man sitting next to him. The man pulled back, as if he didn't want to be touched by this tainted creature, as if Pini had cooties. Some of the donors in the auditorium started laughing, then a lot more joined in, and finally Pini—trying to save his dignity by pretending they were just ribbing him and he could take it—joined in, too, laughing like Pagliacci. Later that afternoon he sat alone in his office for a long time, staring at his desk. I went in to see him. He didn't try to hide what had happened. "They may do that to everybody else, but not to me," he said, and I was glad to see that his pride wasn't broken.

The Technion's "message" that I was helping to impart was not strictly political; in fact we never made any mention of political issues, certainly not the occupation. But as with Modi'in, the politics of the Technion, to a large degree, was embedded in the foundations of the place—in the research it was conducting, much of which was military-related, and in the supply of top scientists it provided the IDF and the country's arms companies. In other words, whatever opinions individual administrators or professors or students might have, the Technion had a clear institutional interest in Israel remaining militarily engaged—and not just Israel, but the many countries to which Israel sold arms. Also, the message that the Technion was crucial to Israel's defense—to its "very survival," as the deathless cliché goes—was, of course, a guaranteed winner with the donors. And so the PR I was writing stressed over and over that the Technion was "vital to Israel's readiness for the 21st century technological battlefield." And that the Technion was a proud subcontractor in America's Star Wars project. And that the Technion was central to the development of Israel's first homemade fighter jet, the Lavie (which ended up being scrapped). One of my colleagues told me that when she saw the Lavie's maiden test flight on TV, she shed tears of pride.

The inherent politics of the Technion, as a major Israeli institution, one that truly is vital to the country's military-industrial complex, and one whose overseas fundraising and academic connections depend greatly on Israel's image, was made explicit to me on the eve of Passover 1988. A few months before, the first intifada had begun, and Israel's image was taking a battering overseas like never before, with continual televised scenes of heavily armed soldiers and tanks putting down a rebellion by teenagers with slingshots. The employees in the administration building gathered for the traditional pre-Passover toast with the president. In his remarks, Dr. Max Reis, previously head of Israel Chemicals Ltd., noted that many of us would be going abroad for the holiday and that the issue of Israel's battle with the Palestinians could well come up in our conversations with people who wanted to hear what actual Israelis had to say. "Remember," the president told us. "Speak in one voice." All around me, people were nodding their heads.

Since then, not much seems to have changed politically at the Technion. In December 2014, the new president, Professor Peretz Lavie, wrote an op-ed telling of his dismay at all the BDS (boycott, divestment, and sanctions) activity he'd encountered on a tour of US and Canadian campuses. It was so bad, he wrote, that "the Jewish students themselves hardly take part in events on campus and are not showing much interest in workshops and programs aimed at training them to represent Israel on the PR level."[1] Shocking.

There was one thing, though, that I loved about working at the Technion: interviewing the academics about the research they were doing. Not the military stuff, but the non-military stuff, especially the medical- and health-related projects. Talking with them about their work, about the moments of scientific discovery, and about the potential their research held for helping cure diseases or helping people cope with disabilities—I left a few of those interviews feeling inspired. One medical researcher, Ella Lindenbaum, was working on a method for growing new tissue from a person's existing, healthy tissue, the aim of which was to heal burn victims without the need for skin grafts. She spoke drily and cautiously at first, but after a while she revealed the big dream that lay in the back of her mind: that the results of this project could be a breakthrough to curing a wide range of diseases, including cancer and heart disease. When I walked out of her office, I felt almost high.

Inside the administration building, though, where the work was all bureaucracy, I felt like I was getting a faint, non-violent impression of what living under Stalinism might have been like. Everyone was afraid of everyone else, not only of those above them but of those below them, of anybody who could spread unflattering stories about them and damage their standing. Everyone was ferociously protective of their standing. And by accidentally doing something that someone in power considered a slight to his standing, I, too, learned what it was to get humiliated.

_____

1. Peretz Lavie, "'Eviction Notice' for Israel on US Campuses," www.ynet news.com, December 22, 2014.

In a newsletter that went out to the donors, I mistakenly identified the dean of the graduate school as the "dean of graduate students." It seemed to me an error of no serious consequence. The dean, however, went to complain in person to the president. The spokeswoman, looking down at me as she descended the stairs to our floor, announced, "You blundered." The president told my boss that I had to apologize in person to the dean. And so I went to the dean's office, apologized, stayed for a couple minutes for a polite chat, then went back to my office and sat alone for a long time, staring at my desk. Pini tried to buck me up. A woman in the department told me how a very influential lady in fundraising, an Israeli this time, once treated her like her chauffeur, and how she ended up sitting in the car by herself, crying. This whole experience firmed up my intention to finish my self-apportioned two years in PR and get a job as a reporter, which is what would happen.

The Technion has since gone on to bigger things. Three of its professors have won, among them, two Nobel prizes. The university is partners with Cornell in a $2 billion technological grad school/ research center being built in New York City. The Technion is a great school. When I was there, I edited a book of papers on the future of engineering education presented by professors from many of the world's best technological institutes, including MIT; the paper by Ze'ev Tadmor, who would later become the Technion's president, was by far the best. I felt proud to be able to say that, and still do. As an Israeli, I'm proud of the Technion's academic prowess. I just wish it wasn't so closely wedded to the arms industry. And to these Sheldon Adelson-type donors. But then the Technion isn't unique for being in either of those marriages; the entire Israeli establishment is in them, and very happy to be.

When the intifada broke out in December 1987, it was a complete surprise to Israelis, me included. Yitzhak Rabin, the defense minister, put it down to "outside agitators," as if he was a Mississippi sheriff during the civil rights movement. The Palestinians had been so peaceful. My immigrant friends used to go to Hebron to buy the lovely, locally made crystal from the city's market. Once I took a shortcut through Hebron on the way back from the Negev to Jerusalem, without a thought. We all wandered freely through the Muslim Quarter of Jerusalem's Old City. I can't count the number of settlers who've told me they had the most wonderful relations with their Palestinian neighbors, how they used to visit each other's homes, until the intifada went and ruined everything. It was the "Jibril deal," the exchange of 1,150 Palestinian prisoners for 3 Israeli POWs, that filled the territories with radical terrorist leaders and ruined everything. It was the "Night of the Gliders," the deadly invasion of an IDF base by Palestinians flying in from Lebanon, that went to the Palestinians' heads. Anything, as Israeli historian Benny Morris put it, but the "all-pervading element of humiliation" that Israel was visiting on the Palestinians. Anything, as Morris wrote, but the "brute force, repression and fear, collaboration and treachery, beatings and torture chambers, and daily intimidation, humiliation, and manipulation"[2] that Israel had subjected them to for 20 years. In that way, Israelis were no different then than now: They're acutely aware of every assault they suffer at Arab hands, and dead to the incomparably greater assaults they inflict on Arabs. When I read now about those pre-intifada days, I'm struck by two things: how little we knew, or wanted to know, about what Israeli soldiers were actually doing in the West Bank and Gaza, and how much more brutal Israeli rule was in those days when the Palestinians were actually quite peaceful, and everyone seemed to get along not too badly.

Day after day that December, the headlines told of two, three, four Palestinians being shot to death by the army. There were full-scale riots across the West Bank and Gaza, and they weren't simmering down. A few years later, on my first day of army reserve duty in the Gaza Strip, one of the commanders told us, "When the first intifada started, the heads of the army thought that if we killed a

---

2. Benny Morris, *Righteous Victims* (New York: Vintage, 2001), 341.

lot of them right at the beginning, it would stop. But it only made them madder."

At first, at least, there was a substantial Israeli reaction against what the army was doing and a good deal of "understanding" for the Palestinians, even though they were throwing stones and at times Molotov cocktails. The reason for that show of sympathy by Israeli liberals, which is unimaginable now, was that Israel had never shown the Palestinians anything but its fist. As of that time, it had not made an attempt to negotiate peace with them. The clampdown on the West Bank and Gaza was total: Israeli soldiers ruled every alley of every refugee camp; Palestinian teenagers got arrested and tortured for hanging PLO flags or spraying pro-PLO graffiti on their own walls. Nobody outside the furthest fringe of the left had ever suggested recognizing the PLO or countenancing a Palestinian state. The prime minister was Yitzhak Shamir, a rigid ultra-nationalist zealot. The late journalist Eric Silver told me of the time he sat in on an interview between a BBC reporter and Shamir, and during a break in the taping, "Shamir turned to the BBC reporter with the most terrifying look on his face, and said, 'You want to *destroy* us, but we won't *let* you!'" So for at least the two decades that preceded the intifada, the period since the 1967 Six-Day War, Israeli liberals couldn't say that the Palestinians had missed any opportunities.

Another reason Israeli doves "understood" the first intifada was that it came just a few years after the debut of the Israeli antiwar movement, during the Lebanon War, which had rightly been called Israel's Vietnam. Also, there was a range of liberal, critical newspapers reporting on Israeli abominations, not just *Haaretz* as there is now; there were also *Davar, Al Hamishmar, Hadashot,* and the then-Labor-oriented *Jerusalem Post.* The sole TV station, the state-run Channel 1, was dominated by liberal journalists, notably Ehud Ya'ari, who co-authored highly critical books on Israel's conduct of the Lebanon War and the first intifada. The last but not least reason for the peace camp's reaction to the intifada was that in the first months of clashes, the overwhelming majority of the casualties—including all but one of the deaths—were on the Palestinian side.

As a result, protests were held every Saturday night in Tel Aviv's Kings of Israel (later renamed Rabin) Square. At first they drew tens of thousands, and for a long while afterward still drew thousands. Allen Ginsberg spoke at one, reading a poem that included references to Golda Meir (which he pronounced "Myer") and David Ben-Gurion (which he pronounced "Gur-AYE-on"). I was living in Haifa and driving to and from Tel Aviv every Saturday evening in the winter rain because I felt a duty to be at those demonstrations; there was a feeling of urgency in the air.

Yet nothing changed on the ground, and within a few months Israelis became inured to the new status quo, and the protests petered out while the daily intifada news, including the Palestinian deaths, moved further and further inside the pages of the newspapers.

Five months after it began, however, the uprising returned to the front pages. In those early months, 122 Palestinians had been killed—along with one Israeli, a soldier. On April 6, 1988, Tirza Porat, a 15-year-old girl from a West Bank settlement, became the first Israeli civilian to be killed in the fighting. The first Israeli news reports, according to the *New York Times,* said Porat and about 20 other teenage settlers had been hiking through the West Bank when Palestinians in the village of Beita began throwing rocks at them, with one of the rocks crushing Porat's skull.[3] "The hike of death," read the front-page headline of the *Ma'ariv* daily, which "published a grisly picture across almost half of its front page," the *Times* noted.[4] Thousands of settlers attended her funeral, shouting for revenge. Shamir told the mourners, "The heart of the entire nation is boiling. God will avenge her blood."[5] In the cabinet, Ariel Sharon recommended that all of Beita's houses be blown up.[6]

---

3. John Kifner, "West Bank Settlers Turn Anger Against the Army," *New York Times,* www.nytimes.com, April 11, 1988.
4. John Kifner, "On Sabbath in Israel, Silence over Girl's Killing in Village," *New York Times,* www.nytimes.com, April 10, 1988.
5. Joel Brinkley, "Beita Journal; Where the Hot Rage of April Is Now Cold Fury," *New York Times,* www.nytimes.com, August 23, 1988.
6. "West Bank Settlers," op. cit.

But a day later, the army announced that it wasn't Palestinian stone-throwers who'd killed the girl. It was one of the hikers' two security guards, who accidentally shot her in the head while he himself was getting stoned by villagers. It turned out, too, that the security guard wasn't getting pelted just because he was an Israeli, or a settler, or a Jew on their turf; he had gotten into an argument with a Beita resident and shot him to death, and only afterward did the stoning begin. What's more, the security guard, Ronen Aldubi, wasn't just any security guard; he was a violent Kachnik whose movements had been restricted by the army. And his fellow security guard had been convicted of destroying evidence in the killing by a settler of an 11-year-old Palestinian girl.[7]

Furthermore, the head of the Israeli army, Dan Shomron, announced, "It's a fact—the youngsters, apart from the girl, got out of there alive not because of rescue by military force, but because some villagers did not allow them to be harmed."[8] This did not calm people's fury, though—just the opposite: Settler leaders and other rightists called for Shomron to be fired. And even though the army had disclosed that a violent Kachnik, not Palestinians, had killed Tirza Porat, and that Beita villagers had protected the other teenage settlers on the hike, the political climate in Israel was such that the army destroyed 14 houses in Beita, bulldozed acres of almond and olive trees, deported 6 villagers to Lebanon, and killed a Palestinian boy during the action.[9]

All this went unnoticed; it was routine IDF intifada duty, hardly even newsworthy. By the end of Israel's vengeance on Beita, the Palestinian death toll in the intifada was "at least 145," the *New York Times* reported.[10] For Israelis, it was now two. Nonetheless, the heart of the nation was boiling.

---

7. "Beita Journal," op. cit; Anthony Lewis, "Abroad at Home; A Fateful Choice," *New York Times*, April 17, 1988.
8. "Abroad at Home," op. cit.
9. Ibid.
10. John Kifner, "Israel Deports 8 From West Bank Tied to Violence," *New York Times,* www.nytimes.com, April 20, 1988.

My own heart was anguished (though less and less as time passed) over the brutality of Israel's actions. Yet it was not a hopeless period, not for Israeli liberals, because it was still very possible to believe, after 20 years of Israeli rule over the Palestinians, that this was a transitory thing—and the intifada heavily reinforced that belief. The Likud couldn't run the country forever; Labor would be back before too long. There weren't more than about 15,000 settlers living deep in the heart of the West Bank and a couple thousand more in Gaza. How hard could it be to move them out? As for the 100,000-plus then living in East Jerusalem, they didn't count because Israel was going to keep all of the capital permanently; talk of giving back any part of Jerusalem was taboo, and I certainly wasn't entertaining such ideas. Evacuating any of the large, "quality of life," "suburban," "security" settlements was taboo as well. Why one Israeli colony on conquered Palestinian land was expendable and another sacrosanct I couldn't say with much conviction, but I was not about to accept that Israel was all wrong and the Palestinians were all right; it was very important for me to believe that the Palestinians bore the larger part of the blame for the situation. Their terrorism and refusal to compromise were the greatest obstacles to peace, I maintained. Meanwhile, we couldn't just pack up and leave the West Bank and Gaza, or any part of it; that would be showing weakness. We had to stay on, stop the settlement expansion, stop the brutality (while staying tough in the face of terror), get the Labor Party back in power, then make a deal with the Palestinians for us to get out of Gaza, divide the West Bank, and keep all of Jerusalem. (Palestinian refugees? Who were they, where were they, what did they have to do with anything?) It all seemed eminently doable. So I was hopeful for the future. Naturally, that made it much easier to live with—and to a great extent ignore—our humiliation, torture, and killing of Palestinians, which was embarking on its third decade.

Ten days after Tirza Porat's death, the Mossad assassinated Abu Jihad, the PLO's military chief, in Tunis. I was enraged by the emotional blackmail and brutality surrounding the incident in Beita—but 10 days later I was saying that Abu Jihad had gotten what he deserved. Yes, the occupation was a grave injustice against the Palestinians, but they had no right to use terrorism. It would be impossible for me now to hold those two opinions at the same time, but I managed it then. Millions of Israeli Jews still do.

A few months shy of my 38th birthday, I got drafted into the Israeli army. It was mid-1989, I was living in Tel Aviv and working for the *Jerusalem Post,* and the army wanted me for a month of basic training—basic training for *alteh cockers,* not 18-year-olds—to be followed immediately by a month of reserve duty, then a month of reserve every year until they put me out to pasture. I was so eager; in those days, at least, you weren't an Israeli until you did the army, and I was getting the chance to make up, if only in very small part, for my shameless end-around the Vietnam-era US draft, and all Israel wanted from me was a few months, not years. At the army physical, I once again came in a little overweight, and once again, amazingly, a friendly draft board clerk, this time Israeli, told me that if I wanted, I could have an exemption. This time, an exemption was the last thing I wanted.

We trained at Training Base 4 in the West Bank, near Ramallah. It had been a Jordanian army base before Israel took it over in 1967. The only toilets it had were "Turkish toilets"—a basin with a hole that you were supposed to squat over. I wasn't going for that and would walk over to the officers' section, nonchalantly, as if I belonged there, and use a decent toilet. Other than the Turkish toilets, though, the army was quite bearable. The commanders were not much more than half the age of most of the soldiers in our unit, and they treated us decently. From my own limited experience, and from everything I know about the IDF, I get the impression it probably looks out for its soldiers' welfare more than just about any other army. In fact it gets criticized by some old-timers for mollycoddling— for paying too much attention to the complaints and concerns of soldiers' parents, all of whom get the commander's phone number and email once their sons and daughters are assigned to their units. I did a story in 2007 on suicides in the army, and none of the three parents I interviewed blamed IDF negligence or harshness for their sons' deaths. "There was no harassment—the opposite, they cared for him more than for the others," said a mother whose awkward, slow-learning, troubled son killed himself during a weekend furlough. "I have only the highest regard for the IDF's aid to families of soldiers who commit suicide," said a father whose "very, very lonely" son also killed himself during a weekend home. So this is another contradiction, along with the "new Israeli niceness" I cited earlier, of the leftist admonition that Israeli Jewish callousness toward Palestinians is "coming home." No, it's staying in the occupied territories.

Toward the end of my month of basic training, the IDF general in charge of manpower was due to visit the base, and for three days before his arrival, all training stopped and everyone in my unit was put on full-time clean-up duty. We were in the middle of the West Bank, the intifada was going on all around us, and never in my month at Training Base 4 did I see such a sense of urgency take hold as in those three days before the general's visit. The master sergeant went crazy, barking at us all day. We scoured every utensil and every inch of that kitchen. We must have picked up 10,000 cigarette butts off the ground. Another recruit, a Moroccan immigrant, and I were told to get in the back of a truck and ride around the base, picking up the big, awkward hunks of metal, wood, and plastic that wouldn't fit neatly in the bins and so had to be dumped somewhere. We filled up the truck bed and rode out of the base, through the West Bank, until the driver, a young, angry-looking soldier not from our unit, pulled up at the very edge of a vegetable garden in front of a house. He told us to unload the debris right there.

And the other soldier and I began unloading it, standing in the truck bed, he thrusting a big shovel into the hunks of junk and dumping them over the side, onto the edge of the vegetable garden, while I did the same with a big, unwieldy pitchfork. We didn't ask any questions. Without thinking, I assumed that if this driver in an

IDF uniform wanted us to shovel this stuff right next to somebody's vegetable garden, it must be all right.

Soon a Palestinian woman came out of the front door and started shrieking at us in Arabic. The driver yelled something back at her in Arabic. I asked the Moroccan immigrant soldier what he'd said. "He said, 'Shut up. Get back inside, you old whore,'" the soldier told me, looking as uncomfortable as I was. A couple of Palestinian boys appeared in the distance, throwing stones, shouting curses, and cackling at us. We had to hurry up. Feeling the boys' eyes on me, my overriding concern was that when I picked up a pitchfork-full of debris (not the sort of work I was used to), I would manage to actually dump it over the side, because if the debris fell back onto the truck bed as I was swinging the pitchfork out toward the vegetable garden, I would look like an idiot and the Palestinian boys would laugh their asses off at me. Whatever I thought of the occupation, I wasn't going to go about my duty, fucked up as it was, in an IDF uniform and let these Palestinian *shebab* laugh at me. So I stuck the pitchfork in the pile surely and decisively, and dumped load after load of junk onto the edge of the hysterical woman's garden until we finished and got out of there. (It was only much later that I would think of Orwell's famous essay, "Shooting an Elephant," about when, as a British imperial policeman in Burma, he killed an elephant unnecessarily because otherwise the crowd of Burmese onlookers would have laughed at him. "A sahib has got to act like a sahib; he has got to appear resolute, to know his own mind and do definite things. . . . And my whole life, every white man's life in the East, was one long struggle not to be laughed at.")

Neither the Moroccan immigrant soldier nor I complained to our commanders against the driver, or confessed to anything. I knew what we'd done wasn't right, yet while I saw it as something that had obviously angered the woman and would be an inconvenience for her to clean up, I didn't realize, I couldn't allow myself to see, what an awful insult, what a—I can't avoid using this word again— humiliation we'd put her through. And I was a peacenik; I'd voted for Ratz, the forerunner to Meretz. And I wasn't 18, either; I was 37.

But above all, I was an immigrant recruit in the army, determined to prove myself, and I wasn't going to open up a front against a fellow soldier, even a pig like the truck driver, on behalf of a Palestinian. The army is all about team spirit, and I wanted to be a loyal member of the team.

The next summer, 1990, the reserve unit I was assigned to got called up to Gaza. I felt this dull dread—that I was going to end up killing a Palestinian kid. I had this image of crouching with other soldiers behind a barricade of sandbags, Palestinian teenagers showering us with stones, we're under orders to shoot, and I kill one of them. The first day in Gaza City, we gathered in a clearing in the late afternoon, muezzins in mosques all over the Strip were calling people over loudspeakers to prayer, and the Arabic din was intimidating. "Welcome to Gaza," said one of the commanders, smiling. Continuing on from the point that killing Palestinians had backfired at the start of the intifada, the commanders, one after another, told us not to shoot unless our lives were in immediate danger—if somebody was pointing a gun at us or was about to stab us or throw a Molotov cocktail at us. Otherwise, don't shoot, don't shoot, don't shoot. Ride around, patrol, if they throw rocks at your vehicle, don't shoot; just keep driving. Let them stew in their own juice. We're not going to put out the intifada in the next month, so let's just get through it. Our mission was to finish out the month with no casualties on our side and none on the other side, we were told. And my dread began to lift.

We were stationed in the middle of Gaza City, at Medina Square, in an old, bleak concrete compound that covered a square block, and that Israel had conquered from Egypt in 1967. It sat on a main drag, and the intersection was perpetually gridlocked with taxis and cars, their horns blaring, the drivers lurching their way forward on fearlessness and aggression. If there wasn't a traffic light at that corner, it was pretty safe to assume there wasn't a traffic light anywhere in the Gaza Strip. My impression of the whole place was of a disaster area—dirt, garbage, rubble, and chaos everywhere, the smell of sewage, packs of howling, wild dogs running the streets in the middle of the night. One time I heard the loud, agitated braying of a donkey and followed the sound to a cemetery, where the animal was standing alongside the boy tending it. My uncharitable thought was that Gaza was beyond rehabilitation, no matter who ran it. A quarter-century later, the jury's still out on that.

Most of the guys in our unit were in their thirties with families, which tends to put a damper on one's killer instinct; we were a relatively mind-mannered bunch. But not so the young Border Policemen who were working the area with us. The Border Police are one of the most notoriously brutal units in the IDF, made up mainly of boys from working-class, usually Mizrahi (Jews of Middle Eastern heritage) neighborhoods where hatred of Arabs is common and violence isn't uncommon. My platoon commander, Haim, a nice guy, a liberal, told us that he and the other officers in our unit had authority over the Border Police, so that if any of us saw them beating up on random Palestinians, we should tell one of the officers and they would deal with it. "We're in control of them," Haim stressed.

The Gazan taxi cabs would always park across the street from our compound and wait for fares, until some soldier would get on the bullhorn and yell at them to drive away. Usually the cabbies took their time about it, and one day somebody ordered two Border Policemen to go hurry them up. I was guarding the entrance to the base with a Danish immigrant soldier, and we watched two Border Policeman storm the line of cabs, smashing them with billy clubs, ripping off antennas, screaming and cursing. One of them went up to the open window of a driver and punched him in the face. I looked at the Danish immigrant soldier. His mouth was literally hanging open. "They're like Germans," he murmured. A third Border Policemen sitting in a jeep motioned a Palestinian teenager sitting on a bench to come over, and when the boy got close enough, he slammed open the door of the jeep in the boy's face. By this time the cabbies were driving off, and the two Border Policemen who'd gone wild on them were in the middle of the street, hugging each other and jumping up and down, roaring in triumph, as if they were soccer players who'd just scored a goal.

The next day I told Haim what I'd seen, just like he told us to do. A little defensively, he said there was nothing he could or should do, and mumbled something about the challenge of handling wild horses.

Stones have always been the Palestinians' staple weapon against Israelis on their turf, and Israelis trying to justify the killing of stone-throwers are fond of saying that "stones kill." I understand very well that stones can kill and that countless Israelis have been hit, injured, and—on extremely rare occasions, usually when they're in a passing car—killed by Palestinian stones. But in that month that our unit was in Gaza, there were either thousands or tens of thousands of stones aimed our way—and not a single one hit their target. Typically, the teenagers would start out cautiously, launching from too far away to hit us, then little by little they'd move in closer, and once they got too close, a couple of soldiers would chase them back or distance them with tear gas. So yes, stones kill, but 99-point-whatever percent of them hit nothing.

Another time in Gaza City, I was riding in the back of a patrol vehicle with two other soldiers, one of them a British immigrant named Colin who became a friend after the army, the other a spokesman for the most racist party in the Knesset at the time, Moledet (Homeland), which advocated expelling all the Palestinians from the West Bank and Gaza. We were riding along a main street past a row of two-story stone buildings, we got stuck in traffic, and suddenly cement blocks began falling on our rear bumper, a few inches from the feet of Colin and me. We were sitting opposite each other next to the open door, with the Moledet spokesman sitting to Colin's side, further inside the vehicle, away from the door and shielded by him from the falling cement blocks. Colin and I looked up and saw a kid of about eight dropping the blocks on us from the roof. Colin and I, a bit giddy from the mild danger and excitement, and impressed by the audaciousness of this kid, moved further inside the vehicle and closed the door, putting us safely out of the little boy's line of fire. Meanwhile, the Moledet spokesman was frantically shifting himself deeper inside the vehicle, as far from the door as he could get, and shouting at us, "*Tiru bo, tiru bo!*" Thinking we may not have understood, he translated it to English: "Shoot, shoot!" Colin and I just disregarded him. When we got out of the traffic, the Moledet guy defended his reaction. "My life was in danger," he insisted. If he'd been sitting next to the vehicle's door, there's no reason not to think he would have shot the kid.

But I saw other sides of the IDF in occupied Gaza, too. Once when I was on lookout on the roof of a residential building, a soldier came on the walkie-talkie asking for someone to bring him a bunch of penny candies to give to the kids in the neighborhood when he got off his watch. "I told them I would give them candy when I came back, and I don't want to find out what they'll do if I disappoint them," he said. Somebody brought him the candy, too. (At the same time, though, none of the other soldiers nor I gave a second thought to the fact that we were commandeering some Palestinian family's rooftop.) Haim, the platoon commander, was reprimanded by military prosecutors for slapping a Palestinian in the face during questioning. An officer was suspended from duty and tried for firing his rifle in the air, which he said he did in self-defense. So it's not that every soldier and every officer in the Israeli army is a brutal bastard to the Palestinians. Nor is it that the army turns a blind eye to every act of brutality. But I was exposed to the most infinitesimal slice of Israel's presence in the West Bank and Gaza since 1967—with the garbage-dumping caper happening the one time I got beyond the base during my entire month of basic training—and I saw and did enough to belie Israel's gaseous claim of having "the most moral army in the world."

I don't think the IDF is more brutal than Western colonial armies were. But Western armies are no longer busy keeping the "natives" down; the IDF, alone among the armies of democratic countries, still is.

Yet I am so damn glad I served in the army and that I served in Gaza, occupation or not. It is crucial to my self-esteem—to have done my duty, minimal as it was, and to have faced danger, though that, too, was minor. I don't care how left wing you are; it is much better to be able to say you served in the army than to say you didn't—certainly for a man. I have to admit that I don't feel more than mildly guilty about having dumped debris on that Palestinian woman's vegetable garden; I put it down to having been a desperately eager new recruit under orders. And I'm proud that the following year I ratted out those two psychotic Border Policemen in Gaza to my platoon commander, for all the good it did. I'm also greatly relieved that I never fired a bullet at a Palestinian.

On August 2, 1990, we heard in Gaza on the radio that Iraq had invaded Kuwait. The whole world was condemning Saddam Hussein for such a blatant act of aggression. Right away I figured Arafat and the PLO would condemn Saddam; at the time, they were lobbying the United States and Europe to convene an international conference and call for negotiations between them and Israel—obviously they couldn't back Iraq's invasion of Kuwait. As for my immediate surroundings, I figured the Gazans would be embarrassed to come out and show their faces—a fellow Arab had just become the world's new villain.

About an hour after we heard the news of the invasion of Kuwait, we were told that soldiers were needed elsewhere in the Strip to police a spontaneous pro-Iraq demonstration. In a few months we all would be lining up with millions of other Israelis to get our gas masks. The Palestinians, for their part, had already fallen head over heels in love with the Iraqi conqueror.

CHAPTER FOUR

GREETINGS FROM SADDAM

If you go through the archives of the *Jerusalem Post* for the Gulf War of 1991, you'll find almost no human interest stories describing what it was like for people living in Tel Aviv during those six weeks, with the sirens wailing and the Scuds booming and everyone sitting in gas masks in their "sealed rooms" with plastic sheeting taped over the windows—which wasn't there to stop the missiles, of course, but to keep out the poison gas feared to be in their warheads. The reason those stories, a staple of daily war coverage, were all but absent from the *Post* is because the firing of the newspaper's Tel Aviv reporter—me—became effective a couple of days before Saddam started launching his missiles. (Why the *Post* didn't have somebody else write those life-during-wartime stories from Tel Aviv, I have no idea.)

Getting hired at the *Post* a couple of years earlier was thrilling, a major accomplishment for me. The paper had a good reputation and at least a couple dozen highly talented journalists on the staff. Plus, it was liberal, even too liberal for many so-called liberals; Yitzhak Rabin was said to refer to it caustically by its pre-Independence name, the *Palestine Post*. However, as everyone told me it would, the thrill wore off. The *Post* was a grumpy place, the editors often high-handed, concerned first with protecting their turf. I started out covering energy and transportation, seeing it as the shit work I had to do to get to something better, but I was also becoming known as a good writer of human interest stories. The main newsroom, spread out at the bottom of an old, dreary building in an industrial zone of Jerusalem, was grim, with no natural light, while the little Tel Aviv newsroom that I ordinarily worked out of had no more newspaper vibe than an accountant's office. Still, the *Post* was a good paper; I was planning to work there in a series of positions for another 30 years or so until I retired.

But a year after I got there, it became a symbol of Israel's post-1985 transformation from socialism to capitalism. The *Post* was a wasteful company owned by the Histadrut national union, which sold it to a pair of right-wing, anti-union, cutthroat publishers from North America, Conrad Black and David Radler. They installed as "president and publisher" a retired IDF colonel, Yehuda Levy, a deep-voiced, mustachioed man of the soil whose journalistic credentials were that he'd been the army's spokesman during the Lebanon War. Everyone at the paper except the minority of right-wingers were naturally afraid that the new owners and Levy would change its editorial line from liberal to Likud, and throttle its high-profile, gutsy coverage of the intifada. After the new bosses interfered with an editorial they deemed too far left, the editor-in-chief, Erwin Frenkel, quit, and over the space of a few days, 30 reporters and editors followed.

I stayed. It seemed to me that except for Frenkel, whose authority had been directly undermined, people were quitting not because of what the new owners had done to their journalistic freedom, but because of what they might do to it later. I thought the mass resignation was premature, an overreaction. But to the extent that this was a battle between right and left, I was of course completely on the side of the journalists and against the new ownership. This made me very uncomfortable. But even worse was seeing my friends and co-workers quitting their jobs on a matter of principle, while I was keeping mine. I suffered from acute survivor's guilt, to the point that I was sobbing in the mornings on the way to work. But I'd wanted this job at the *Post* so badly: It had been my goal from the beginning. I'd finally gotten it and was just starting out. I imagined trying to explain over the phone to my sister, Suzie, who knew how important the job was to me, why I was quitting—and I couldn't. Plus, I was about to get married, I was paying off a mortgage on my Tel Aviv apartment, and there was no other English-language newspaper in the country, so I wasn't going to leave. But what would I do if Black, Radler, and Levy really did try to turn the reporters and editors into the production staff of a pro-Likud rag? Would I have to give up my integrity to go on being a working journalist? Would I have to sell out completely? One morning I found myself in a bathroom stall at the *Post,* sobbing violently, when the epiphany came: I had an inheritance coming to me. If worst came to worst, if the new powers at the *Post* insisted that I become a flack for the right, I'd quit, take a few thousand dollars' advance on my inheritance, and look for a decent job for two or three months until I found one. I stopped crying and went back to work.

If I had it to do over again, knowing what I knew then, I would do the same thing. But if I'd known then what I know now, I would have quit with the others. The ensuing year was the most depressing one of my professional life. Covering Tel Aviv, I was writing about local issues, not the occupation, but I realized I was happy with that arrangement: It kept me from having to confront the right-wing higher-ups. There was virtually no direct political meddling; the only time I encountered it was when a low-level editor sought to dissuade me from interviewing Abba Eban for a story, saying he was out of favor with the paper's new regime, and I just disregarded her. Also, I remember a reporter complaining that some story had been given a political edit. Otherwise, there wasn't any censorship from above that I was aware of. Instead, there was an atmosphere of timidity, of self-censorship. Several liberals had stayed on, but more and more the key positions at the paper were filled by people whose writing or editing would not offend a right-wing sensibility. And later I would understand that even if it certainly hadn't been my intention to cast my lot with the forces of the right against those of the left, that's the way it played out publicly. That was the political meaning of my decision to stay on. The new owners had made it clear that the *Post*, to one degree or another, would be shifting from left to right, and finally the journalists working there voted "yes" or "no" on that shift with their feet. Since there was no way I was going to become a right-wing reporter, as far as I was concerned I'd voted "no." But as far as the political arena beyond me was concerned, I'd voted "yes."

A year after the walkout, the *Post*'s unionized journalists, myself included, were locked out of work by Yehuda Levy for refusing to quit the union and sign personal contracts. The union eventually came to terms with Levy, but I got fired on the basis of two accusations: 1) that I'd sabotaged the computer system, which was false; anybody familiar with my tech savvy knows the only way I could sabotage a computer system is with a baseball bat, and 2) that I'd written an anonymous note calling Levy a liar, which was true. Getting fired by the *Post* was such a huge relief, such a weight off my heart. I wasn't on their side anymore; they'd cast me out as an enemy. My survivor's guilt vanished. And by then, the *Jerusalem Report* magazine, staffed in large part by *Jerusalem Post* exiles, had started up, and when the Scuds began falling I was right there at the Tel Aviv "front," and I covered it for them. I was a journalist writing about a historic conflict, one in which I had the highest possible personal stake. This was what I'd come to Israel for.

During the build-up to the war, the phone rang at the *Post*'s Tel Aviv office, and I picked it up; it was the host of a Toronto radio talk show calling for a local reaction to Saddam Hussein's statement that if Iraq were attacked by the United States and its allies, his first target for retaliation would be Tel Aviv. I don't remember what I told him, but I imagine it was pretty tough talk; I was completely behind the first President Bush's decision to send in a half-million troops to get Saddam out of Kuwait. My liberal friends and relatives in the United States were against going to war: The Democratic Party, with few exceptions, was against going to war. The hangover from Vietnam still hadn't lifted. As far as I was concerned, this was the West's "Munich moment": A monstrous tyrant with a "million-man army" and oceans of chemical and biological weapons, along with the planes and missiles to carry them to distant targets, had invaded another country, an ally—fine, a puppet—of the United States. This had electrified the "Arab street"—an Arab leader was defying America, humbling it. And much of the world, including half of America, thought the least bad thing to do was to let him get away with this—precisely because he was (or seemed to be) so powerful and dangerous. It seemed clear to me that if Saddam were allowed to keep Kuwait, he wouldn't stop there. And if that happened, the Middle East would be remade in his image, the West's fear of him would grow, it would become that much harder to contain him, and meanwhile he would be on his way to getting nuclear weapons. The best writing on the crisis was being done, I thought, by the supreme neocon Charles Krauthammer, whom I'd never agreed with on anything before and haven't since. Yes, I saw this as a replay of the rise of Nazi Germany and believed it had to be stopped at any cost. And today, with the benefit of hindsight, I see no reason to revise that opinion.

It was a scary time. I'd become sort of an Israeli architecture buff and developed the habit of aesthetically appraising the buildings I walked past, but now the thought kept popping into my head: Will this building still be here much longer? The dangers ahead weren't a topic for casual conversation among Israelis, but one day I began talking with the grocery store owner up the street, and he said, quietly, "Come on, what do you think? Thousands of people are going to get killed." Israelis were being drilled over and over—at the gas mask distribution center, on TV, in the newspapers, in brochures left at the door—on how to use the gas mask and how to inject oneself with the atropine syringe in the kit if the missiles proved to be carrying biological weapons. (How we would know if the missiles were loaded with, say, cholera, anthrax, or plague in time to inject ourselves was a question left unanswered.) We were told that if and when the missiles began falling, we must stay inside our "sealed rooms" and not go down to bomb shelters, because while the shelters would obviously be much more effective than plastic sheeting and masking tape against conventional missiles, they would be death traps in the event of an attack by missiles armed with poison gas, which floats downward.

Philippa and I, now married and living in an old, small apartment near the Tel Aviv beach, were getting calls from our families who, while trying not to increase our fear with theirs, were asking whether we planned to stay put. We did. We were immigrants in Israel, and this would be our first war, and we were not going to run—that was not the Israeli way. (If we'd had children then, maybe we would have thought differently.) Like everyone else in and around Tel Aviv, we believed we were risking our lives. The predictions were for a long, grueling war, with worries raised about Saddam being able to launch not only chemical or biological weapons, but also dirty bombs and "Fuel Air Explosives . . . [which] for all intents and purposes are nuclear weapons without the fallout," as Hirsh Goodman, editor of the *Jerusalem Report,* wrote.[1]

The morning of January 16, 1991, was cold and gray in Tel Aviv. Overnight, the American deadline for Saddam to leave Kuwait had run out. Bush had gone on television to announce that the bombing of Saddam's military in Iraq and Kuwait had begun. The president's mouth seemed to be a little dry during his address, which only made me respect him and empathize with him more. What gave me the most courage that morning, though, was a new Hebrew song on the radio that taunted Saddam, saying he was nothing, that his army wasn't even in America's league. Maybe it was true. Whatever—a shot of Israeli bravado, under the circumstances, was good for my spirits.

---

1. Hirsh Goodman, "An Evil Logic," *The Jerusalem Report,* February 7, 1991.

Nothing happened that day or night. Nothing happened the next day or evening, January 17, and we went to sleep. In the middle of the night, about 2:30, the phone woke Philippa and me up. It was the radio guy from Toronto; I'd given him my number. "They're reporting on CNN that Iraq has fired Scud missiles toward Israel," he said, then asked for my reaction. "I'm sorry. I've got to go," I said and hung up. We got out of bed and put our gas masks on. I felt weighted down, moving very slowly, my heart felt heavy—like in a bad dream, but I was decidedly awake. Two Scuds landed one after another with a tremendous boom that shook the apartment. I thought they must have hit our neighborhood—and wouldn't know until the next day that they had fallen almost two miles away.

The next morning came more Scuds, loud and reverberating but not as bad as the first ones. The day ahead would be one of the worst of my life, certainly the most fearful. The word was spreading that Saddam had just been "getting his range" with conventional missiles, and that night he would fire his WMD. There was a curfew on; no one was supposed to go outside their homes. Philippa and I wouldn't leave the city because that would be cowardly, running under fire. Staying put was still the Israeli prescription, and President Chaim Herzog, who'd gained fame with his morale-boosting radio commentary during the Six-Day War, was doing it again, bucking people up, urging them to be steadfast and remain at home. Tel Aviv Mayor Shlomo "Chich" Lahat was doing the same, citing the example of London during the Blitz, quoting the British slogan of the time: "The king and queen and Mister Brown are all at home in London town." I was talking daily to my friend Arnon, who lived in a kibbutz near the Lebanese border and had stood up under years of Katyusha rockets, not to mention having fought in three wars; I was not going to duck out now that my turn had come.

If the instinct in the face of danger is fight or flight, we couldn't fight and we wouldn't flee, so we just sat there that day in the living room, hour after hour, in ultra-high anxiety. I thought I could actually feel the blood running in my veins. People would call from the States, and we'd swing back and forth between talking and crying.

That night, before we went to bed, the siren sounded again, and we went into the sealed room and put on the gas masks. As I recall, no Scuds landed that time; maybe the Patriot anti-missile system had gotten them. But at the sound of the siren, I found that I functioned perfectly well. Afterward, my anxiety disappeared: The thing I'd been most afraid of, without knowing it, was that I would fall apart, but I hadn't.

The following afternoon we got a call from our neighbors; they were leaving the Tel Aviv area for a while for someplace safer and calmer, and asked if we could take care of their cat. Sorry, we said, it was all we could do to take care of ourselves. But the idea was infectious: to get out of the line of fire and breathe easier for a while. We called our close friends in Jerusalem, which had become the national bomb shelter—there were too many mosques and Palestinians in the city for Saddam to aim at it—and drove down to stay with them, for as long as we wanted. I was thinking of no more than a couple of days, but then that night some Israelis in Eilat who were flying out of the country for the war were interviewed on the news. They seemed a little embarrassed, and I could understand why. We drove back to Tel Aviv the next day.

In retrospect, we were silly, and trying way too hard to be good Israelis. Tens of thousands of people fled Tel Aviv during the war and were duly ridiculed as rootless cosmopolitans by the staunch Israelis, the salt of the earth. But the fact is that if they hadn't left, many more than two Israelis would have been killed by the Scuds. A few hundred apartments were totally destroyed, yet there were only 11 serious injuries. Time after time, entire apartment buildings in Tel Aviv, Ramat Gan, and Haifa were devastated, yet only a few people would be injured, or none at all. It wasn't on account of the plastic sheeting and masking tape on the windows, but the healthy flight instinct of so many residents.

By now it's no longer a shame in any way for Israelis living near the Gazan or Lebanese borders to sit out the wars with relatives at a safe, or relatively safe, distance from the rockets. The view is that this is only logical: Why risk your life for nothing? It's not as if you can fight back. You don't hear these staunch, stiff-necked Israelis declaring anymore, "This is my home and no terrorist is going to run me out of it." That's a vestige of pre-bourgeois Israeli bravado, which my wife and I and hundreds of thousands of others fell victim to in the Gulf War, and good riddance to it.

In Israel's wars of the 21st century, our leaders have become fond of accusing Hamas fighters in Gaza of hiding behind civilian "human shields." They use this claim to illustrate the Palestinians' "culture of death" in contrast to our own "culture of life." Besides being propaganda—Hamas fights Israel no differently than guerrillas have ever fought a stronger, invading army—it is a reminder to me of the Gulf War. When I hear about their human shields and our culture of life, I remember the psychological pressure on Tel Aviv and Haifa residents to keep up the national morale by remaining abjectly vulnerable in their "sealed rooms" while the Scuds came crashing down.

The six weeks of the Gulf War were the most patriotic, most gung ho of my life. On the day after the first Scuds, my friend Steve Rubenstein, a writer for the *San Francisco Chronicle,* called to see how we were doing, and one of the things he quoted me saying about Saddam was, "That son-of-a bitch, we're going to get him." The *San Jose Mercury News,* where Steve's wife, Caroline, was an editor, called me up, and used this remark of mine: "We're going to smash him now and the world is not going to stand in our way." I heard on the news that Zubin Mehta, who conducted the Israel Philharmonic, had been en route to a performance overseas and that when he learned the Scuds were falling on Tel Aviv and Haifa, he canceled his upcoming concerts and got the first plane back to Israel. The news made me weep with gratitude and adoration. Not long after the start of the war, I realized it was best for Israel to stay out of it and let America do the job, but those first days, when I was afraid and my whole being was saying "fight back," were the one time I've ever lost myself in national war fever—and it is a warm, wonderful feeling. I felt the same way after 9/11. I would love to feel that way every time Israel goes to battle, but not every battle finds Israel being bombed by a would-be Hammurabi fresh from conquest, just like not every battle of America's finds the World Trade Center being leveled by jihadists. I've been a hawk in wartime (rarely) and a dove in wartime, and being a hawk, alas, feels so much better.

The *San Jose Mercury News* article from that day continued: "The attacks have also changed Derfner's political views. He said he used to be a liberal who advocated talks with the Palestinians. 'I don't even know if I can qualify as that anymore,' he said. 'Look at these Palestinians. How can they support such a character?' "[2] A decade before the bus bombings of the second intifada, the first Gulf War soured many a liberal on peace with the Palestinians. A friend of mine, a declared socialist who'd led a protest at Ulpan Etzion against a planned field trip to the occupied West Bank, called from the United States to say, "The Palestinians can go fuck themselves." The woman who'd nicknamed me "the voice of the right" at *New Outlook* magazine, and who'd once remarked to me that "the Palestinians have a really good culture," called with this update: "God bless the Palestinians. May they live and be well, but not near me."

The popular Gulf War image of the Palestinians, which has since been discounted by many as a myth, was that they were "dancing on the rooftops" as they watched the Scuds streak overhead toward Tel Aviv. Since many Israeli Jews were also coming out on their rooftops to watch the Scuds duel the Patriots—Tel Aviv Mayor Lahat told me that he himself would go to the roof of City Hall for that purpose—it stands to reason that many Palestinians were doing the same. Whether or not they were dancing, too, it's very safe to assume they were at least cheering. The Palestinians didn't support Saddam;

---

2. Laura Kurtzman and Ruth MacKay, "Israelis' Second Round of Fear," *San Jose Mercury News,* January 19, 1991.

they idolized him. The new chant in the West Bank was "Ya Saddam, ya habib / udrub, udrub Tel Aviv." ("Oh Saddam, oh good friend / smash, smash Tel Aviv.") I saw a photo in a newspaper of a float in the likeness of a Scud missile riding in a Palestinian parade. And it wasn't just Yasser Arafat and the PLO or just the "hardliners" who looked to Saddam as their savior; it was the moderates, too. In a *New Yorker* article[3] after the end of the war, the late Israeli author Amos Elon wrote that Dr. Sari Nusseibeh, an academic and activist seen then and now as the ultimate Palestinian peace-lover, wrote an article in a Palestinian newspaper titled "Saddam Smashes the Six-Day War Myth." But what sticks with me most about wartime Palestinian infatuation with Saddam was another passage in Elon's article, from an interview with another well-known Palestinian liberal:

> Jonathan Kuttab, a prominent civil-rights lawyer in East Jerusalem and a Christian, told me that he had watched a tape of the entire CNN interview with Saddam Hussein. "For the first time in my life, I felt I could relate to Islam," he said. "He seemed like a prophet. His message sounded almost like liberation theology. . . . I am a Christian, but, as an Arab, I now recognize my Islamic roots. Secular Arab nationalism died in this war. Saddam Hussein's message, in two words, was 'Allahu Akbar'—God is great. God is greater than Bush, stronger than his devastating bombs, stronger than the Israeli occupation of our land. Israel and America should be worried. Saddam's victory will be obvious to everyone five years from now."

Today I hold no grudges against the Palestinians for cheering the Scuds that had us quaking in our gas masks. When you treat people like inferior beings, they're going to want revenge, and we'd been treating the Palestinians like inferior beings for a very long time. However, what I still do hold against them—not for how it hurt Israel, but for what it said about the Palestinians—was their wild adulation for this sadistic Iraqi mass murderer. I've heard the

3. Amos Elon, "Report from Jerusalem," *New Yorker,* April 1, 1991.

excuses—that Saddam returned the Palestinians to center stage after they'd been abandoned by everyone else; that they didn't really love Saddam per se, they merely saw him as useful to their fight for freedom—but it won't wash. The Palestinian people, led by Arafat, together with masses of Arabs in other countries, were smart enough to see that Saddam was using the Palestinian cause strictly for his own purposes—to splinter America's war coalition by embarrassing the Arab states into leaving it. Nevertheless, the Palestinians raised him up as a great liberator, a historic Arab-Muslim leader—and he was a monster. Not to Israel or America, but to the millions of Shi'ites, Kurds, and other Muslim "enemies" of his inside Iraq, and to the hundreds of thousands of Muslim Iranians he slaughtered after invading their country. Yes, the Palestinians had their reasons for glorifying Saddam—all of them bad.

But then again, the United States backed Saddam to the hilt throughout his 1980s war of aggression against Iran—to the point of supplying him crucial components for building chemical and biological weapons[4]—and nobody gives a shit; America is still the land of the free, Reagan is still a great American hero, and Carter, who endorsed the Iraqi invasion before leaving the White House, is still a great humanitarian. So why should I or anybody else wag their finger at the Palestinians? The whole world plays "my enemy's enemy is my friend"; why shouldn't they? That their allegiance to Saddam was more than tactical, that it grew out of the vengeance in their heart— well, who can blame them for that, either?

Toward the end of the war, as the Iraqi army began coming apart, the Scuds were landing less frequently and less accurately; some were falling in the Mediterranean Sea. However, the consensus was that the closer Saddam came to defeat and the death that would no

---

4. "United States Support for Iraq During the Iran-Iraq War," *Wikipedia*, last modified November 17, 2016, https://en.wikipedia.org/wiki/United _States_support_for_Iraq_during_the_Iran%E2%80%93Iraq_war.

doubt follow, the more likely he was to go out in a blaze of glory, to fire off his poison and plague at Israel like a last blast of Fourth of July fireworks. It didn't happen. For Israel, the war just sort of petered out. The final day fell on Purim, a gleeful holiday with lots of people in costume, and many news media couldn't resist reporting that Israelis were celebrating the victory over Saddam, but that was no victory celebration, only Purim.

Most Israelis, naturally, felt that Bush "didn't finish the job," that he should have sent the army to catch Saddam and get rid of him. I never believed that for a second. Bush and Secretary of State James Baker had gotten the support they'd sought at home and abroad on the promise that once Saddam was out of Kuwait, the war was over. To breach that promise would not have been a good idea, and lots more people would have been killed; the allied death toll wouldn't have been capped at a miraculous 350 (mostly from non-combat accidents). Everyone who slagged off Bush for not finishing the job were cheering on his son George W. when he tried to do just that a dozen years later—before turning on him when it didn't work out so well.

Bush the elder's conduct of the first Gulf War—from the enlistment (with Baker) of initially unwilling partners in Europe and the Arab world against a terrifying enemy, to the startling success with so few allied casualties, to the immediate pull-out once the war's original goal was achieved—remains to this day the greatest display of US presidential leadership I've seen in my lifetime. What came afterward, though, was something very different. It was only a few years ago that I read in any depth about the hundreds of thousands of deaths to Iraqi children from disease and malnutrition on account of the postwar UN sanctions,[5] even though this story had been widely reported two decades before. But who wants to read such damning stuff about your side when you're convinced that from start to finish, this was one of their finest hours? Not knowing the damning stuff about my side, not wanting to know, then after a while

---

5. "Sanctions Against Iraq," *Wikipedia*, last modified December 5, 2016, https://en.wikipedia.org/wiki/Sanctions_against_Iraq.

deciding to find out about it—in the progression of my views about Israel, that would be a recurring pattern.

A couple of days before the Gulf War had begun, a couple of Knesset members from the left-wing Ratz and Mapam parties proposed that Israel agree to go to an international conference on the Palestinian issue. Saddam had said he would get out of Kuwait if Israel got out of the occupied territories, so the Knesset members' bill (a symbolic gesture that had no chance of passage) meant to show that Israel would go the last mile to prevent a war. An international peace conference had been the goal of the Palestinians and the Israeli peace camp prior to Iraq's invasion of Kuwait, and I'd fully supported it. But I was so disgusted with these two Knesset members for raising the issue now, of all times—Saddam was using the Palestinians cynically, and here these peaceniks were legitimizing his ploy—that I went out to my car and peeled the Ratz sticker off the bumper.

But as the war was forgotten, I recovered from my lurch to the right and antipathy toward the Palestinians, and when Baker's Madrid peace conference convened in the fall I was all for it, even though I figured Shamir wouldn't give an inch, which he didn't. It was an altogether sterile diplomatic exercise (though it did get Israeli and Palestinian representatives talking, a mechanism the Rabin government would use to concoct the Oslo Accords). Throughout the talks, the Shamir government maintained it had won a great diplomatic victory by keeping the PLO out, when it was plain to everyone that the Palestinian delegates could hardly go to the bathroom without Arafat's okay. The image I remember best from the conference is of Arafat greeting Dr. Haider Abdel Shafi, the elderly, dignified head of the delegation's Gazan contingent, and Dr. Hanan Ashrawi, the equally dignified spokeswoman, by pressing their heads down into his shoulder, forcibly, as he embraced them. It was a crude gesture of dominance, of showing them and everyone watching who was boss, and for me an early, off-putting sign of the Palestinian leader's character.

One night in 1990 when I'd been working at the *Jerusalem Post,* I got into a debate with one of the editors about why the great majority of Mizrahim refused to vote Labor, a fact of Israeli political life that was seen as Likud's electoral insurance policy. The editor contended it was because of their formative Israeli experience in the *ma'abarot,* the bleak immigrant transit camps where the Ashkenazi Labor establishment lodged Mizrahi immigrants of the '50s and '60s, treating them, in general, as primitives. I maintained that wasn't the problem, or anyway not the main problem; the main problem was that Labor's leader, Shimon Peres, came off to Mizrahim as a too-clever manipulator, and that if Labor ran Peres's rival, Yitzhak Rabin, for prime minister, he would draw a lot of Mizrahi votes away from Likud with his tough, war hero's image. Catching a cab home with a Mizrahi driver, the editor and I decided to test our opinions: We told the driver we were taking an informal poll, he agreed to be interviewed, and we asked which party he voted for. "Likud," he said. But if Peres weren't Labor's candidate for prime minister, if instead it was Rabin, would he consider voting Labor? "Then, yes, that's a different story, Rabin is a strong leader, he was an army general." I don't recall why, but the driver had to drop us off on the way, so he called another one to pick us up and take us home. The second driver was also Mizrahi, and we gave him the same shpiel, and he gave us the same answers.

This was rather thin anecdotal evidence of Rabin's ability to get elected where Peres had failed, but it illustrated my argument: Labor's image with Peres was gray on gray. A party of old kibitzers, diplomats. They needed a lion, a fighter, and that was Rabin—"Mr. Security." With him, they might be able to drive the right from power.

The Labor Party eventually came around to the same conclusion, putting Rabin at the top of its ticket for the June 1992 election. The right ran its usual brutish campaign, following Rabin from speech to speech with platoons of hecklers carrying whistles who would send up an ear-splitting shriek as soon as he opened his mouth. "Rabin go home, have a whiskey and go to sleep," they chanted, referring to old rumors that he was an alcoholic. (I always figured those rumors started when he was seen at a party having two or, God forbid, three drinks; through the '80s, Israel was a teetotaling country, in line with its pinched rectitude during its earlier decades.)

On the day that unofficially kicked off the election campaign, I got a preview of the fascist mob fury that would prefigure Rabin's assassination. It was Mimouna, the traditional post-Passover, North African Jewish holiday that sees Israeli politicians going from one *mufleta* pastry-laden gathering to another. At Jerusalem's Sacher Park, the left-wing Meretz tent, with party leader Shulamith Aloni inside, was getting hit with stones and bottles. "They defend the Arabs," shouted one guy being pushed away by police. "As far as I'm concerned, all the leftists should die," a kid of about 13 told me. People were chanting, "death to the Arabs," "death to the left-ists," "Kahane." The chants continued when Rabin, Shamir, and the other politicians spoke from a platform. Rabin tried to score points with the crowd by recalling the Six-Day War and "reunification" of Jerusalem, when he had been head of the military, but the booing got louder. The biggest cheer of the day came when Shamir took the podium. "Only with our love for Eretz Yisrael, the complete Eretz Yisrael, all of it, every part of it, will we overcome our enemies and all the hatred against us in the world," he said. Rabin left the park immediately after speaking; Shamir was mobbed so tumultuously that police on horseback had to drive people off.

Rabin didn't win the election as a peace candidate; he ran mainly as the more proficient warrior against terror, which was scaring Israelis badly. "Gaza in Tel Aviv!" went the onscreen text of one Labor commercial, focusing on the brutal stabbing death of a girl outside the city. And while Rabin derided Shamir's "political settlements" in the heart of the West Bank, he promised to build up "security settlements" in the West Bank's Jordan Valley and near Jerusalem. In all, he wasn't exactly a bleeding heart.

I didn't think Rabin would win, even in the last days before the election when all the pollsters were making him the next prime minister; I had been traumatized by Likud's power in the "Israeli street." But Labor's coalition squeaked through, and on the elation-filled night of June 23, 1992, Labor supporters poured champagne on each other, chanting about how the Likud had just "eaten it." At Likud headquarters in Tel Aviv, the depressed crowd watched the scene on a big screen, with Shamir and other party leaders seated at a long dais. Hearing the chant, the VIPs either stared grimly ahead or tried without success to smile like good sports. Only one man sitting up there was laughing out loud; only he was confident enough of his future to do so: the Madrid conference's media star, the Gulf War's media star, the UN ambassador who took on the whole Muslim world, the younger brother of a modern Jewish hero and martyr, the 42-year-old, movie-star handsome, matchless communicator who was already known simply as Bibi.

CHAPTER FIVE

NETANYAHU UNPLUGGED

One afternoon in mid-1993, Binyamin Netanyahu was standing in shirtsleeves in a downtown Jerusalem square, exhorting a crowd of right-wingers against the abomination of the week being committed in Washington by the Rabin government. His voice was raw and raspy to convey uncontrollable rage and intolerable insult, as if he was telling his listeners, *"They're raping our daughters!"* The rawness in his voice, though, sounded false; Netanyahu's natural speaking voice was rich and smooth. But the right-wing politicians and settler leaders who'd preceded him at the microphone had spoken in that hoarse tone, which for them was indeed natural; for Netanyahu it was an affectation, an attempt to show the Greater Israel faithful that even though he didn't wear a yarmulke and beard, he was, no less than they, in the grip of a wild, burning fury over the government's bargaining with their land and lives. (The issue at hand had something to do with "Baker's three points," or "Mubarak's five points," or some other long-forgotten detail of the going "peace process" of the time.) After the rally, a crowd of kids followed Netanyahu to his car, chanting, "Bee-*BEE*, Bee-*BEE*." Visibly pleased with the wave of enthusiasm welling up around him, Netanyahu strode ahead, maintaining his erect, regal carriage, acknowledging his young fans with flashes of his confident grin.

It was the first time I'd ever seen him in person. I'd come to the rally to set up a meeting for a profile I wanted to write about him for the American Jewish magazine *Moment*. He'd recently become the leader of the Likud, and thus head of the Israeli opposition, by easily winning the Likud primary following Shamir's retirement. American Jews interested in Israel knew him very well in English from his years of media appearances and speaking engagements; I meant to show them Netanyahu at home with his countrymen, in his mother tongue. I told his spokesman I wanted to follow him around and interview him; a couple of days later I was told I could meet him on an upcoming bus tour by Likud Knesset members of the rocket-stressed communities near the northern border.

Along the way, the bus stopped at an industrial zone in the town of Kiryat Shmona, and a young female employee who'd heard he was there started shouting, "Bibi Netanyahu! Bibi Netanyahu!" as he passed, like he was a movie star. At a lookout post on the Golan Heights, which are considered Israel's "high ground" against Syria, Netanyahu observed how much higher the mountains were on the Syrian side. "Look at the command they've got!" he exclaimed to the other Likudniks. Posing for pictures with the Syrian mountains in the background, Netanyahu, an expression of foreboding set on his face, suddenly told the photographer to switch positions and take his profile from the other side. After a visit to the "Good Fence," where Lebanese domestics and farm workers came across the border daily to work in Israel, Ron Nachman, a Likud Knesset member and long-time mayor of the West Bank settlement Ariel, muttered to Netanyahu, "These shits make money off of us from this." Netanyahu didn't respond.

Later he came to my seat on the bus, and I introduced myself and told him I wanted to do a profile of him. "Why, whatever for?" he said, evidently unaware that this wasn't an expression of modesty but a parody of one. He picked up the book lying next to me on the seat, *Hiroshima* by John Hersey, and said, "This was his first big one." He may have been trying to impress me with his erudition, but he didn't need to: I knew he was a very well-read individual, the son of an accomplished historian. I asked if I could interview him in his home, and he said he liked to keep his private life private but would sit down with me in his Jerusalem office.

I'd first heard of him some years before as Israel's highly impressive representative at the UN. Later, when he started his political career, I saw he was obviously capable, clearly had a bright future, and while he could be overbearing in his black-and-white view of the conflict, the Likudniks I respected—including his mentor, Moshe Arens—were no different in that regard, and Netanyahu had not shown himself to be one of the "bad guys," the Arab-bashers, the rabble rousers. He didn't traitor-bait the left like Shamir or radiate violence like Sharon; the worst I could say of him was that he was a fearmonger. So I went into my research for the profile having no reason to think of Netanyahu as dishonest, or unprincipled, or unscrupulous, or racist. I had no evidence of his being a man of poor character—except for one thing: his handling of "Bibigate."

In the scandal surrounding his extramarital affair, Netanyahu had succeeded in slandering his bitterest Likud rival as a blackmailer, a criminal, a man of "mafia tactics"—without ever mentioning the man's name. The reason for this omission, plainly, was that if he had named the name, he would have had to prove his accusation: that this rival of his was behind the telephone threat to release a video of Netanyahu's sexual relations with his paramour unless he dropped out of the Likud leadership race. So instead of naming names, Netanyahu used innuendo. "I know who is behind this blackmail," he said on January 14, 1993, at the top of the nightly news. "It is one person, a senior figure in the Likud who is surrounded by a gang of criminals." And so his work was done: Everyone instantly knew he meant David Levy, the ex–foreign minister whom he'd upstaged as deputy foreign minister, a Mizrahi who had some rough characters among his supporters, who was stereotyped as a working-class primitive, the kind of politician who might be "surrounded by a gang of criminals." Months later the police closed their investigation of Netanyahu's complaint, announcing that they'd found no criminals and no crime. When reporters asked Netanyahu if he planned to apologize to Levy, he reminded them that he "never mentioned any names" and said he wanted Likud "to move forward into the future, not backward into the past."

A pretty slimy performance, even for a politician. A black mark—but still only his first; not nearly enough, in my mind, to write him off as a louse. It would be years later before I asked myself: What kind of guy rushes onto the evening news, one day after a blackmail attempt, and discloses to the whole country, the whole world, that he cheated on his wife—and does this to save his political career? It's one thing for a politician to inadvertently humiliate his wife publicly by being exposed for having an affair—but to humiliate her by taking the initiative to expose it himself? On prime time TV? That's a politician of rare, uncanny ruthlessness, one "who has no God," as the Hebrew expression goes. But I didn't understand that when I was going in for the interview; at the time I had a serious problem only with Netanyahu's politics, nothing else.

In his office, which was unremarkable except for its pretty view of Jerusalem, we first made some small talk, then sat down across his desk, and I put my cassette recorder between us. Without a word, he reached over, popped it open and pulled the cassette out. Holding it in his hand, he said, "I don't work with these." I protested, but he made it clear he wouldn't do the interview if I insisted on recording it. I told him there was no way I could take reliable notes by hand—how would I quote him at length accurately? He agreed to let me record him for the sake of accuracy—but I would have to submit for his approval or disapproval any quotes I wanted to use in the story. Those were his conditions. I've written hundreds of profiles, plenty of them on VIPs, and nobody ever made such a demand on me. It was his right, of course, but the most minimal sense of fairness would have dictated that he present those unusual conditions when we set the time and place for the interview, not when I show up for it. But he had me over a barrel; it was his way or no way, and I agreed to his terms.

At that point he got up from his chair. "There's something I'd like to do now," he said, "but only if you agree to keep it off the record." Sure, I said, what do you want to do? "I'd like to smoke a pipe," he said. Now it can be revealed: Bibi Netanyahu liked to smoke a pipe. I was beginning to see that he had a thing about secrecy. And control.

I'd spent two days in the *Ma'ariv* newspaper archive going over his voluminous clippings file, and I came away knowing next to nothing about his life before he went into politics. I wanted to bring this out in the story, to let readers learn something about Bibi Netanyahu the person. He told me that in high school he'd been a "jock-nerd," a member of the wrestling team and near the top of his class academically. He talked about "breaking up the furniture" wrestling at home with his brother Yoni. This was great; this was the sort of thing I was looking for. But when I finished transcribing the cassettes, I saw that his personal reminiscences were all saccharine and self-serving; the story that I ended up writing contained none of them. I had, however, wanted to use the stuff about him being a "jock-nerd" and about him and Yoni "breaking up the furniture," but he didn't approve it for publication.

While I didn't find any stories about his early life in his clippings file, I did find the names of some of his friends from his Jerusalem childhood. One of them agreed to talk to me anonymously about Netanyahu in his youth. "He was always very dominant in expressing his ideas, even as a child," the friend said. "He's had the same political opinions since elementary school. They've deepened and developed, but essentially they're the same."

Uzi Landau, then a Likud Knesset member, told me he was present at the creation of Netanyahu the politico. It was when they were both attending M.I.T. shortly after the Yom Kippur War, and Landau, as head of the Israeli Students Association in the Boston area, was handing out leaflets, trying to counter the anti-Israeli influence of local left-wing and Arab organizations. "Bibi walked up to me and asked who we represented, and said he had a lot of ideas. He came to one of our meetings and was critical of our tactics, saying that we should not just show that Israel is a democracy, and that we're nice people, and that we suffered in the Holocaust, but should also try to show the mutual interests of the US and Israel." Netanyahu took over the organization's information campaign and began speaking to local Jewish audiences and lobbying politicians. "He had exactly the same self-confidence that he has today," Landau said. "I don't think there's any difference in what you see of him today from what he was then."

Fine, he doesn't change, he hasn't demonstrated a moment's doubt about his ideas or himself in his entire life; that's very interesting. But what's underneath?

Landau, who described himself as a "personal friend" of Netanyahu's going back 20 years: "We would get together with our families and some additional friends. As a matter of fact we are still good friends. Do I know him very closely as a person? No."

The anonymous childhood friend: "In my opinion, he can be described as a loner. He's very serious, very well developed intellectually, he can discuss any subject. But sensitivity, feeling for people—these aren't his outstanding traits."

Would you say he is a loyal friend?

"I would say he is loyal to himself."

In May 1993, just before I started working on the profile, Netanyahu published *A Place Among the Nations—Israel and the World*, a 467-page book that, as the jacket says, "traces the origins, history, and politics of Israel's relationship with the Arab world and the West." It's very interesting, very well-written, but no different in its essential view of Israel's past and present than a Zionist Organization of America brochure. Before our interview, which was held over two hour-long sessions in Netanyahu's office, I naturally read it. During the second session, I began asking him about his stand on this issue and that one, and he said repeatedly, "Read my book." Finally, I told him that I had read his book. He tilted his head sideways and said, "Did you read it or skim it?" No, I read it, I said, and we continued the interview.

David Horovitz, editor of the *Times of Israel* and previously editor of the *Jerusalem Post,* has written of Netanyahu's technique of "giving the voters those extra two seconds of full-on, ultra-sincere eye contact to lock up their support."[1] A few minutes after telling Netanyahu I'd read his book, I got my two seconds. During the Q&A, he paused, fixed me with the look, and said, "Larry, I think you understand my vision better than any Israeli journalist." I recall lowering my eyes and trying to make the wince on my lips look like a smile of appreciation, and went on to the next question.

This was nothing new, a politician feeding a journalist some flattering nonsense in the hope of getting sympathetic coverage. But what nonsense! He didn't know who I was, I'm sure he'd never read anything I'd ever written, I'd been talking to him for maybe an hour and a half total, and he tells me he thinks no Israeli journalist has ever plumbed his depths like I have. He was telling me a lie, but it was such a bad lie, such a ridiculous one. How could he expect that it would work, that it would get me on his side? Later I thought about that and asked myself: What sort of person tells ridiculously bad lies? A stupid person. But stupid is one thing Netanyahu definitely isn't. So what sort of intelligent person tells really bad lies? Answer: one who thinks the person he's lying to is stupid—stupid enough to believe him. I don't think I gave Netanyahu any reason to think I was stupid. So why would he feed me such obvious baloney? It wasn't until much later, when Netanyahu's insincerity became as visible and audible as Nixon's had been, when his reputation as a habitual teller of whoppers was cemented, that I understood why he'd tried to con me with such patent hogwash about my understanding of his vision. It was, I concluded, because he assumes that people in general are stupid—that until proven different, everyone is a gullible simpleton, and he can tell them anything he wants and get away with it. And when I realized that, I realized what it was, well beyond his politics,

---

1. David Horovitz, *A Little Too Close to God* (New York: Knopf, 2000), 139.

that made him (like Nixon, again) so infuriating to watch on TV: It wasn't just the preening that shows he has such a high opinion of himself, it was the outrageousness of his bullshit that shows he has such a low opinion of his audience. Watching Netanyahu do his selling job on TV, or in person, is to have your intelligence insulted.

When I look back on the interview and my reading of Netanyahu's book, there were things I chose to overlook because I didn't want to think of him as a racist. His antagonism toward Arabs hadn't yet come into focus, and I suppose I was still too much of an immigrant and too timid an "objective journalist" to want to reach such a conclusion. But there's no reason to overlook those things now.

In *A Place Among the Nations,* first published in English, he warned Americans that if what he called the "Palestinian Principle"—that an ethnic minority is entitled to carve out a state anywhere it has a local majority—spreads to the United States, Mexican immigrants could take over the American Southwest.

> The United States is not exempt from this potential nightmare. In a decade or two the southwestern region of America is likely to be predominantly Hispanic, mainly as a result of continuous emigration from Mexico. It is not inconceivable that in this community, champions of the Palestinian Principle could emerge. These would demand not merely equality before the law, or naturalization, or even Spanish as a first language. Instead, they would say that since they form a local majority in the territory (which was forcibly taken from Mexico in the war of 1848), they deserve a state of their own. . . .
>
> [This scenario] may sound farfetched today. But it will not necessarily appear that way tomorrow. . . .[2]

---

2. Benjamin Netanyahu, *A Place Among the Nations* (New York: Bantam, 1993), 150.

If a white American said that now—or in 1993, when Netanyahu published it—he would be called a racist, a white, anti-Hispanic racist. But I let that passage go, and didn't mention it to him during the interview or write about it in the profile. But he returned to the theme of the Mexican peril again, in 2002, and in a much cruder way. Netanyahu was speaking to an audience in Dallas, at an event sponsored by the National Center for Policy Analysis. Ruben Navarrette, Jr., a columnist for the *Washington Post,* wrote:

The idea was to get Americans to feel Israel's pain. But, as a Mexican American in the audience, all I felt was nauseated. . . .

When asked for a historical overview of Middle East turmoil, Netanyahu mentioned how Jews migrated back to the Holy Land in the early years of the 20th century, set up farms and businesses and turned a desert into a desirable destination. So desirable that soon there were hordes of Palestinians trying to get in and enjoy the fruits of Israeli labor. Then, Netanyahu turned to the crowd and offered this bit of sarcasm: "Now, you here in Texas wouldn't know anything about this phenomenon.". . .

Asked about why Israel is reluctant to allow Palestinians living in refugee camps to enter into Israeli society, Netanyahu mentioned security concerns but also said that a mass migration would "flood" Israel. "You know about this," he said. "This is the reason you have an INS."[3]

However, this Dallas audience must have been a liberal Democratic one, not exactly Bibi's crowd. Navarrette:

The good news is that, judging from the audience's reaction, Bibi made a boo-boo. The ethnic pitch got no applause, only uncomfortable looks and nervous laughter.[4]

3. Ruben Navarrette, Jr., "Bibi Bombs in Dallas," *Washington Post,* April 20, 2002.
4. Ibid.

So much for Netanyahu's views of Mexican Americans. The other red flag I saw, but decided to ignore, was something he said when I first came into his office and we were making small talk, getting acquainted before the start of the interview. I mentioned the high school he'd gone to in a suburb of Philadelphia, Cheltenham High.[5] He said it had been a very good school when he was there in the mid-'60s. Then, with a conspiratorial smirk on his face, he added:

"It's changed."

His meaning was clear to me: Cheltenham had been a good, white school when he was there, then the blacks moved in and it went to hell. There's no other reasonable interpretation of those words coming from a person who lived in America in the 1960s and 1970s, especially when they're directed in private, presumably off the record, to an American immigrant of roughly the same age, and more especially when they're accompanied by a "you get my meaning?" look on the speaker's face. In January 2015, I recounted this anecdote on *+972 Magazine*, and a reader identifying himself as "Merlot" made this comment:

> I live in Cheltenham and I hear this same sentiment expressed all the time. At times it is clear that the sentiment comes with racial undertones and that the person saying the school has gone downhill is saying this due to changes in demographics. However, at present it is more often true that people are referring to actual problems in the district. However, in 1993 the current administrative problems in the district did not exist. It was a very good school district and despite its administrative problems remains a pretty good, certainly above average, school district. In 1993 the idea that the change being referred to could be anything other than racial integration is hard to believe.[6]

---

5. "Cheltenham High School," *Wikipedia*, last modified December 8, 2016, https://en.wikipedia.org/wiki/Cheltenham_High_School.
6. Comment by Merlot to Larry Derfner, "Netanyahu On How His Old U.S. High School 'Changed,'" www.972mag.com, January 25, 2015.

Why would Netanyahu make that remark, "It's changed," with that expression on his face during the warm-up for our interview? I figure it was because he wanted to gauge whether he was going to be talking to his kind of Jewish immigrant to Israel, or to a liberal. As I remember, I responded by nodding without expression. But just like he did with that audience in Dallas, he gambled that he could get me on his side with a bit of racist pandering, and he lost. His catalogue of bigoted remarks about Arabs, his scaremongering about Mexican Americans, his verbal wink to me about American blacks, his affinity for old, rich ultra-conservatives, and his superior attitude all tell me that in Bibi Netanyahu, what we've got is a genuine, old-fashioned white man.

When the interview was over, I stood in front of his desk and said goodbye. "Bye," he said, without lifting his head to look at me, an edge of impatience in his voice, his attention turned immediately and fully to something he was writing. Nope, sensitivity to people didn't seem to be one of his outstanding traits, but workaholism did. (Not that workaholism in a political leader is a bad or unusual thing.) He didn't find time to go over the quotes with me before leaving for vacation with his family and parents, so he took time during his vacation to do it by phone. But unfortunately, his efforts, not to mention mine, proved futile: At the end of August, a few days before I sent the story in to *Moment* magazine, news began to appear about a secret agreement between Israel and the PLO. A couple of weeks after that, Arafat and Rabin shook hands on the White House lawn, and with the Israeli government breaking so dramatically with the past and launching the country into a new era, no American Jewish bimonthly magazine was going to run a 5,000-word profile on the leader of Israel's opposition. So the story never got published.

The irony is that I'd actually written a few nice things about Netanyahu. I described him as a "fundamentally decent man," which was the product of my timidity at recognizing his racism and ruthlessness, the latter having led him to slander his chief party rival as a mafia-style criminal in the most gutless way, and to voluntarily humiliate his wife in public. I also wrote:

> [L]ike Shamir and Sharon, Netanyahu whips up elemental Jewish fears, and will describe the most apocalyptic visions to drive home his message. . . . But in certain important ways, Netanyahu is better than Shamir or Sharon. He is much more the democrat, and did not go in for their dissent-is-treason line when the Likud was in power. And, unlike Shamir and Sharon, Netanyahu makes it a point to warn against vigilante attacks on Palestinians, and calls to arms by the lawless wing of the Jewish right (although he's not nearly as outspoken about it as the best of the Likud "princes," Benny Begin and former justice minister Dan Meridor).

That was true at the time of the writing. But in the coming two years, as leader of the opposition to the Oslo Accord, a period that culminated in the assassination of Rabin, Netanyahu would sell his soul to the devil. In hindsight, I don't think the devil had to bargain too hard.

CHAPTER SIX

"WE HAVE TO KILL RABIN"

The day after Rabin and Arafat signed the Oslo Accord in Washington, an Israeli settler was stabbed to death in a West Bank orchard. I thought, *Wait a minute. This wasn't supposed to happen. It's one thing to kill Israelis when you see no hope, but now?* And I quickly put that idea out of my mind, for the sake of my own hope. Besides, Hamas took responsibility for the killing, and everybody knew the Hamasniks weren't going to give up terror now; if anything, they were going to intensify it. But that murder in the orchard was a harbinger of things to come: The killings of Israelis continued at a steady pace, mainly by Hamas, but not only by them. And Israelis were getting mad. Support for the peace deal with the PLO, which ran about three to two right after it was signed, was imploding. Right-wingers were beyond mad; they felt their government was handing them and the whole country over to a pack of sworn Jew-killers.

Five months after the ceremony on the White House lawn, I went to the funeral of Zippora Sasson, a pregnant Ariel settler who was shot to death in her car on a West Bank highway by Hamas gunmen. This was the 23rd fatal Palestinian attack of the new Oslo era, and Sasson was the 29th Israeli killed. Before the burial, people were gathered near her shrouded body, and Ariel's mayor, Ron Nachman, told how the murderers must have been so thrilled to see that they were killing not only a Jew, but her unborn Jewish child as well, and he blamed it on "this cowardly government." Men and women were moaning with grief and rage, rage at the government no less than at the killers, and the atmosphere was choking.

Six days later, on February 25, an 80-year-old Israeli man was axed to death in the middle of the city of Kfar Saba—another Hamas job. And that same day in Hebron, Dr. Baruch Goldstein emptied his army rifle, magazine after magazine, into a crowd of Muslim men and boys kneeling in prayer in a mosque, killing 29 of them and wounding over 100, before his gun jammed and he was beaten to death by survivors.

The Hebron massacre set off a cycle of Palestinian suicide bombings and Israeli displays of lethal force, including targeted assassinations, from which the "spirit of Oslo" never recovered. I've heard left-wingers describe Goldstein's slaughter as the original sin of the peace process—the impetus to the chain reaction of massive violence—in answer to the consensus Israeli view that Palestinian terror was responsible for Oslo's failure. But Goldstein's rampage didn't come out of nowhere. He was a true-believing Kachnik— "super-Kach," as one of his neighbors described him to me. But his friends Mordechai and son Shalom Lapid, shot by Hamas men two and a half months earlier, had died in his arms as he was trying to save them; a lot of Jewish blood was being spilled. Would Goldstein have gone on the rampage if the Palestinians had kept the peace? No one can say, of course, but it's impossible to say that the terror of those months following the signing of the peace agreement played no part in his decision to mow down Muslims at prayer. So even if the Hebron massacre did produce the Palestinian suicide bombings that set the stage for the ultimate failure of the peace process, it may be that the five-month drumbeat of Palestinian killings had produced, or at least had helped produce, the Hebron massacre.

At the time, I saw both Goldstein's and the Palestinians' terrorism as unprovoked and unjustifiable. But like Israelis in general, I was leaving out one big part of the picture, really the elephant in the living room: the acts Israel and its army were perpetrating against the Palestinians on a routine, ongoing basis, even after that sunny day on the White House lawn when Rabin declared "enough!" An example of these acts was described by "Taisir Salman" (not his real name), a Palestinian from the Ramallah area, to Israel's B'Tselem human rights organization following his 43-day interrogation by Shin Bet agents in mid-1994:

> He began beating me with his fists and with kicks. He grabbed me by the neck and kicked me in the testicles. That went on for an hour and forty-five minutes. Then the interrogator went out and two other[s] came in. They sat me on a chair and tied my hands behind the backrest of the chair. One of the interrogators took a plastic ruler and began to hit me with the end of the ruler, and told me to confess.[1]

After a month and a half of Shin Bet treatment, Salman was put in "administrative detention" (a euphemism for imprisonment without charges) for two months, then released. He was one of nine Palestinian arrestees who gave testimony to B'Tselem for its 1994 report on torture. Seven of them were released without ever being charged, one was awaiting trial when the report came out, and only one actually got convicted and served prison time for the crime that led to his arrest. Wrote B'Tselem: "The repeated claim that

---

1. From the testimony of Taisir Salman, "Torture During Interrogation: Testimony of Palestinian Detainees, Testimony of Interrogators— Information Sheet, November 1994," B'Tselem—The Israel Information Center for Human Rights in the Occupied Territories.

'pressure' was used against detainees because of the need to prevent murderous attacks is a mere pretext in these cases; the same is true of the overwhelming majority of the cases in which detainees are tortured." The report's lone arrestee who was convicted of a crime—Mahdi Shahrur, who lived near Nablus—gave this description of his questioning by the Shin Bet:

> Then someone came and dragged me when my hands were tied (they were tied behind) and took me in to be interrogated. They did not remove the blindfold even during the interrogation. He said, "Do you want to go the good way or the bad way?" He began to beat me all over. . . . It went on for maybe two hours. Beating the whole time. He would leave the room for fifteen minutes and come back and beat me. The blows were mainly in the face, the knees, and kicks in the testicles. I was screaming. There were also fists in the stomach, they pulled my hair. . . .[2]

At the time, Mahdi Shahrur was 15. He'd been arrested for throwing stones. He was sentenced to a year and three months in prison, which was reduced on appeal to seven months.

From the start of the intifada in December 1987 through 1994, the Shin Bet interrogated some 23,000 Palestinians, according to the Israeli Attorney General's Office. B'Tselem stated: "GSS [Shin Bet] interrogation methods did not change after the [September 1993] Oslo Accords."

But torture was just one of the conditions of Palestinian life that survived the dawning of the Oslo era. When the peace accord was

---

2. From the testimony of Mahdi Shahrur, "Torture During Interrogation: Testimony of Palestinian Detainees, Testimony of Interrogators—Information Sheet, November 1994," B'Tselem—The Israel Information Center for Human Rights in the Occupied Territories.

signed, about 8,700 Palestinians were in Israeli jails as security prisoners—for fighting the occupation, violently or non-violently, during the previous quarter-century, in which time Israel showed no inclination whatsoever to give up its military dictatorship over the West Bank and Gaza. How would Israeli society handle 8,700 Israeli soldiers being in enemy prisons, likely after having been tortured? It's unthinkable. The whole country turns upside down for one prisoner in enemy hands, Gilad Shalit; imagine Israel living with 8,700 Gilad Shalits. No, you can't imagine it. But that was the Palestinians' reality when the Oslo Accord burst upon the world—another reason the incantation *peace* may not have had the same resonance for them that it did for so many others.

Furthermore, after the Oslo Accord went into effect, Palestinians still weren't allowed to travel between the West Bank and Gaza, or to East Jerusalem. (They still aren't.) Israeli soldiers didn't budge from an inch of Palestinian territory for eight months, and at that point they only got out of Jericho and the population centers of the Gaza Strip; they remained in place throughout the remainder of the West Bank for two years before pulling out of six other major cities besides Jericho. Meanwhile, they never gave up control of the West Bank's roads (or those in Gaza until the "disengagement" of 2005), and a steady, dependable supply of soldiers among them never stopped brutalizing and humiliating Palestinians at the army checkpoints, on patrol and during raids. In his bitter, self-lacerating book *Tismonet Machsom* (*Checkpoint Syndrome*), Liran Ron Furer describes what he did as a soldier at a Gazan checkpoint one afternoon in 1998, when he and his partner Boaz stopped a Palestinian from Khan Yunis refugee camp taking his wife and three children to the beach, and the Palestinian told them he'd forgotten his Israeli-issue permit to pass through. Furer, pissed off from lack of sleep, boredom, the heat, and the hatefulness of his job, decided to teach the man and his family a lesson:

> "Get out, get out of the car! Stand over there!" The father gets out and stands off to the side, Boaz takes the bags with the

towels, the sacks of grapes and the inflatable tube out of the car. The father goes up to Boaz. "What's the problem, soldier?" Boaz tells him to wait there and goes on pulling out bags of towels, and the father takes Boaz by the hand. "Why are you doing this, soldier, what's the problem?'"

Boaz tells him something, I can't hear what, but this upstart of an Arab is still holding onto his hand and Boaz, the faggot, just keeps on talking to him normally, and I went up to them and smacked the Arab in the face so hard, with my whole hand, and grabbed him by the shirt and pushed him into the car. "Get the hell out of here, you're not getting through without a permit!" The father didn't even say anything, he was completely in shock, and suddenly he started to cry, really hard, tears coming down and everything, and he turned the car around and drove back into Khan Yunis.

I was surprised, he actually looked tough, self-respecting, how could he allow himself to do that without being ashamed? To cry like that in front of everybody? Even his kids, who were sitting there quietly in the backseat, didn't cry.[3]

The checkpoint syndrome didn't end with the Oslo Accord. The killings by soldiers and settlers didn't end either. While Palestinians killed 30 Israelis in the first five and a half months of the peace process (up until Goldstein's mass murder), Israelis killed 28 Palestinians in less than the first two months. The takeover of Palestinian land for the expansion of settlements likewise continued—during Rabin's term, the number of settlers grew by about 25 percent.

The year after the peace process began, Human Rights Watch (HRW) published a 300-page report on what it called Israel's "conveyor-belt-quality" torture of Palestinians. HRW took testimony from 4 Israeli soldiers and 36 former Palestinian prisoners—including 10 who said they'd been tortured in the months after Rabin shook hands with Arafat. "The peace process, we found, has yet to

---

3. Liran Ron Furer, *Tismonet Machsom* (*Checkpoint Syndrome*) (Tel Aviv: Gevanim, 2003), 57–58.

trickle into the interrogation rooms," the report's authors wrote. Asked by journalists for his reaction to HRW's findings, Foreign Minister Shimon Peres put everyone's mind at ease: "I'm sure that with the new agreement, human rights problems will disappear."[4]

This is what we Oslo supporters decided to believe: that the ongoing, day-to-day reality for the Palestinians didn't matter because it was all going to be washed away by peace. Which made it that much easier to ignore the Palestinians' ongoing, day-to-day reality. And so when terror attacks happened, we told ourselves they were unprovoked, except by the malicious desire on the part of Hamasniks and other rejectionists to destroy the chance for peace. But in fact the provocations were there during the early days of the Oslo Accord no less than they had been before. So if the great majority of Israeli Jews say it was Palestinian terror that killed the peace process, and some left-wingers say it was Baruch Goldstein, I would say it was Israel's occupation, the routine of tyranny that continued unabated long after the peace process began, that did it.

Yet the Oslo Accord was presented as the answer to the Palestinians' problems. Did Hamas have the right to use terror as it did for the goal of torpedoing the accord, when Arafat and the PLO, the Palestinians' mainstream leadership, had accepted it and put down their guns? Did Oslo offer the promise of justice to the Palestinians, such that they no longer had a *casus belli* against Israel? Well, for starters, not only did Hamas, Islamic Jihad, and the other "rejectionist front" groups see the Oslo Accord as an abandonment of even the Palestinians' minimum demand of an end to occupation, so did democrats like Noam Chomsky, who described Israel's deal with the PLO this way:

> To illustrate with an analogy, it is somewhat as if New York State were to cede responsibility for the slums of South Bronx and Buffalo to local authorities while keeping the financial, industrial, and commercial sectors, wealthy residential areas, virtually all of the usable land and resources, indeed everything except

---

4. Larry Derfner, "Torture on Television," *The Jewish Week*, July 1–7, 1994.

for scattered areas it would be happy to hand over to someone else, just as Israel is delighted to free itself from the burden of controlling downtown Nablus and Gaza City directly.[5]

Another democrat, Edward Said, called the agreement "an instrument of Palestinian surrender, a Palestinian Versailles."[6] But they're leftists, and Said was a Palestinian leftist, so let's look at what Richard Nixon, a conservative and admirer of Israel (though not of American Jews) told Rabin after the White House ceremony, according to a posthumous quote provided by Nixon's interlocutor (and former speechwriter), William Safire. Nixon said: "I told [Rabin] later that it takes a strong man to make peace; he's able to do what he's doing because Arafat is weak. . . ."[7] So not only the Palestinian "rejectionists" but Nixon, the ultimate realist, recognized that Arafat's signing of the Oslo Accord grew out of his political weakness (which Arafat himself exacerbated greatly by backing Saddam in the Gulf War). And nearly 20 years later, a very shrewd Israeli attorney, Dov Weisglass, who had been Ariel Sharon's right-hand man in the prime minister's office, looked at the situation and wrote an op-ed titled "Oslo Deal Was Good for the Jews."

Today, as a result of the Oslo Accords, the PA, not Israel, is responsible for the daily life of some 3.5 million Palestinians in the West Bank and Gaza. . . . Before "Oslo" Israel was responsible for the daily life of the Palestinians, in accordance with international law. Israel built the infrastructure, supplied electricity and water, and sustained health services, education, transportation, public order, policing and the courts. Israel also paid the salaries of thousands of Palestinian civil administration employees. . . .

---

5. Noam Chomsky, "A Painful Peace," *Z Magazine,* January 1996.
6. Edward Said, "The Morning After," *London Review of Books,* October 1993.
7. William Safire, "A Conversation with Nixon," *New York Times,* May 2, 1994.

A Palestinian once told me that the Oslo deal was a "brilliant Israeli arrangement." How so? I asked him. "It created the only prison in the world where the prisoners have to provide for themselves, without the management's participation." Israel has the authority of the sovereign in the territories—without the obligations. This situation is a direct result of the Oslo Accords.[8]

The Oslo Accord didn't mention anything about the Palestinians getting a state, or a square inch of Jerusalem, or the return of a single refugee, or the removal of any settlement, or even a halt to settlement expansion, which never let up. Later, during peace negotiations, the best offers of Ehud Barak and Ehud Olmert would have left the Palestinians with a state, all right—a vassal state, one with no right to a military force or control of its own borders or airspace, with its West Bank territory pincered by Israeli settlements and highways, and its would-be capital, Arab East Jerusalem, all but isolated from the rest of "Palestine." So at best, the Palestinians were never offered a state during the peace process, but rather a Bantustan within the borders of Israel. And at any rate, Barak and Olmert were each so terminally weak politically when they made those offers that I don't believe either of them could have gone through with it even if Arafat or Abbas, respectively, had agreed. So for the Palestinians, from the beginning, the Oslo Accord meant a continuation of life under Israeli rule, with no more than a hope of independence, a hope that remains barren a generation later.

So can I blame Hamas and the secular rejectionist groups for refusing to put down their guns and bombs in the face of that? I can't, not today. But I sure could then. I figured if Yasser Arafat and the PLO accepted the deal, for God's sake, how could anybody say it was unfair to the Palestinians? And either way, how could terror ever be justified?

---

8. Dov Weisglass, "Oslo Deal Was Good for the Jews," www.ynetnews.com, August 21, 2012.

But then again, it's not as if the Palestinians only turned to terror because of what the Israelis were doing to them. The Palestinians have a history of using terror against one another, too. In the six years of the first intifada, about 750 to 950 of them were killed as "collaborators" by Hamas, Islamic Jihad, Fatah, and the Popular Front for the Liberation of Palestine, according to B'Tselem. The victims were commonly tortured as well. Many of the targets were indeed collaborators for the Shin Bet, but a great many more just worked for Israeli employers, or were, in Hamas and Islamic Jihad's judgment, "moral collaborators"—pimps, prostitutes, merchants of alcohol or of what the Islamists considered pornography—or they were just unfortunates who'd rubbed the wrong people the wrong way.

B'Tselem's report on this feature of the intifada tells the story, based on an eyewitness's testimony, of Munir Ahmad Ali a-Ra'i,[9] a furniture painter and father of five in a Gazan refugee camp. Even though he'd had his arm broken by Israeli soldiers during the intifada, he was stigmatized in the camp because he claimed to be a communist, he'd smoked hashish, and, according to "Y.A.," the eyewitness, "since he asked many questions, he also made people suspicious." His neighbors accused him of throwing stones at their houses. One day in 1991, a group of masked men saying they were from the intifada's Unified Central Command dragged Munir from his home to a square "where a large crowd had gathered to see what would happen." The enforcers accused him of writing slogans on walls under orders from the Shin Bet. A member of Munir's family told his captors that if they could show any proof he was a collaborator, the family would kill him themselves. The men of the Unified Central Command didn't answer, and went on with their work, said Y.A.:

> The masked men began to beat Munir with axes and rods. He shouted, "I repent . . . I repent," and managed to escape from

---

9. All Y.A. quotes from the case of Munir Ahmad 'Ali a-Ra'i, "Collaborators in the Occupied Territories: Human Rights Abuses and Violations," B'Tselem, January 1994.

them in the direction of the market. He tried to hide underneath one of the stalls, but one of the masked men managed to grab him and carried on giving him ax blows on his legs, accompanied by encouraging cries from the curious onlookers.

Munir survived, but a few months later three men came to his workplace and one of them shot him in the chest. He survived that, too, laying in Gaza's main hospital, Shifa, for two days—"until a member of the [Popular Front's] Red Eagles group came to the hospital and shot him in the head. He died instantly," said Y.A.

The phenomenon of Palestinian collaborator-killings was well-known by mid-1993, a few months before Oslo, when I raised the issue during the Q&A at a day-long Tel Aviv conference held by the Public Committee Against Torture in Israel. Until that point, the only topic of discussion in the conference room had been the torture of Palestinians by the Shin Bet. When I asked the panel's reaction to the torture-murder of Palestinians by their own, Palestinians in the audience turned and glared at me. From the panel, the Israeli lady who headed the Public Committee also glared at me. I don't remember getting a straight answer to my question. But during the break that followed, a middle-aged Palestinian activist came up to me with a stern, reproachful expression and said, "That will be a legitimate question—*after* we have our own state."

As people headed out to the lobby, the Israeli emcee looked at me a little sheepishly and said in a low voice, "These people aren't comfortable with self-criticism."

The disintegration of a popular uprising into rampant internecine violence was nothing new for the Palestinian national movement, either; its activists had indulged in this same sort of thing and worse during the original intifada, the Arab Revolt against the British and Zionists in 1936–39. Benny Morris, an early Israeli "new historian," wrote in his book *Righteous Victims* (just before his shift to the right during the second intifada) that by its final year, "The rebellion had deteriorated into a free-for-all among the rebels themselves. More Arabs were being killed by fellow Palestinians than by

the British or the Jews."[10] He quotes a rebel commander's letter that
year to the *Times of London*:

> Complaints are received from the villages in the Jerusalem area
> regarding robbery, extortion, torture and murder committed
> by several people wearing the uniform of the Jihad. . . . How
> did the innocent sin so that their money is stolen, their cattle
> robbed, their women raped and their jewellery extorted? Our
> rebellion has become a rebellion against the villages and not
> against the government or the Jews.[11]

Everyone has the right to fight for their freedom and independence. But the Palestinians also have a long habit of fighting, often cruelly, for the sake of forcing their will on one another. That doesn't erase their national right to self-defense, or to a sovereign state of their own; all sorts of peoples with violent histories have statehood. But it does erase the notion that self-defense is the only reason Palestinians turn to political violence. And it raises the question of how they would conduct their domestic affairs if they ever did get their own state.

The Oslo Accord was a whole new deal. For Jews, both in Israel and the Diaspora (or those in the Diaspora who cared about Israel), it caused an undeclared schism, one that has never been repaired. What has changed, though, is that since the bloody second intifada killed the peace process in late 2000, the left side of the Jewish schism has weakened decisively while the right side has had the field to itself. But during the seven years of the Oslo peace process, the two sides were roughly equal in numbers and power.

---

10. Benny Morris, *Righteous Victims* (New York: Knopf, 2011), 152.
11. Ibid.

For me, the right's reaction to Oslo acted as a cure for a great deal of my immigrant's Zionist sentimentality. I no longer tried to think of myself as part of *Am Yisrael* in a way that I never would have thought of myself in relation to the American people. Now it wasn't just the fringe—Goldstein, Kach, the crazy rabbis, and settlers—who'd become alien to me, hateful to me; now it was the entire ideological right, beginning with Netanyahu and much of Likud, that had turned toxic, that was filling the streets in rallies where posters showed Rabin wearing an Arab keffiyeh (head scarf) and mobs chanted, "Rabin is a traitor." And these were only the most conspicuous signs of the poison that had spread through the country.

Millions of words have been written about the Rabin assassination, its prelude, and its aftermath. But there are a few things I still want to say about that period that I think bear saying.

To begin with, the consensus view is that the culmination of the incitement against Rabin came at the rally in Jerusalem's Zion Square a month before his murder, the rally where Netanyahu and other right-wing leaders spoke from the balcony while below, among the rabid crowd, teenagers gleefully held up for the TV cameras copies of a photomontage showing Rabin in an SS uniform. At the edges of the mammoth demonstration, protesters stoned and jumped on Rabin's car (he wasn't inside) as it inched its way toward the government compound, and did the same to the car carrying Housing Minister Binyamin Ben-Eliezer.

That was a month before the assassination. However, the venom had already reached that strength 15 months earlier, as I saw and heard at that same spot in downtown Jerusalem on July 2, 1994, during a rally called to protest Yasser Arafat's triumphant entry to Gaza. Hours before the demonstration began, while hundreds of right-wingers noisily set up a tent camp near the government compound, a couple of other reporters and I asked Benny Katsover, a long-time settler leader, about the wildness and menace that now marked the anti-Oslo movement. Blaming the government for inciting people to such extremes, Katsover said he was worried by the mood and the things he'd been hearing.

"I hear it from people, not just in Judea and Samaria, but all over," he told us. "It's against Arabs, but also against Jews. It's getting stronger and stronger. Some people say, 'We have to blow things up. We have to kill.' People have a rage in their belly.

"I feel it," he went on. "Too many people, to my regret, are saying, 'We have to kill Rabin.' "

Going by the journalist's rule of thumb that the size of a gigantic crowd is halfway between the police's conservative estimate and the organizers' liberal one, there were 175,000 people at the rally that night. At the start, when the main thoroughfare, Jaffa Road, was still filling up, a few dozen teenagers, many wearing "Likud Youth" T-shirts, began chanting "Death to Rabin." Some adults joined in. Nobody said anything to stop it.

A man held up a placard with a caricature showing Arafat sodomizing Rabin; the caption read, "The process must continue." People laughed. Some told the cartoonist, "Good for you." Nobody said it was out of bounds. I found a Likud Knesset member, Eliyahu Ben-Elissar, in the crowd and told him about the caricature, and asked if he planned to do anything. "This is not our way," Ben-Elissar said, "but it's not for me to tell him to take it down, and it wouldn't do any good anyway. Besides, that is not the issue."

Another man in the crowd, a solid, all-Israeli type with a sly smile, saw me walking around with a notebook and a pen, and said, "You're with Meretz, right?" I asked what gave him that idea. "You just look like one of them," he said. Since I don't have a high forehead and wasn't wearing little wire-rim glasses, I didn't fit the Meretz physical stereotype, so the guy was likely talking about the expression on my face, which evidently gave away the shock and contempt I felt for what I was seeing.

Once the speeches got underway, the roar of "Rabin is a traitor" became deafening; either thousands or tens of thousands were chanting it. Netanyahu, Sharon, Shamir, and the other speakers had to pause from time to time because they couldn't hear themselves above the din. None of them offered a word of objection to the incitement being blasted at them from below.

Afterward, thousands in the crowd went on a march and report-edly about 200 of them broke off and rampaged through the Muslim Quarter of the Old City, torching one Palestinian car, smashing the windows of many others, and breaking windows of Arab shops. Elsewhere, a minimob broke windows of the US Consulate and sev-eral consular cars.

After the rally, I spoke to Elyakim Haetzni, a former Knesset member and leading settler ideologue, who likened the government to "kapos," only worse. "The kapos were forced to collaborate [with the Nazis]; this government does it willingly," he said.

The protest took place on a Saturday night. The following morn-ing, security forces escorted the ministers to the weekly cabinet meeting, while thousands of police surrounded the government compound to protect it from the surging tent dwellers.

Again, all this happened 16 months before Rabin was shot.

I went to the fatal Tel Aviv rally on the night of November 4, 1995. The cheers for Peres were much more enthusiastic than those for Rabin. We of the peace camp saw Peres as the idealistic initiator of the Oslo Accord, Rabin as the flinty pragmatist who'd had to be persuaded to go along with it. In life, Rabin was not loved by the mass of his supporters; he was too distant, authoritarian, crusty, and famously "analytical." Peres was much warmer and seen as a true-believing dove, not a *bitkhonist*, a security freak, like his boss. In retrospect, our affections were misplaced. Rabin was carrying the whole thing on his back; he was the one being cursed by fascists outside his Tel Aviv home, he was the one leading the verbal counterattack against the right, he was the one in danger—or certainly the main one.

I left the rally after the speeches; I could hear Ahinoam Nini singing in the background as I started the half-hour walk home. Not long after I arrived, I got a telephone call from Chicago from a col-league at one of the American Jewish newspapers I was writing for. He told me Rabin had been shot and that a Jew had been arrested.

"A Jewish pig!" I informed my sister, who called from L.A. as I was on my way out. I hailed a cab in the street. "You heard, Rabin was shot," I said to the driver. "I know. Good that he was shot," he said. "Good that he was shot?" I replied, somewhere between disbelief, anger, and journalistic curiosity. "Sure it's good. He gave everything to the [new-immigrant] Russians; what did he do for us?" said the big Mizrahi driver. I told myself I didn't want to start cursing him because he might throw me out of the cab and I needed to get as close to the hospital as I could, as fast as I could. But when he let me out in the traffic jam, I paid him and didn't say anything, purely out of cowardice.

I started walking fast up the block toward Ichilov Hospital, along with a lot of other people. I fell in line with a couple of young Orthodox Jews in white shirts and black pants, one of whom was listening to the news on a portable radio. The news said Rabin was in "fair" condition. "That's good. They were saying before that he was in critical, maybe he's improving," I said to the two guys. Across the street a stylish young woman was getting into her sports car, and she'd heard me. In a weary voice, she called out to us, "No, no, he's dead." I stopped in my tracks and said loudly to no one, "Damn it, damn it, damn it" over and over.

I went to Ichilov, where a crowd was standing outside. I didn't interview anyone. Later, a friend asked me why I didn't; it was because the people were obviously thinking and feeling things that were far beyond their ability to put into words, certainly at that moment, so any answer they gave to a journalist's questions would have been banal. I heard one man say, "That's it. This country's finished." Another man began to faint, but the woman he was with grabbed him. For me, it didn't sink in that Rabin was dead until the radio announcer stopped reading the news. There was a silence, and then came that deep, grave, searing symphonic music associated with the deaths of Soviet dictators. I went over to the square, which was covered with the torn posters and other trash left over from the giant rally. A few thousand people were still standing around, not knowing what to do. Others knelt and lit candles. I felt cold and empty and what I wanted very badly was to go home to my wife and infant son.

In the days afterward, I called Benny Katsover and reminded him that he'd told me over a year before that he was hearing people talk about the need to kill Rabin. "I never stopped hearing people talk like this—how we have to assault, murder, assassinate," he said. "Sometimes I'd be sitting at a red light, and the driver next to me would yell, 'We've got to kill him.' You heard it from every stratum of the population."

Noam Federman, a notorious Kach leader, told me that people used to come up to him and say, " 'We've got to kill Rabin.' I heard it so many times, not from 100 people, and not from 200 people, but many more. I heard it from people in Judea and Samaria, but more so in Jerusalem, and in other places too, from religious people and from secular people."

No, it wasn't half the country—the half that opposed the peace process—that killed him. A few of the national camp's notables— Likud Knesset members Benny Begin, Dan Meridor, and David Levy—were even heroes of that terrible time for speaking out so urgently and repeatedly against the incitement. The great majority of Israelis who opposed Oslo were bystanders—they neither fed the fire nor tried to put it out. But a large minority, I'd say hundreds of thousands of Israeli Jews, backed by lots of American Jews, made up a movement obsessed by the idea that Rabin was a traitor, an eager collaborator with those who were out to kill Jews and destroy Israel. The inescapable logic of this message was that Rabin deserved to be executed. And the movement bearing this message was the lifeblood of the broader opposition to the Oslo peace process. After the assassination, the state-run Channel 1 news reran a pre-assassination clip several times of a politician saying in an interview that "a very reliable source" had told him that the Rabin government was "signaling" Hamas, via the PLO, that it would not object to the murder of Jewish settlers.[12] That claim was likewise tantamount to incitement

---

12. Larry Derfner, "Forgetting Rabin," *Atlanta Jewish Times,* October 25, 1996.

to Rabin's murder. The politician who made it—without backing it up in the slightest, of course—was Binyamin Netanyahu, the leader of the opposition, the headliner at those monstrous rallies.

A month before the murder, after the attack on Rabin's car and the display of the SS posters, after a man had rushed at Rabin during his appearance at a park, after the danger had become too palpable to ignore anymore, President Ezer Weizman said, "This is an unprecedented phenomenon. It cannot be allowed to spread. There are forces that can stop it if they wish." Did Netanyahu want Rabin to be killed? No. Could Netanyahu have stopped it if he'd wished? At the very least, he could have disassociated himself and the party he led from a movement that radiated bloodlust. He could have gotten off the balcony.

No political event ever affected me anywhere near as powerfully as Rabin's murder. First the shock and anger, then the grief, then the love for the martyred leader—not only of one's nation, but of one's cause—then the rebirth of hope. Walking through the square in the days afterward and seeing all the people, especially the young, and all the candles and heartbroken graffiti messages—I felt such love for my country and for the better part of my countrymen. A week afterward, I wrote that Israel had gone through "a catharsis, a purifying experience. . . . The decent majority emerged from the week of mourning like someone who has survived a life-threatening illness: with a resolution to take much better care of themselves from now on." In retrospect, the main thing Israel learned from the Rabin assassination was to beef up the security detail around the prime minister.

A popular theory, associated most closely with Bill Clinton and clung to by many disenchanted Israeli and American Jewish doves, is that Yigal Amir didn't just kill Rabin, he also killed the peace process. But the truth is the exact opposite: The peace process died *despite* the assassination, which gave the policy of the slain prime minister the strongest boost, by far, it had ever received. A week before the murder, Israel's most trusted pollster, Dr. Mina Tsemach, found Rabin leading Netanyahu in popularity 40 to 39 percent, a statistical tie, although the government was not popular. (This, incidentally, disproves a favorite theory of the right: that at the time of the assassination Netanyahu was leading Rabin in the polls.) A week after the murder, Tsemach's poll found Peres, the new premier, leading Netanyahu by the extraordinary margin of 54 to 23 percent.[13] Asked if they thought the government should continue the peace process with the Palestinians, a staggering 74 percent of people said yes, while 23 percent said no.

So what happened? How did Netanyahu end up beating Peres, albeit by only 1 percent, in the prime ministerial election six and a half months later?

The shift was set in motion at the beginning of 1996, when Peres ordered the assassination of Yahya Ayyash, "The Engineer," Hamas's military chief and master bombmaker, responsible for the deaths of scores of Israelis. When I heard the news of Ayyash's death on my living room TV, I literally leapt for joy. And how short-sighted I was. In the previous four and a half months, a total of one Israeli had been killed in a terror attack—but Ayyash had it coming, so Peres ordered the hit in Gaza and it was a happy day in Israel. The blowback began late the next month, when Hamas bombed a Jerusalem bus, then a week later blew up another one, then the day after that sent a suicide bomber to Tel Aviv's Dizengoff Center mall. Between those three explosions and two individual murders, 60 Israelis were killed in the course of nine days.

Aside from the size of the death toll, that murder spree was historic for several reasons. It neutralized the political effect of the Rabin assassination, getting the right wing off the defensive and back on the warpath. It cut dramatically into Peres's lead in the polls over Netanyahu, putting the challenger within striking distance with the election less than three months away. It forced Arafat to start cracking down severely on Hamas, since he knew that if this kind of

---

13. "Poll," *Yediot Ahronot,* November, 10, 1995.

terror continued, the peace process was over and he would no longer be the *rais*, the president, of any place.

Yet at the same time, despite Arafat's dramatic shift in approach toward Hamas, the bombings marked the closing of the window, opened on the White House lawn two and a half years before, when much of mainstream Israel became ready, for the first time, to suspend its distrust of the Palestinians and "give peace a chance." After that traumatic, nine-day outburst of terror, "peace" for Israelis would mean nothing more than security, and their deep resentment and spitefulness toward the Palestinians, from Hamas to Fatah to everyone in between, would be back to stay.

Hours after the Dizengoff Center bombing, the crowd across the street was dominated by the same sort of "soccer hooligan" types who, together with the religious far right, had set the atmosphere at the anti-Oslo rallies. Israeli broadcast journalists have always, automatically, described the mood at such post-terror gatherings as being filled with "pain and rage," but it's bullshit. I've been to them—the people in pain and rage are quiet, and they're the minority. Instead, the crowds at the scenes of terror attacks in major Israeli cities are dominated by the soccer hooligans, who get high on the mob malevolence. They're gleeful, laughing, jumping up and down, bouncing against their squealing girlfriends, singing their fight songs with new lyrics. *"Baruch Goldstein, Baruch Goldstein, there's no one like you in the world . . ."* Across from Dizengoff Center that evening, a couple of people were holding up a new caricature—of Peres's face as a skull on crossbones, with blood dripping out of his mouth, and it was captioned "Traitor." The soccer fans "sang" in their braying, hoarse voices, *"He's a traitor, he's a traitor, he's a traitor. . . ."* When I first got there, I saw a middle-age man shouting, "They don't give a damn about us. Peres does what Arafat tells him to." He wasn't smiling, he was genuinely incensed, someone to at least be taken seriously. Later on I saw him standing on a car, chanting with the crowd, "Death to the Arabs," with a crazy little smile at the corners of his mouth. These crowds are so intimidating. I saw a couple of brave souls trying to suggest, delicately, that maybe Peres wasn't a murderer, maybe he didn't want Jews to get killed. It didn't go over well. One elderly, mild dissenter was warned, "Get out of here. This is no place for leftists." Such was the scene in the heart of Tel Aviv, a half-mile from what was now Rabin Square, four months after the assassination. The same fascist orgy all over again.

But those were the wild men of the right; most Israelis, including middle-of-the-roaders, wanted the peace process to continue—not because they believed in it, but because they were afraid that if it ended, all hell would break loose with the Palestinians, and maybe with the Arab states as well. But the bombardment of terror had to stop. The status quo had become untenable. Everyone, me included, agreed that if things went on like this, the peace process was over and whatever happened, happened. In Ramallah, Arafat got the message, he went after Hamas, and while the terror didn't end, it began to diminish steadily.

As for candidate Netanyahu, since most Israelis wanted the peace process to continue, he was in a dilemma. He'd done nothing but denounce the Oslo Accord as a national suicide pact, but if he campaigned against it, the voters would reject him. So he came up with a brilliant solution: "Secure Peace." That became his slogan. He would continue the peace process, he would make peace, but peace with security, secure peace, not Peres's peace with terror. Over and over, in his jingle, his campaign ads, his speeches: Secure Peace. At the same time, he modulated his tone; he didn't want to scare people, to remind them of his pre-assassination self. But he definitely wanted to scare them about Peres, and that he did: In dark, foreboding, Hitchcock-style TV ads, he linked Peres with terror, with Arafat, and with "dividing Jerusalem." Through it all, Peres stuck to his Rose Garden strategy, as if it was beneath him to acknowledge these accusations—which were eating away at his lead. During the televised debate in the week before the election, Netanyahu played a younger version of Reagan to Peres's older version of Carter: Instead of "there you go again," it was "don't tell me your stories."

Another thing that contributed to Peres's defeat was his decision a month and a half before the election to launch "Operation

Grapes of Wrath" in Lebanon, whose southern region was still occupied by Israeli troops. Israeli tank shells killed over 100 civilians
in a UN shelter in the village of Qana. As a result, a campaign to
cast a blank ballot for prime minister spread among Israeli Arabs,
which cost Peres (who got 94 percent support from the Arabs who
did cast their ballots) an untold number of votes. And since he only
lost by 30,000 votes, his decision to escalate the war in Lebanon was
decisive—though certainly not as decisive as his order to assassinate
Yahya Ayyash.

On Election Day, May 29, 1996, the exit polls put Peres ahead
by 1 percent. A friend of mine lay in bed all that night listening to
the returns on the radio, and as Netanyahu got closer and closer, he
would recall later, "I had a gut feeling like my life was in danger." In
a little while it was morning in Israel.

A week later I wrote, "This has been like a death. . . . For days
after the election I would wake up and immediately go into a funk
on remembering that Netanyahu had won." Leah Rabin, speaking
for any number of peaceniks, said, "I feel like packing my bags and
flying as quickly as possible away from here."[14] She also spoke for
many of them in criticizing the Peres campaign for not pounding
away at Netanyahu and the right for paving the way to her husband's
murder. But Peres's campaign chairman, Labor's Haim Ramon,
explained that his people had tested a set of anti-Netanyahu,
incitement-themed ads on focus groups, and they didn't go over well.
That line of attack was too divisive, too incendiary—voters did not
want to hear it, Ramon said. I have no doubt he was right and that if
Peres had run those ads and campaigned on that message, he would
have lost the election by a bigger margin. Ever since that nine-day
terror spree erased the political effect of Rabin's assassination, the
Israeli public has made it very clear that it does not want to discuss
who, beyond Yigal Amir, was responsible, because this is truly so
divisive, so incendiary a question. In electing Netanyahu, a slight but
nonetheless triumphant majority of the public sent a message about
that great crime: Case closed.

---

14. "Israeli Election Draws Mixed Reactions," www.cnn.com, May 30, 1996.

A good friend of mine who'd come from France with a TV crew to cover the election, Ed Goldstein, whose earlier move to Israel had inspired my own, and who had spent years debating whether to move back, decided to cancel his plans to hang around the country a little while after Election Day. "I want to get out of here," he said. "This is ugly."

CHAPTER SEVEN

AMONG THE JEWISH UNDERCLASS

A t heart, I am a 1930s socialist, a comrade of the poor and the minorities fighting the rich and powerful. I'm extremely proud of my father's communist-prisoner past—and I have always regretted terribly that by the time I reached adolescence, he'd made enough money to move us to West L.A. and that I came of age as a middle-class kid, always wishing I was poor so I could live a heroic life, too, like a character in a novel by Steinbeck, or James Baldwin, or any of those idealistic writers who shaped my sensibility and whom I still love. Becoming a journalist (seeing as how, unfortunately, I didn't have a fiction writer's imagination) was a way to at least glimpse other, more exciting lives, and, given my inclinations, that meant being drawn, always, to the underclass.

But while I have a socialist's heart and am moved most of all by stories of the poor rising up in a righteous cause, I do not have a socialist's mind anymore. I root for the poor, but I no longer "believe" in them. I don't think being weak necessarily makes you good, and neither does it necessarily make you blameless for your problems— or for the problems you may cause others. In fact, poverty, from what I've seen, tends to make you angry and miserable and either passive or aggressive. That's the reason I believe in fighting it: because it's bad for people. If the poor were as heroic and inspiring as I once believed, and as my heart still wants to believe, poverty might be something to fight *for*, not against.

In Israel, as in many other countries, poverty has an ethnic dimension: It afflicts mainly Mizrahim, Arabs, and Jews of Ethiopian background. (Also ultra-Orthodox or haredi Jews, but that's a matter of choice: Most of them choose religious study, financed by welfare and charity, over work.)

And not only is Israel's circle of poverty made up largely of Mizrahim, Arabs, and Ethiopians, the circle of Israeli crime and violence is, too.

For a true-blue Jewish liberal, this is extremely hard to swallow. But it's a fact. In May 2015, the Israel Prison Service reported that at Israel's all-juvenile prison, nearly half the detainees were Arabs (who make up 20 percent of the national population), and over 40 percent of the Jewish detainees were Ethiopians (who make up less than 2 percent of the national population).[1] As for Mizrahim, a Hebrew University criminologist who asked the prison service, at my behest, for figures on Mizrahi and Ashkenazi inmates said he was told there were no such statistics. But I've read journalists and Mizrahi academics—who blame the situation on Ashkenazi discrimination—say Mizrahim, who make up about 40 percent of the national population, make up "60 percent" or "an absolute majority" of Israel's prison population.[2]

---

1. Telem Yahav, "Prison Service: Almost Half of Jewish Teen Detainees Are of Ethiopian Descent," www.ynetnews.com, May 30, 2015.
2. Michal Zak, "Mizrahi Jews Remind Israel of its Hidden Other," *Middle East Eye*, March 16, 2015; "Encyclopedia Judaica: Crime," Jewish Virtual Library, 2008; Anat Georgi, "The Israeli Melting Pot and its Discontents," *Haaretz*, May 14, 2013.

I want to be very clear: The overwhelming majority of Mizrahim, Arabs, and Ethiopians are peaceable, law-abiding citizens. However, the overwhelming majority of violent criminals in Israel are Mizrahi, Arab, and Ethiopian.

Who's to blame for this? There is a taboo against paying more than lip service to the idea that the poor bear a substantial part of the responsibility for their own problems, and there's a good reason for that taboo: Putting much of the blame on the poor for being poor is hurtful. They're already suffering; blaming them for it, or for a good deal of it, seems like adding insult to injury. And for a middle-class Ashkenazi (like me) to do it also amounts to "punching down."

Furthermore, it's one thing when the ethnic dimension of the "culture of poverty" coincides with systematic Ashkenazi discrimination, as it did in the '50s and '60s when the waves of Mizrahi immigrants arrived. (The discrimination continued into the '80s, though in a lower gear, as "development town" and inner-city Mizrahi kids were routinely funneled into vocational rather than academic high schools.) But when such discrimination and prejudice subsides—as it has, drastically, toward Mizrahim (though much less so toward Ethiopians and not at all toward Arabs)—then at some point you have to entertain the possibility that the Ashkenazim aren't completely to blame and that at least the Mizrahi members of the underclass, who by now face only incidental prejudice, bear some if not most of the responsibility for their situation themselves.

This strikes at the heart of left-liberal ideology. It means that the solution to poverty is not entirely in society or the government's hands. But if you don't consider the possibility that at least the Mizrahim of Israel's underclass bear a good deal of the responsibility for their own condition, if you continue to put all the blame on the "Ashkenazi elite"—no matter that by now most Mizrahim have entered the middle class, no matter that the residual prejudice against them is minuscule compared to that faced by Ethiopian Jews, and nothing at all compared to that faced by Arabs and African refugees—then you may not be as progressive as you think. Then you may be guilty of what an otherwise-unenlightening president, George W. Bush, once called "the soft bigotry of low expectations."[3]

And just as there is a taboo against blaming the non-Ashkenazi underclass to any significant degree for their social problems, so there is a taboo against blaming the Mizrahim among them for their conspicuous presence in the ranks of Israeli racists and fascists, and for their crucial contribution to keeping Israel's anti-Arab right wing in power. Again, I want to be clear: Israel's cardinal sins—harsh discrimination against Arab citizens, military dictatorship over the Palestinians, and military aggression against Arab states—are obviously not the fault of the Mizrahi poor. As a matter of fact, they are all the fault of the one-time Ashkenazi "socialist" elite, who inaugurated each of these three miserable, ongoing traditions during times when they really did run the show all by themselves. (Israel's other cardinal sin, the extremely callous treatment of African refugees, is a 21st-century development and represents a collaboration of all Israeli ethnic groups.)

Another caveat: Racism and fascism among West Bank settlers are dominated by Ashkenazim, not Mizrahim, because in the settlements these diseases grow out of ideology, and Ashkenazim have always dominated the ideological settler movement, which grows out of the broader religious nationalist movement, whose elite has likewise always been Ashkenazi.

But there is no taboo against blaming settlers for racist ultranationalism (one reason being that they're mainly, conveniently Ashkenazi). Yet there is a taboo against recognizing that in Israel proper, the biggest reservoir of violent, mob-style racism and fascism lies in the relatively poor "development towns" of the Negev and Galilee and in the poor neighborhoods of the cities—all of which are populated primarily by Mizrahim.

---

3. "Text: George W. Bush's Speech to the NAACP," www.washingtonpost.com, July 10, 2010.

As any poll will reveal, racist and fascist attitudes have become pretty well entrenched throughout Israeli Jewish society, especially among the young, and so has the popularity of the right wing; Mizrahim and Ashkenazim are both part of this trend. To add yet another disclaimer: The huge majority of Mizrahim in Israeli cities and towns are, of course, not mob fascists. And one final caveat: The voting pattern of the Mizrahi professional middle class is probably much closer to that of the Ashkenazi middle class than to that of the Mizrahi poor.

Having said all that, though, the fact remains: Aside from veteran Russian immigrants (who are an anomaly on the Israeli right, being both highly educated and secular), the Orthodox Jewish middle class, and the haredim, the hard core of the Israeli right's political support comes from the Mizrahi underclass (who, not incidentally, are also Orthodox).

There's nothing unusual about them in this regard; they're part of a global pattern. Poor Mizrahim are right wing with a strong tendency to racism just like poor whites are all over the West, and just like poor Muslims are in the Middle East, where they dependably support the most militant nationalist or religious-nationalist candidates. In every society I know of, the poorer classes of the dominant group—in Israel, Jews; in the West, whites; in the Middle East, Muslims—are drawn to demagogues who promise them power, because they have so little of it. And they tend to hate the people who are on the rung below them—in Israel, Arabs; in the West, blacks and other people of color; in the Middle East, blacks (as black Sudanese refugees in Israel have attested from their experiences in their Arab-run homeland and their sojourn in Egypt).

Yes, for me to say these sorts of things counts as punching down. But unfortunately, from everything I've seen and learned, this is the lay of the land. And one thing my words aren't is racist, because for something to be racist it has to be a lie, and what I've written is no lie. For me to say that the problems of anti-Arab and anti-black racism, ultra-nationalism, crime, and violence in Israel have no connection with ethnicity and economic class, or that they do but they're wholly the fault of the Ashkenazi elite, would indeed be a lie, and a cowardly one.

The late 1990s, the period of Netanyahu's first term as prime minister, was a time when Israeli society split into the elites and the *amcha*, the salt of the earth. The division was whipped up by Netanyahu and Aryeh Deri, leader of the Mizrahi ultra-Orthodox Shas party, and went into high gear after they both came under criminal investigation and sought to rally public support to their side. (They, Avigdor Lieberman, and Likud fixer David Appel were suspected of trying to corrupt the office of attorney general; only Deri was indicted, and the charges against him were later dropped.) The late '90s were also a time of high unemployment and deepening poverty and inequality, which Netanyahu dealt with like the good Republican supply-sider, trickle-downer he is: He slashed away at the welfare state. Nevertheless, the poor remained loyal to him. Writing again now for the *Jerusalem Post* (the chief executive I'd called a liar was gone, a couple of friends at the paper convinced the new editor-in-chief that I hadn't sabotaged the computer system, and to some extent I swallowed my pride), I went out to cover the story of poverty in Israel. I found myself torn between sympathy for these people because of the hardships of their lives and antipathy for them because of the hatred I kept hearing toward leftists and Arabs. (I also wrote a lot about Israeli Arabs, who dominate the ranks of Israeli poverty, but the Arab poor are a separate issue that I'll get into later.)

They didn't look bad, the 30 or so development towns in the "periphery"—like Beit Shean and Kiryat Shmona in the Galilee up north and Sderot, Ofakim, and Yerucham in the Negev down south. The streets were clean, the beige and pastel tenements and private houses were generally in decent shape, and inside the families kept them very nicely. There wasn't hunger or much alcoholism, drug abuse, or violent crime; you could walk the streets at night without a worry. What hit you, though, was the stagnation in the atmosphere.

The only "action" was in the beauty parlors, little restaurants, and candy stores where people sat around killing time. It seemed like everyone played the lottery. There were virtually no good jobs in these towns; the textile factories that once kept them going were closing one after another, victims of globalization, and the residents lived too far away from the job-rich center of the country to commute. Hardly anybody had a college degree, the only books seemingly being read were holy ones, and the schools were lousy; just about anybody with ambition left for Tel Aviv, or Haifa, or Jerusalem, or America, or someplace where they might have a future.

Yet with all that, the main political struggle in the development towns, and in the inner-city neighborhoods likewise dominated by poor Mizrahim, was between Likud and Shas. The left-wing Meretz party always fought the hardest against poverty, yet the Jewish poor hated them. It was Meretz that led the fight to allow over 100,000 poor families, mainly Mizrahim, to pay a minimal price to buy the public housing flats they'd been paying rent on for decades. The spearhead of that campaign was a Meretz Knesset member who was even born in Iraq. And who opposed the idea? Netanyahu. In the development towns and poor urban neighborhoods, masses of these hard-up families became homeowners thanks to the Meretz-led campaign—and they went right on hating Meretz and cheering Netanyahu.

"I'm very, very much against Meretz. They're for peace and equality between the Jews and Arabs, and I hate the Arabs," an 18-year-old girl in Ofakim told me. "Besides, Meretz has no Jewish content. As far as I'm concerned, they behave like heretics." The girl would be voting for the first time in the next election—for Netanyahu, she said.

Once I went with Eli Ben Menachem, a likable, energetic, Mizrahi backbencher with the Labor Party, on his rounds in south Tel Aviv's seedy but lively, colorful Hatikva Quarter, the old-time Harlem of Israel, where he lived in the same old building he was born in. We went to the apartment of a struggling single mother and he promised to see if he could help her. "I do this because I believe in it, but I know they're not going to vote for Labor. They're going to vote

Likud," he said, grinning like a good sport. The woman nodded. "I have the highest respect for Eli, but I'm Likud in my blood."

In Jerusalem's Katamon Tet neighborhood, I talked to a Mizrahi man who'd been paying rent on a public housing flat for 33 years, and now the Netanyahu government was talking about selling these apartments to private management companies, which would raise the rents. "I want to leave my apartment to my children and grand-children. And if anybody tries to move me out, I'll kill him," the man said. He ran a candy store out of a tent. He had three grown children at home: two unemployed, one in the army. I asked him who he blamed for the threat to sell his home out from under him. "I don't blame Netanyahu. When he came in, the government was broke. He's just trying to raise some money. I blame the Labor Party. They're the ones who ruined our lives in the first place."

By the election campaign of 2015, I thought the poor Mizrahim had given up on Likud and Netanyahu. If they were still poor after yet another generation of this same bunch being in power, I figured they wouldn't vote for them again; they'd either vote for a party even further to the right or not vote at all. But I was wrong. On the mid-afternoon of Election Day, it was to these people whom Netanyahu aimed his Hail Mary appeal for votes—to the poor and badly edu-cated, who are the least diligent voters in every country, and who, among Israel's Jews, are largely Mizrahim. "The Arabs are going to the polls in droves, the leftist NGOs are bringing them in buses," Netanyahu warned.[4] And it worked: The votes came pouring in, with 40 percent of those from the development towns going for Likud, compared to 26 percent of Jewish voters nationwide. (All told, these towns, along with the poor urban neighborhoods, gave a completely lopsided majority of votes to the bloc of right-wing/religious parties

---

4. Ishaan Tharoor, "On Israeli Election Day, Netanyahu Warns of Arabs Voting 'In Droves'," *Washington Post*, March 17, 2015.

over that of the center/left bloc.[5]) *Haaretz* reporter Roy Arad heard from some of these people, such as a 59-year-old unemployed man in the Negev town Kiryat Gat:

> Netanyahu seems honest with the Mizrahim, like Begin. I am a Likud voter since childhood. . . . There are serious social problems and Bibi made mistakes and didn't help the poor, but it seems to me this time he learned. The truth is that I can't *not* vote Likud, just like I haven't switched soccer teams since I was 10, Maccabi Tel Aviv always. The vote for Bibi is from here [pats his heart].[6]

The unemployed Mizrahi guy from a development town who loves Likud and his soccer team—it's a basic Israeli stereotype but one rooted in reality. The phenomenon of racist hooliganism at Israeli soccer games, directed mainly at Arab players but also at blacks, is concentrated almost solely among poorly educated Mizrahi fans. Betar Jerusalem, the legendary team of Israel's capital, a team historically aligned with Likud, has to this day an unwritten but ironclad policy against hiring Arab players—because its Hitler Youth–style fan club, La Familia, has threatened all manner of violence to prevent it. When Betar's owners signed two Chechen Muslim players—not Arabs, but still Muslims—a couple of Betar fans burned down the team's clubhouse. After one Betar game, a gang of La Familia types attacked Arab workers and patrons in a shopping mall near the stadium. Once I sat in the stands among 2,000 Betar fans for a game in Tel Aviv, and all around me people were chanting "Death to the Arabs" and singing a team song that ends "I hate all the Arabs." The strange thing was that they didn't even look angry. They looked almost bored; they were so used to it, like they were singing the national anthem or mumbling their prayers.

---

5. "Results of 20th Knesset Election," Central Elections Committee (Hebrew), March 17, 2015.

6. Roy Arad, "Staunch Supporters and Swing Voters: Meet the People Who Chose Netanyahu," *Haaretz*, www.haaretz.com, May 21, 2015.

And while Betar Jerusalem exhibits the most virulent case of racism, the disease infects all of Israeli soccer. It's quite an experience to sit with your two young sons in the stands of a Maccabi Tel Aviv home game in the 21st century and hear an entire section of fans roaring monkey noises—"*Hoo-hoo-hoo!! Hoo-hoo-hoo!!*"—at a black player after he's scored a goal.

This behavior, of course, isn't unique to Israel; soccer seems to bring out the inner fascist in masses of people all over the world. But in Israel such behavior is the special preserve of the Mizrahi lower middle class.

Likewise, the most notoriously brutal of Israel's fighting units against the Palestinians, the Border Police, is top-heavy with soldiers from this same population. I spent a month of army reserve guarding the Border Police base in Gaza, and one quiet Shabbat I was talking to this skinny Mizrahi soldier and he shared this with me: "You know, if you show me the most beautiful Arab girl in the world, really a knock-out, and you tell me I can either rape her or kill her, I'd rather kill her." That was what he wanted to tell me. Now it was my turn to say something. So I asked why he had to rape the girl or kill her—why couldn't he just, you know, not do either? His face went blank. "I hate Arabs," he shrugged, and went on his way. That evening as we were all heading into the dining room, he trotted toward the entrance, saw me, pantomimed shooting me with a machine gun, grinned to show he was just kidding, kissed the mezuzah on the doorpost, and went in to eat with his high-spirited brothers in arms.

The large proportion of poor and lower-middle-class Mizrahim in the most abusive army units, like their near-exclusivity in the ranks of soccer hooligans, goes nearly unmentioned publicly, but it's one of the ABCs of Israeli society and politics. An even harder-to-miss elephant in the salon is the near wall-to-wall presence of Mizrahim in Jewish violent crime. Virtually all of the country's Jewish mafia families have Mizrahi names: Abergil, Abutbul, Alperon, Ben Harush, Shirazi, Harari, Domrani. (Ze'ev Rosenstein, now in prison, was an exception, but his troops were Mizrahim.)

They came up in rough Mizrahi neighborhoods and remain success stories to many of the people who stayed there. In 1993, thousands of mourners attended the funeral in south Tel Aviv's Hatikva
Quarter for Yehezkel Aslan, a neighborhood kid who grew up to be
Israel's number-one mafioso by selling heroin and having his rivals
killed, before getting shot to death by someone from the competition. A few days afterward I walked up and down Hatikva's main drag,
Etzel Street, past the popular Middle Eastern grill restaurant where
Aslan conducted business, and asked people their opinion of him.

"The kids used to point to him and say, 'That's Yehezkel Aslan.'
Everybody looked up to him," said a young counterman at a candy
store. "Everyone gave him respect. He'd pass by and people would
wave to him and say, "Shalom, Yehezkel,' and he'd wave back," said
the owner of another Etzel Street grill. Like a good mafia leader,
Aslan took care of his old neighborhood, donating money to fix up
synagogues, finance the local soccer team, feed the elderly, give new-
lyweds a financial stake. He even donated to a Hatikva drug rehab
center, which seemed only fair, since he'd made so much money off
its clients. I only heard one person speak badly about Aslan. "He was
a dirty rag. A lot of people died because of him. Some people walk
around here half dead because of heroin, and he brought it in," said
a high school kid arguing with the pro-Aslan counterman at the
candy store. Everybody else I talked to said, "He was a good man,"
"He was the best," "He had a good heart, he helped everyone," "I was
heartsick over his death."

Nine years later, in 2002, another mafia leader, Felix Abutbul, the
crime boss in Netanya, got shot to death outside his casino in Prague.
For his funeral in Netanya's Independence Square, "thousands and
thousands of people came out, everybody was crying. He was like the
mayor here," the owner of an outdoor café in the square told me. A
laborer in the city's produce market who'd gotten to know Abutbul in
prison said, "Even a prime minister wouldn't get a funeral like that.
You have no idea how people in this city loved him." The deceased
was said by police to have run a local extortion racket—notably at
the expense of merchants in the produce market and Independence

Square. His gang was also into gambling, loan-sharking, arson, and, of course, murdering rivals. But finding witnesses brave enough to testify against Abutbul was next to impossible, so police only managed to keep him in jail a couple of times, and for no more than a few months, once for beating up an employee and once for beating up a building contractor. Abutbul's skill at dodging the law only raised his stature among his legions of Netanya fans.

"Who are the police?" sneered a watermelon vendor in the market. "They make a mountain out of a molehill. He was a wonderful man, a man with a heart of gold; he built a synagogue; he gave money to the poor. His whole family is wonderful. The police go after a fine man like that instead of all the drug addicts and bums." What Yehezkel Aslan was to the Hatikva Quarter, Felix Abutbul was to old Netanya. Said the café owner in Independence Square: "Whenever he walked down the street, people would come up to shake his hand. He settled feuds between the businessmen. He always dressed elegantly. Everybody admired him; they wanted to be like him."

What on earth is going on here? These people are not children; they raise children. Where did they get these ideas? And as the saying goes, they all love their mothers, not to mention the Blessed Holy One. There is a serious problem among the Mizrahi underclass and among those who climbed out of it economically but not mentally—and this cannot all be put down to the Ashkenazi elite.

So what can it be put down to? I think the first question that has to be asked is: Why is there a Mizrahi underclass, a Mizrahi subculture of poverty, crime, and violence, when there is no parallel among Ashkenazim—and when most Mizrahim are not poor and only a miniscule proportion of them are violent criminals?

There is no objective explanation for this. But I'll give mine.

One part of the answer is the traumatic legacy of the *ma'abarot,* the immigrant "transit camps" where hundreds of thousands of immigrants from the Middle East lived in tents, then sheds, for years, and where they were often treated by Ashkenazi authorities like lesser beings. I had a friend when I first came to Israel, an immigrant from Wales, who told me his Indian-born father had gone to

Israel in the mid-'50s after he got his engineering degree, hoping to help build the Jewish state. "But he saw they looked at him as just another one of these dark-skinned Jews, and they were going to throw him into one of those *ma'abarot*, and he left the country," my friend said. Many of today's "development towns" grew out of those "transit camps" (such optimistic, forward-looking terms the Ashkenazi authorities came up with), and the residual effects were naturally felt in the towns long after the transit camps closed down.

But they've been closed now for three generations; the *ma'abarot* do not by themselves explain why there are still so many poor Mizrahi neighborhoods in 2016 Israel.

Another part of the answer is enduring, free-floating Ashkenazi prejudice. When my mother came to live in Israel, she rented an apartment from an old Ashkenazi man who wanted to write into the contract that she was forbidden to sublet to a Mizrahi tenant. (We convinced him to leave that clause out.) I have a friend, a good-looking, dark-skinned man of Yemenite heritage, whom my wife tried to set up with one of her Ashkenazi friends, and after her friend met him at our house, she told my wife, "Why did you want to set me up with him? He's black." When we went looking for an apartment in Modi'in, one of the agents tried to woo us by saying, "This project is for quality people, not shleppers from Lod," referring to the run-down, mainly Mizrahi town nearby. We have Ashkenazi friends at a moshav who told us the community's leaders have an unwritten rule against accepting Mizrahim as members. There is a good deal of this garden-variety type prejudice against Mizrahim in Israel, and I have no doubt it results in some of them running into closed doors, professionally and socially.

Yet at the same time, I have no doubt that being Mizrahi has opened some doors, too; there are plenty of liberal, well-intentioned Ashkenazim in positions of power in this country who will bend over backward to help Mizrahim. In any case, the level of contemporary Ashkenazi prejudice, or certainly of discrimination, cannot fully account for the persistence of a Mizrahi underclass.

One of the long-standing explanations, which makes sense to me, is that during the Jews' mass exodus from the Middle East from the late '40s through early '60s, the educational and economic elites of the communities tended to go to Britain, France, and the United States, while the poorer, less-educated masses went to Israel. In the West, Mizrahim are every bit as successful as Ashkenazim, often more so. And the "pure Sephardim," those who trace their heritage back to the 1492 expulsion from Spain and Portugal, are a Jewish aristocracy in Israel. I had a "pure Sephardi" friend whose family was Syrian, and he told of his parents' extreme displeasure over his "marrying down" to a Polish Jewish woman. Also, there's evidence that the Mizrahim who came from monied, well-educated families continued the family tradition in Israel; the Iraqi immigration of the early '50s was notable for its high proportion of highly educated, prosperous people, and they founded what is by now a permanent Iraqi Jewish elite in this country.

So socioeconomic background matters. But so does national background. I cannot look at the educational and economic standards of the Middle Eastern countries the Mizrahim came from and say this has no connection whatsoever to the staying power of a Mizrahi culture of poverty in Israel.

The relevance of national background becomes even clearer when you look at the so-called Russian immigrants, more accurately called immigrants from the former Soviet Union (FSU). Those from Russia, Ukraine, and other countries in the western part of the FSU have become known here as world-beaters in education and the professions, while a large proportion from the FSU's Caucasus mountain regions and southern Asian countries such as Kazakhstan and Uzbekistan have joined the Israeli poor and lower middle class. In 2000, researchers and social workers from the Joint Distribution Committee told me the "Mizrahim" from the FSU generally came here with relatively little education and continued their insular, religious lifestyle—in contrast to the Western-oriented, individualistic ways of FSU Ashkenazi immigrants. A study done at the time by the "Joint" found that the high school drop-out rate among Caucasus immigrants was 25 percent. Zehava Shimon, a social worker in charge of the Joint's programs for Bukharan immigrants, told me that in this community, the boys are expected to work, to bring home money, and they'll go to work in the souks of south Tel Aviv, a real snake pit, when they're only 13 or 14. The girls are expected to be modest, stay at home, and their parents will marry them off as young as 16 or 17. Some of them are pregnant by the time they're in the 12th grade.

There is a sad fact in the world: On the whole, countries in the "greater" Middle East (including the homelands of the FSU "Mizrahim") lag behind those in "greater" Europe (such as the homelands of the FSU "Ashkenazim") in educational and economic development. I believe this is the decisive reason—though, as I said before, not the only one—why the communities in Israel's Jewish underclass are Mizrahi (except for the communities of Ethiopians): because Mizrahim came from cultures that landed most of them in this country at a developmental disadvantage, and while over the generations the majority found the resources to overcome it and enter the middle class, many didn't. And in my opinion, the main difference between Middle Eastern and European culture, in terms of equipping people for life in a modern, Western-oriented society like Israel's, is the importance families place on their children's education. For whatever reasons, and the main one is probably the relative wealth of Europe over that of the Middle East for nearly the last millennium, education for education's sake tends to be a bigger deal for Ashkenazi families in Israel than for Mizrahi families, who tend to be more concerned with making money quickly, thus viewing education in a more utilitarian way.

If you look at the immigrants of the 1990s from the Middle Eastern–oriented countries of the former Soviet Union, they were not housed in worse conditions or met with any more discrimination in Israel than those from the European-oriented countries did. So why is there widespread poverty and poor academic performance among "Mizrahi Russians" and not among "Ashkenazi Russians," who are known mainly for their academic success? I can't find any other reason except national-cultural background—mainly the difference in the value placed on education.

Michael Ben Sheetrit, principal of Branco Weiss High School in Modi'in, which does great work with kids who've dropped out or been kicked out of school, was himself a high school dropout from a destitute Mizrahi family in a development town. He turned his life around after the army upon meeting a young bank manager who came from the same sort of background. "The difference is that his parents placed an emphasis on his studies, and made sure he had a matriculation certificate and would go to college," Ben Sheetrit told *Haaretz* last year. He also pointed out, "Immigrants from the former Soviet Union will live two families to a home and work in low-paying jobs, [but they] see study and after-school enrichment classes as sacrosanct."[7]

Yet the socioeconomic influence of culture in Israel can be seen most clearly within Israel's Arab minority, roughly 90 percent of whom are Muslims and 10 percent Christians. All Arabs in Israel face racism and systematic discrimination from the Jewish powers-that-be—and, in a situation analogous to that of FSU Jewish immigrants, there's no evidence that Arab Christians suffer substantially more racism and discrimination, if any more at all, than Arab Muslims do. Yet Christians have established themselves as the "Jews" or "Asian Americans" of Israel's Arab population in terms of achievement—especially educational, where they outdo Israel's Jewish population, too—while Arab Muslims dominate the ranks of the national culture of poverty. (One of the Muslims' most vital ladders out is the Christian high schools, which are legendary for their excellence and whose student bodies are now mostly Muslim.)

Within the Arab community, Christians also play the role of the Jews when it comes to crime and violence. They number almost solely among the victims, while the perpetrators typically come from the Muslim underclass. An Arab Muslim researcher in Jerusalem explained this to me (very off the record):

---

7. Rotem Starkman, "The School Principal Who Learned How to Succeed the Hard Way," *Haaretz,* January 17, 2016.

A bunch of young roughnecks aren't going to start up with a Muslim girl because they know they could get killed by her *hamula* [extended family or clan], but they figure if they start up with a Christian girl, they've got nothing to worry about. Christians also have an image of being quiet, of turning the other cheek, of being more refined, and to the criminals and thugs, all that makes them an easy target.

As the saying goes, culture matters. But on the other hand, culture is not everything. If it were, then any Ashkenazi Jew or Arab Christian would be more knowledgeable, prosperous, law-abiding, and peaceable than any Mizrahi Jew or Arab Muslim, and that, needless to say, is light years from the way things are. The majority of Israel's Mizrahim are in the middle class, and only a relative very few are involved in crime. And while most Arab Muslims in Israel are poor, likewise only a tiny proportion are criminals. Furthermore, Mizrahim and Muslims on the whole are rising academically and economically as opportunities for higher education have expanded dramatically in the last generation, with scores of new colleges opening, and as Mizrahi and Muslim women enter the workforce in much larger numbers and have significantly fewer children than before.

However, for Israeli Arabs, Muslim and Christian alike, economic advancement lags well behind academic achievement because of the basically Jewish-only profile of the professional ranks in the Jewish economic sector, all except in medicine, the related field of pharmacology, and higher education. (School-teaching is also fully open to Arabs, as they have a separate, Arabic-language public school system.) Even the almighty Israeli high-tech sector, a young, supposed meritocracy, was until the last few years nearly off-limits to Arabs, including those who graduated from the Technion, Tel Aviv University, or Hebrew University. In 2009, the Israeli high-tech manpower company MIT did an experiment, taking the CVs of 180 Arab engineers and mailing them to various Israeli companies in two batches, one listing the applicant's Arab name and usually Arab hometown, the other with the name and hometown left blank.

"Out of 180 applicants, the companies wanted to interview only four whose CVs included the names and hometowns. But of those whose CVs were anonymous, the companies wanted to interview about 50 of them," the head of MIT told me. Lately, however, there has been a good deal of awareness and will in the industry to fix the system, and things have improved, with the proportion of Arabs in Israeli high-tech reportedly growing from 0.5 percent in 2008 to 2 percent in 2015.[8] But there is still a very long way to go—in high-tech as in the rest of Israel's economy.

So in all, while discrimination accounts for part of why Mizrahi Jews and Arab Muslims make up the hard core of Israel's underclass (along with Ethiopian Jews, who came here much more recently than the Mizrahim and with even greater cultural disadvantages), and why there is a socioeconomic gap between those groups on the one hand and Ashkenazi Jews and Arab Christians on the other, cultural background seems to me the main reason. (Except in the case of the economic gap between Arab Christians and Jews, whose only explanation, in view of the Christians' academic edge, is Jewish discrimination.)

How to close this socioeconomic gap? Nothing original. Regarding Arabs, both Muslim and Christian, Israel has to stop being racist, plain and simple. To a lesser extent, this is true regarding Ethiopian Jews, too. And taking Arabs, Ethiopians, and poor Mizrahim together, Israel has to invest more and more to help them make it into the middle class. The answer, in short, is social democracy. It works—which can be seen in the massive Mizrahi entry into the Israeli middle class in recent decades—if not as thoroughly or as fast as taxpayers expect.

But for the Mizrahim of the underclass, discrimination is not remotely the problem that it is for Arabs and Ethiopian Jews. Most Mizrahim have made it: They've taken their places at every level of mainstream society—notably in government, which controls funding

---

8. Inbal Orpaz and Rotem Starkman, "A New Innovation for Startup Nation: Employing Israeli Arabs," *Haaretz*, www.haaretz.com, July 27, 2015.

to the poor—so it's not that the Ashkenazim have closed the doors to them. Instead, I think the main problem among the Mizrahi poor is a victim's mentality—an abiding sense of being wronged and of being helpless, together with habitual seeking of handouts and of blaming everyone but themselves. This is an old, "conservative" critique of the Mizrahi underclass that is rarely heard in public anymore, but from what I've seen, it's accurate.

I witnessed it again and again in the early '90s, when the sudden influx of hundreds of thousands of Russian immigrants needing housing had the effect of cranking up rents, which landed large numbers of poor, mainly Mizrahi Israelis in tent camps in parks around the country, and later in the temporary bungalow camps the government set up. Going to these places and introducing yourself as a journalist was like walking into a beehive. Suddenly people were crowding around you, pouring out their rage and frustration at every possible government official and agency, asking if you could help them get a state-subsidized apartment. It was a mounting cacophony of complaint and supplication—yet the people there were young and healthy, mainly in their 30s, as often as not on welfare, and parents of little children.

By 1996 the bungalow camps had all but shut down as thousands of families had by then found low-cost, subsidized apartments to move their families into. I went to one of the few camps still standing, in Bat Yam, south of Tel Aviv. The homes were shabby, with what seemed a permanent layer of junk and trash on the grounds, and little dogs running around wild. From among the 50-odd down-in-the-mouth householders still there, I heard the old familiar story. "The country threw us to the dogs," said one woman. "They left us here to live like Bedouin," said one man.

The park's assistant manager was a Mizrahi from Bat Yam named Avi Ninio, who'd been one of the leaders of the homeless movement when it began with barricades and Molotov cocktails in 1990. Six years later, he said he'd changed his view of his old comrades:

> I've lost my patience with them. Most of these people are spoiled, they think they deserve everything. You don't know how many

low-income families are dying to get the kind of mortgages we're offering the people here. . . . They bitch to me that they can't afford an apartment, they want a better deal. You have to understand the chutzpah of these people.

I know them, I know them too well. I tell them, "Instead of riding in taxis all the time, why don't you ride the bus? Instead of spending so much money talking on your cell phone, why don't you spend less? Instead of smoking Marlboros, why don't you smoke [much cheaper] Israeli cigarettes?" You show me one person here who doesn't smoke American cigarettes. I tell them to their face, "Pal, as far as I'm concerned, you can stay here another 20 years."[9]

The park manager, Dov Malick, an Ashkenazi, added:

I heard these people's parents complaining all the time that they were victims, unfortunates, that everyone was against them, that the country owed them everything. Now you've got a second generation with this mentality. Even some of the solid, hard-working people who came here eventually fell into this kind of thinking. They absorbed it from the environment.

For the Mizrahi poor, the way out begins with something that is too often missing among them: self-reliance. In the mid-'90s, an example was being set in Yerucham, a well-maintained Mizrahi development town of 10,000 in the Negev that, despite suffering some of the worst unemployment in Israel, was outdistancing most of the country's middle-class towns in the percentage of pupils matriculating high school. If this isolated desert town couldn't offer its children much of an economic future, it would at least give them the education to pursue their future elsewhere. The mayor, Motti Avisror, a Mizrahi Likudnik who was widely credited with

---

9. Larry Derfner, "No Place Like Home," *The Jerusalem Post Magazine*, May 10, 1996.

transforming Yerucham's schools, told me the solution was to instill self-confidence and motivation in the teachers, parents, and kids, and to stay on the case every day. The locals made up their minds "to stop crying," said Avisror:

> We decided to see the glass as half full, to take responsibility, to believe that we could make the change ourselves. When you keep telling people they're victims, even a person who used to believe in himself becomes convinced that he's a victim—that this, evidently, is his fate and there's nothing he can do about it.

Israel's Ashkenazi leftists aren't doing the Mizrahi underclass any favors by infantilizing them—by turning a blind eye to their self-defeating habits and blaming everything on the Ashkenazi establishment. Without self-reliance, all the government help in the world isn't going to get people a good education, a good job, and a good life. If Ashkenazi leftists care about these people like they say they do, they would do well to start by treating them as adults.

My family moved to Modi'in in 1997, and one of the city's great successes, especially in the beginning when apartments were cheap, was in attracting many upwardly mobile Mizrahim from the poor nearby towns of Lod and Ramle, and for "putting the ethnic genie back in the bottle," as the Israeli saying goes. With 85,000 people in town now, I honestly couldn't guess if the majority are Ashkenazi or Mizrahi. I'm pretty sure the mayor is Mizrahi, or at least of mixed Ashkenazi-Mizrahi parentage (which is altogether common in Israel), but I wouldn't swear to it. My kids have Mizrahi friends, we go to the bar mitzvahs of our Mizrahi neighbors, and it was 18 years before I found out that the woman downstairs, one of our closest neighbors, whose husband is Ashkenazi, was herself Mizrahi.

One evening I went to heckle the supporters of a popular Mizrahi ultra-Orthodox rabbi who'd come to town to brainwash the young people, and a Mizrahi neighbor up the block (also married to an Ashkenazi) told me, "Give it to them!" Another evening I went to listen to a popular Ashkenazi rabbi, likewise a preacher of drivel, and I sat down next to yet another Mizrahi neighbor in the sparse audience, and we ridiculed the rabbi between ourselves; like me, my Mizrahi neighbor had come for a hate fix.

In Israel's Jewish middle class, there is no ethnic genie, certainly not one of any consequence; there are Ashkenazim mixed with Mizrahim, including within families. And this Jewish middle class is fully open to poor but ambitious Mizrahim who want to join it; the proof is in the great masses of those who already have.

During our first years in Modi'in, in the late '90s, I was pretty optimistic, despite having to hear Prime Minister Netanyahu every day. I loved my work, running around the country and writing stories, we were getting ready to have another kid, and there was something special about being one of the "founders' generation" of this new city being carved out of the hills. It was like being a settler but in a place that was good. Before moving there, I had this idea of Modi'in being an environment that would stimulate our little boy Alon's mind, and when I saw the complex, expansive jungle gym in the main park, it immediately struck me as the embodiment of that idea—the sort of image I'd had in mind. There was a special, hopeful, community feeling among the parents. We were in this together. We made friends. I was a very proud suburban pioneer; I used to drive around town, which was covered with construction sites, and just marvel.

Politically, things in Israel were depressing but not at all hopeless. The Oslo Accord was still alive, not even Bibi wanted it to die altogether—for fear of what would take its place—and Labor's Ehud Barak had a chance, at least, to remove him from power. Meanwhile, terror had steadily gone down until it wasn't a pressing day-to-day issue anymore. (Thanks, above all, to Arafat and his troops, who were arresting Hamasniks in droves, torturing and often humiliating them in prison by shaving off their beards.) And this, I believe, was the main reason Bibi lost the 1999 election to Barak: Because terror went down too early in his term, so that by the time the election came, Israelis had gotten used to the calm and were asking, *What have you done for us lately?* And the objective answer was: not much. The economy was hurting. The peace process was stalled. And with his innate disdain for other people once he doesn't need them anymore, Netanyahu had alienated so many Likud politicians and activists at every level that he didn't have much of an army behind him in the campaign.

Barak, meanwhile, came out fighting. I heard him say somewhere that a political campaign "is like boxing. You just keep punching until the other guy falls." And I read one of his allies tell *Yediot Ahronot*'s Nahum Barnea that the campaign's turning point came in the traditional trial by fire for prime ministerial candidates—whether they can "make it through the souk," meaning whether their entourage can literally out-punch, out-shove, and out-roar the opposition's during the mandatory candidate's appearance in the rough, loud, traditionally pro-Likud, big-city produce market. In an appearance in one of these arenas, that's exactly what Barak's team did, the ally said: They physically kicked ass on the brawlers whom Bibi's campaign had sent out to bully Barak, which can be fatal to a peace candidate's campaign, confirming him as a weakling. It didn't happen to Barak, and from that point on, said the ally, they knew their man was the toughest and Netanyahu's people knew it, too. Primitive, but that's Israeli politics.

I got a kick out of Barak's growling, warrior spirit, the way he got dead in the right wing's face and took two eyes for an eye. What do you know, a fighting liberal. He'd been touted for prime minister, as Labor's successor to the Rabin-Peres generation, for a long time. In 1986, political analyst Hanan Kristal made the most extraordinary forecast in Israeli political history, predicting that Barak, who was then one of the army's top generals, and Netanyahu, who was then ambassador to the United Nations, would face each other 10 years later in the 1996 race for prime minister. Kristal hit one out of two in 1996 and two out of two in 1999. Bibi and Barak were Israel's two most likely to succeed politicians—and Barak wiped the floor with him in the 1999 election. What a man—he could do anything. Other Labor hopefuls claimed Rabin's mantle, but Barak claimed Ben-Gurion's. He was going to reinvent the country as one at peace with the Arabs, he was the De Gaulle whom the Israeli left, myself included, had been waiting for.

As it turned out, we were standing at the abyss.

CHAPTER EIGHT

IMPLOSION

The 15 months between the swearing-in of the Barak government and the outbreak of the second intifada were a laboratory test of the fond old claim that if the Palestinians would only give up terror, Israelis would readily give up the occupied territories, or almost all of them. The test showed that claim to be false.

Those 15 months were some of the safest, most peaceful that Israel has ever known. A total of five Israelis were killed by Palestinians in that period. Ever since the spasm of suicide bombings in late February–early March 1996 that had threatened his rule, Arafat was clamping down harder and harder on Islamic terrorists. Yet it was politically impossible in Israel to give him a shred of even grudging credit. Meanwhile, among many Palestinians and in much of the Arab world, Arafat was seen as Israel's collaborator. During Barak's brief diplomatic attempt at peace with Syria, I asked Middle East historian Dr. Yossi Olmert (a Likudnik and brother of ex–prime minister Ehud Olmert) his view of Hafez Assad's mindset in the negotiations. He said that above all, Assad did not want to let Israel and the United States lead him around by the nose. "He does not want to be like Arafat, this is very important to understand," Olmert stressed. Israelis didn't understand and didn't want to understand that Arafat was going after Hamasniks like they'd always demanded; no matter, he was back to being the "arch terrorist," the "mass murderer," and nothing he did could change it.

I have no great love for Barak anymore, to say the least, but in retrospect he never really had a chance to make peace with the Palestinians or the Syrians: the majority of Israelis were firmly against it. He took office as a consensus leader, he had an unusually broad government with parties of the right, left, and center, secular and religious, Russians and Mizrahim—and the more he talked about making "painful concessions" for peace, the more his popularity drained. He started off with a brawny coalition including 75 of the Knesset's 120 members—and by the time he came back from the Camp David peace talks with Arafat a year later, it had withered to a clinically dead 30. Would he have been able to uproot tens of thousands of settlers, as per his Camp David offer, to make way for a Palestinian state, when even suggesting such a thing had crippled him politically? And all this time, Arafat was doing a brutally efficient job of helping keep Israel safe. No, the Palestinians' fight against terror wasn't reciprocated by the promised Israeli readiness to give back conquered land, because Israelis were psychologically incapable of acknowledging that the Palestinians were fighting terror. In the Israeli public's eyes the glass of safety and security was not 95 percent full now, it was 5 percent empty. Thus, a pattern was set: The more peace the Palestinians gave Israel, the more peace Israelis demanded. As for getting land in return, the Palestinians could whistle for it.

On Nakba Day, May 15, 2000, marking their "catastrophe" (in Arabic, *nakba*) of 1948, the Palestinians rebelled. During the day's violent protests, Palestinian Authority police, for the first time in nearly four years, fired on Israeli soldiers. No IDF troops were killed, but a dozen were wounded by bullets and rocks. Naturally, the Palestinians got much, much the worst of it: Thousands joined in the stone-throwing, and the army injured hundreds of them, while killing two policemen and four protesters.

What had gotten into these people? Didn't they know that Barak was for the two-state solution? Didn't they realize that the good guys were in power in Israel, and that we were trying our best?

Later, Ron Pundak, one of the architects of the Oslo Accord, would describe in *Yediot Ahronot* what it was like for the Palestinians in those pre-intifada days under Barak:

> Existing settlements grow at a faster pace, new settlements the size of small cities are built to the east and west of Ramallah, creating a new reality on the ground, in contradiction of the Oslo Accord. The water shortage is 10 times worse than ours, due to limitations Israel places on routing of water. Denial of freedom of worship to Muslims and Christians (in the last seven years every Palestinian in the territories is barred from praying at Haram al-Sharif). Effective continuation of the occupation on 80 percent of the West Bank and 25 percent of Gaza. Continual, varied means of abuse, including outright violence, by border policemen at IDF checkpoints in the territories, and this is just a partial list.

To flesh out Pundak's first point, about settlement growth: In 2000, Barak's only full year as prime minister, some 5,000 settlement homes were built—three times the annual rate under his successors Sharon, Olmert, or Netanyahu.

But who knew? And if you knew, who cared? The peace camp was in the saddle, the endgame of Oslo was at hand, this was all temporary, the whole rotten business was on its way out.

I went to Ramallah the day after the riots and saw that the Palestinian Authority police, whatever they had done the day before, were keeping order now. They turned back a crowd of young marchers chanting about the "blood of the martyrs" well before they could reach their destination, the IDF checkpoint at the northern entrance to the city, where the rioting had been the worst. This had been a Nakba Day eruption, and now it was over. Downtown Ramallah looked so prosperous, with car dealerships and a giant fitness center and stately, two-story stone villas with satellite dishes on the roofs. Why would they want to endanger this?

Near the checkpoint at the entrance to Ramallah, Israeli soldiers were carrying sandbags into the sparkling City Inn hotel, which they had commandeered during the fighting. Standing outside, dressed in a green, double-breasted suit and brown brogues, was Odeh, the hotel manager. In his early 30s with a round, smiling face, a neatly-clipped mustache, a wife, three kids, and a house, he seemed like the picture of domestic propriety. When I asked him what kind of life he'd had before the hotel, he laughed off the questions at first. Then, still grinning, he said, "I was arrested and put in Israeli jails plenty of times. I was in the streets in 1982 when they invaded Lebanon, and I was in the streets, of course, during the [first] intifada." His opinion of Arafat? "No comment."

For the last three years Odeh had managed the City Inn, saying he'd "decided to seek stability, to build my career." He didn't want to go back to the intifada and still believed that little by little the Palestinians would achieve their goals at the negotiating table. But witnessing the Nakba Day riots at the junction had stirred something in him. They'd upset his stability:

> I don't want to say I was happy about the violence. I know there are mothers waiting for their sons to come home—on the Israeli side, too. We don't need violence, we need peace. But I must say that inside, what I was feeling was this: My people aren't dead. They're still alive, and they'll fight for freedom."[1]

---

1. Larry Derfner, "Ramallah's Uncertain Quiet," *The Jerusalem Post*, May 19, 2000.

Five and a half months later, on a Saturday evening marking the end of Rosh Hashana, some of my neighbors were sitting on the stoop in front of our building, but this time we weren't making the usual holiday small talk. The Palestinians in East Jerusalem, the West Bank, and Gaza had gone wild. Even more shocking was that the Israeli Arabs in the Galilee had gone wild with them. The latter were blocking major highways; Israeli police were mobilizing to defend kibbutzim. The day before, seven Palestinian rioters had been killed by police on the Temple Mount, which was a continuation of the riots that had greeted Sharon's visit to the Mount with 1,000 cops the day before that—but what was this? An insurrection? Why? Why now, after Camp David? Hadn't the Palestinians done enough damage there by walking away from Barak's peace offer; now they were starting an all-out war?

Some of my neighbors were furious, saying the army should just mow them down. I was stunned. And bewildered. I wasn't mad, not yet, but underneath I was starting to feel that the Palestinians had betrayed me. Me and the whole Israeli peace camp.

Once this new, second intifada started, I knew that for the Palestinians there was no going back. After this stunt, after their police had opened fire at Israeli soldiers and killed a few of them in those first days, if the Palestinians went back to the negotiating table, they would get nothing. The Israeli public's loathing for them was now absolute. Meanwhile, Barak was finished; the Likud was coming back to power.

Like other peaceniks, I couldn't make up my mind which side, Israel or the Palestinians, was at fault. I could blame Sharon for lighting the spark, but the Palestinians had gone way beyond reacting to Sharon's walk on the Temple Mount. It's a terrible, anxious, bottled-up feeling to be an Israeli when this country is at war and you're not sure it should be.

Then something happened that decided it for me. Two weeks into the fighting, I saw on the TV news a festive crowd in Ramallah clapping their hands in time to music, children sitting on their fathers' shoulders. They were celebrating the lynching of two Israeli reserve soldiers who'd taken a wrong turn into the city. Footage of Vadim Norzich's body being thrown out the window of the Ramallah police station to the mob below was broadcast over and over. The *New York Times*' Deborah Sontag wrote: "With a fellow reserve soldier, Yossi Avrahami, he was stabbed, stomped, beaten and burned to death at a Palestinian police station. Afterward, cheering Palestinians paraded his pummeled body down a main street."[2]

A couple of hours afterward I was downstairs getting something out of the trunk of my car. On the rear bumper was my Peace Now sticker. My neighbor Nadav, an easygoing fellow and a political moderate, was standing nearby. In the friendliest of voices, he said, "Larry, Peace Now isn't really relevant anymore, is it?" I looked at the sticker. "No, it isn't," I said. My belief in peace now was gone. At some point—I don't remember if Nadav was still down there or not—I peeled the sticker off my bumper and crumpled it up. It was a wrenching moment; it felt like something inside me died. Yet it was also a moment of clarity. I wasn't ready, though, for this gesture to be my final word. That would be too bleak. I took the crumpled-up peace sticker and stuck it on my bulletin board for a day when it would be relevant again. (And only after a couple more years of intifada would I finally throw it in the trash.)

For the first time, I felt hopeless. One cold, wet, winter day in Jerusalem, I bought two framed, sepia photos of happy Independence Day crowd scenes from the early '50s and hung them on the wall in my workroom. I was desperate for some antidote, even if it was Zionist kitsch, to this thick malaise that had paralyzed me and the rest of the country (except for those on the hard-charging right, who were getting ready to take over, and promising victory over the Palestinians). In Modi'in, I imagined a heavy, yellowish-gray cloud hanging low in the sky, blocking out the future. Nobody talked about "the situation"; it was too depressing. When you saw your neighbor, it was still *Hi, How are you doing, Fine.* But once, after going through

---

2. Deborah Sontag, "Whose Holy Land?: The Victims; Israel in Shock as It Buries Mob's Victim," *New York Times*, October 14, 2000.

this routine while passing one of the dads on our street, out of curiosity I stopped and asked him, "You're fine, really? Is that right?" Immediately, he replied, "Couldn't be worse. I'm afraid to go out for lunch in Jerusalem. I'm afraid to drive places with my kids. I can live with being in danger myself, but my kids have to be in danger, too?"

By spring, I'd had it. I'd thought about leaving Israel countless times—it's a habit here with most leftists and Western immigrants—but it had never been more than an inner gripe or sigh. This time I made up my mind. I had a boy of six and a boy of two, and I didn't want to bring them up in such an environment. Part of it was the danger: Life was beginning to feel like Russian roulette; I figured it was a matter of time until something or someone blew up in Modi'in. But worse was the atmosphere they would grow up in. Who wanted to raise boys in a country that was constantly at war? Worst of all, I didn't believe it would ever change: Israel and the Palestinians weren't going to make peace, and even Sharon, by now the prime minister, wasn't able to put down the terror, which was no surprise to me. This second intifada, I was convinced, would become, in today's language, the new normal.

I was 49, so we weren't going to just pack up and leave; it was too much of a risk. But Philippa and I agreed that if I could find a job overseas, we'd go. Mentally, I was ready; I'd thought it through and crossed the necessary line. I talked about it with my sister, brother, and a few close friends, and nobody suggested I was making a mistake. "You've given up. You've lost hope," said an American immigrant friend, making an observation, not a judgment, and I agreed. In my heart, I was saying goodbye to this place, and was surprisingly broken up about it, and already pledging inwardly to remain connected to Israel from abroad. But I was going. Our first choice was Toronto, and I made telephone calls to the *Toronto Star* and the *Globe and Mail,* and put together a batch of clips and a CV and a cover letter. It was all a waste of time. One of the papers sent me a form email saying they weren't hiring; the other misunderstood my letter and directed me to the foreign editor to whom I could pitch freelance articles from Israel. This took the wind out of my sails altogether, and I gave up looking. In retrospect, it was probably a good thing; given what the Internet was about to do to newspapers, if somebody had hired me they probably would have fired me before long, and at my age I would have been unemployable in a new country and our lives would have been ruined. But if one of those Toronto newspapers had offered me what looked like a solid job, and we didn't get cold feet, it's likely we would have been gone. Such thinking was, of course, discouraged by official Israel, but it seemed to me I had a choice: Either try to be a good Israeli or try to be a good father, and I feel no shame at all that I chose the latter.

Morally, the bottom line for me in the second intifada was that Barak had offered the Palestinians independence and they'd turned it down and gone to war, which meant we were the ones fighting in self-defense. I became tough-minded. But little by little these cracks started appearing in the edifice of my moral clarity: We were so much stronger than the Palestinians. And we'd been ruling their lives so harshly for so long. Plus, it was one thing when you're talking about "the Palestinians," another when you're talking about a Palestinian individual whom you know. Then it wasn't so easy to be tough-minded, as I found out in getting to know a Palestinian I'll call Taher.

I met him not long after the second intifada began, in a nursery in Modi'in where he'd been working for over 20 years, coming in without an Israeli permit, illegally, by whatever way he took from the village of Beit Sira, only a couple of hundred yards away on the other side of the Green Line. A slight, lean guy with a thick mustache and toothy smile, the same age as me and with 10 kids, he did landscaping jobs at Jewish homes in the area. The first time I saw him, the little daughter of one of his customers was sitting in his lap as he talked to the mother, who then carried on shopping, leaving her daughter curled up in Taher's arms. Not your typical intifada-era tableau.

Over the coming year I saw him a few more times, quoting him anonymously in a couple of stories. As the violence escalated, it got increasingly hard for him to evade the Israeli patrols on his way to work. Once, he said, his son got arrested trying to get to work in Modi'in, and when Taher went to plead for his release, the soldier smacked him in the face, right in front of his son. Taher said he was against Palestinian terror but equally against IDF assassinations of intifada leaders, which I saw at the time as a false moral equivalence. But I didn't expect a Palestinian to see things my way, so I didn't let it change my opinion of him. Giving me his cell phone number, he invited me to Beit Sira. "You can't come into the village by yourself, but tell me when you want to come and I'll meet you at the entrance." It was impossible not to like him.

After a couple of particularly horrific terror attacks, he stayed home from work for weeks on end for fear of getting caught, jailed, and heavily fined. He told me over the phone he was tearing branches off trees for firewood. His sister, who'd had a heart condition, had died after soldiers turned her car back at the entrance to Ramallah, where she was trying to get to the hospital. To go to her funeral, Taher had to walk along dirt back roads and duck IDF patrols for four hours. "I was covered with dirt," he said, "but I made it."

Idle and destitute at home, he was beginning to sound more militant and more desperate. The intifada was futile but justified, he said: Settlers were killing Palestinians so Palestinians had the right to kill settlers, though not civilians in Israel. He felt himself on the verge of going out to steal to feed his family.

His boss told me that some people were putting together food packages for his family, leaving the bags off the shoulder of Route 443, where Taher would sneak over and pick them up. I donated, of course. I didn't consider it charity—he had supplied me raw material for stories, which made me money, so why shouldn't he get paid too? Especially since the subject of those stories, the intifada, was proving great for my income and devastating for his.

I felt bad for all the illegal Palestinian laborers getting arrested. As I wrote in the Introduction, I would pass the police station on my morning walk and see them in the yard behind the fence (before the fence was covered in green so people wouldn't see them anymore).

Once, early in the new intifada, I stopped on my route and asked a couple of the Palestinian detainees, sympathetically, what had happened. I knew these were poor, put-upon men who only wanted to work and that getting arrested would cost them weeks or even months in jail and hundreds of dollars in fines, which was obviously unjust. But I figured it was much, much less unjust than for Israelis to be getting killed by the one in 20,000 of them, or whatever the proportion might be, who had other things in mind besides work. So I fully supported the Israeli crackdown. In fact, after one terror attack, I strode into the police station next to the yard and demanded to know why building contractors in Modi'in weren't getting arrested or at least fined prohibitively for hiring illegal Palestinian workers. The desk cop said they were doing their best. I said it wasn't good enough and stormed out. After a while, as the detainees behind the fence began multiplying, I felt like they were looking at me, thinking malicious thoughts, and I began putting a slight thrust of defiance in my stride when I passed them. I understood their sentiments, but I'm sorry: We didn't start this war, friends. You did, and this is the price. I am not a settler, I am walking on internationally recognized Israeli land, and I am willing to compromise for peace even more than Ehud Barak. You are not going to make me feel guilty.

Then, walking past the police yard one morning, I glanced at the detainees, and there was Taher, sitting on the ground with the others. I stopped. He saw me staring and heard me say, "Unbelievable, unbelievable." By habit, he smiled hello. Seeing that I was trying to be sympathetic, he shook his head and smiled ruefully, as if to say, *Yeah, can you believe how they treat me?* Then, his courtesy paid, he turned hard and quiet again.

He'd come with his boss to collect some debts from customers he'd done jobs for; his boss had gotten busted too and was sitting miserably inside the police station. I talked to a couple of plain-clothes cops on Taher's behalf, and after jawing back and forth with me, they said that if he was as solid and trustworthy as I claimed, nothing would happen to him. And nothing did. The next day I called him and he said he'd been released without a fine, and would be going to Amman for his son's wedding as planned. "That's fantastic. Congratulations," I said. "I'm sorry all this happened to you, but thank God it worked out." "Thank you, thank you," he said, sounding rushed, and since I could hear people in the background, I just said goodbye. I didn't call him again, and stopped going into the nursery where he worked. Our friendly alliance had become too awkward for me, too polluted by current events that magnified our inequality.

As the intifada churned on, I continued to feel bad for the innocent Palestinian laborers getting arrested. But I also continued to endorse their arrests. We had to put an end to this constant killing and pressing danger; everything else was secondary. And I didn't change the route of my morning walk. When I'd pass the police yard, I'd take a quick look through the fence at the detained men—turning away before any of them could look me in the eye—and keep walking.

As the fighting continued, my politics changed. At first, on the eve of Sharon's wipeout of Barak in the election (Likud Knesset member Limor Livnat said, correctly, that her party "could have run a broomstick for prime minister and still won"), I wrote an op-ed, "Intifada of Fools," in the *Jerusalem Post* about what the Palestinians had let themselves in for:

> The Palestinians will be going it alone against Sharon and a fed-up Israeli public, and they will have brought it on themselves. They will have elected the man. Myself, I won't be voting for Sharon; I don't like him and I don't trust him. But after seeing the distance Barak went for peace, and the crazy war the Palestinians launched in response, I can't help feeling some grim satisfaction that they're now going to have the ol' bulldozer to deal with. For Arafat and his flock, it'll amount to rough justice.[3]

3. Larry Derfner, "Intifada of Fools," *International Jerusalem Post*, January 26, 2001.

I was mad. I blamed the Palestinians for the war and gave up on peace negotiations with them, certainly with Arafat, now the *rais* of the intifada, as their leader. But I still knew that the occupation was wrong and had to be dismantled to the greatest extent possible, so I became a convert to unilateral withdrawal. I had moved right—but the Israeli public had moved much further right; it wanted to "let the IDF win." After a Hamas suicide bomber killed 30 Israelis at a Passover seder in Netanya, the public got its wish: Sharon made Arafat a prisoner for life in his Ramallah compound, mauled the West Bank and Gaza far more lethally and destructively than before, and assassinated Hamas leaders in the Strip one after the other. I thought it was crazy; the Palestinians would just fight back more fiercely and the bloodshed would rise on both sides, while Israel would slide back to its pre-Oslo policy of patrolling every alley in every city, village, and refugee camp indefinitely. Writing in *U.S. News and World Report,* I approvingly quoted the dean of Israeli military affairs journalists, Ze'ev Schiff: "What is left for Israel to do that it has not already done to prevent terror?"

Then, as the war lengthened and Israel began to grind the Palestinians down, and the "kill ratio" widened in Israel's favor, I became more sensitive, or at least less callous, to Palestinian losses. The infrequent trips I made to the West Bank to meet with Palestinians reminded me of how much I wasn't seeing. Once, on a story about settler destruction of Palestinian olive groves, I saw a field of ruins, mounds of debris stretching for acres just on the other side of the Green Line. "Those were Palestinian shops, make-shift shops, hundreds of them. They were torn down to make way for the security fence," said Rabbi Arik Ascherman, head of Rabbis for Human Rights, who was driving. I'd never heard about this, and if I had, I wouldn't have cared; I was against building the separation fence/wall on the Palestinian side of the Green Line, but better there than nowhere, because we had to keep terrorists out of Israeli cities. Seeing that vista of flattened shops, though, made the problem of building the fence on Palestinian land a lot more real. Another time, on a miserably hot, humid August day, I went to the

Jewish settler enclave in Hebron, where I'd been a few times before, only this time it was different: There wasn't a Palestinian to be seen on the streets. "Curfew," an Israeli soldier told me. I wrote in the *Jerusalem Post*:

> Curfew. It's one of those words I hear all the time. Like closure, encirclement, demolition, detention, wounded, dead. Curfew sounds pretty mild compared to all those, so it never made much of an impression on me. Then I saw what curfew means: a city of silent, deserted streets with 150,000 people, mainly dirt-poor families with lots of children, locked unwillingly inside their cramped homes in August, for who knows how long.

Even former Shin Bet leaders began to speak out against the Israeli onslaught. In a foreshadowing of the famed 2012 documentary *The Gatekeepers,* four ex-Shin Bet chiefs told *Yediot Ahronot* that the war against the Palestinians had gone too far. "We are treating them in a disgraceful manner," said Avraham Shalom. "To this day I don't understand why a tank that's driving on the streets of Ramallah also has to crush the cars parked on the sides," said Yaakov Perry.

Three years into the war, 27 active and reserve Air Force pilots signed a public letter declaring their "refus[al] to take part in Air Force attacks on civilian population centers," meaning they would not fly missions in the West Bank or Gaza. They joined some 1,000 combat soldiers who'd publicly refused to serve in the territories. On the op-ed page of the *Jerusalem Post,* then-Knesset member Isaac Herzog wrote that the pilots' letter "fires a missile straight into the heart of IDF camaraderie." Underneath his piece, I wrote in defense of the "refusers":

> If every soldier began refusing to fight in the territories, the government would see that it couldn't hold onto the territories any longer, and at some point it would have to start getting out—by negotiations if possible, unilaterally if necessary. . . . The refusers are putting themselves on the line for a just and

crucial cause. That makes them even braver Israelis, and makes this at least a marginally more spirited country.

Throughout the second intifada (whose end can be marked by Arafat's death in November 2004), I believed we were fighting in self-defense. Years later, I would see that Barak had never offered the Palestinians more than vassal statehood at Camp David and that his actions on the ground up until then were those of a determined colonial ruler. He'd given the Palestinians no reason to trust him, and his disdainful treatment of Arafat during the two weeks at Camp David certainly did nothing to change that. Put all this together with President Bill Clinton's heaping of all the blame on the Palestinian leader, with Sharon's humiliating show of force on the Temple Mount, with the police's killing of seven stone-throwing rioters there the day afterward, and, above all, with the Palestinians' unrelieved subjugation, and I can't say anymore that they started the war and that Israel was fighting back. No, we provoked the second intifada. We expected the Palestinians to peacefully accept a present and a future under the enemy's thumb, something Israelis would fight to the death against. We shouldn't have been surprised when the people under our thumb, for whom we are the enemy, took that route themselves.

But the justice of their cause is one thing; how they pursue it is another. There are still impressions I formed of Palestinians during the second intifada, negative ones, that I've had no cause to revise. One was of Arafat, who reigned as their national leader for 35 years, and who became like a Palestinian king, or pope, a holy symbol of the nation and its cause. I only saw him in person once, and it was an appalling scene. Early in the fighting, US Secretary of State Colin Powell came to visit, and I went with a swarm of reporters to the presidential compound, the Muqata'a in Ramallah. We were hustled up the stairs by a large contingent of glowering, conspicuously armed security forces dressed in black. I told Khaled Abu Toameh, my partner in covering Israel-Palestine for *U.S. News and World Report,* that "I feel like I'm in a police state." Khaled replied, "You are in a police state." We entered a large hall, with Arafat's men sitting in front as their boss introduced his guest. "I would like to welcome General Powell," Arafat said, then joked, "but of course I am a general too!" His henchmen in the front rows erupted in loud, appreciative laughter—such inspired wit, such masterful one-upmanship: Is there anyone like our *rais*? It was a clichéd picture of a megalomaniacal dictator and the fear he struck in his subjects.

This is something I find hard to understand: In life and in death, Arafat is held up as the father of the Palestinian people, yet the regime he ran for a decade in Gaza and the West Bank was a plague on their lives, a mafia that ruled by violence, threats, and extortion. In a story for *U.S. News and World Report,* "A State of Corruption," based largely on Khaled's reporting, we wrote:

> Arafat has no known material desires, though he supports his wife and daughter living in France and Switzerland. Instead, he uses money to corrupt those around him. "He locks in people's loyalty by giving them material advantages," says a Western diplomat. "And none of his beneficiaries will dare go against him because he'll expose them."[4]

The owner of a West Bank chain of food stores said he had been paying "taxes" regularly to a PA security force, whose men threatened to jail his children and denounce him as an Israeli collaborator—effectively a death sentence—if he didn't pay up. "When I went to complain to more senior officials in the PA, they also asked for money," the businessman said. About the PA's court system, a former judge in the West Bank city of Nablus called it "a big joke," saying many judges were "subject to intimidation and threats from PA security commanders and senior officials in Arafat's office."

Another impression of the Palestinians at war that won't go away was the way the leadership and much of the public—though by no

---

4. Khaled Abu Toameh and Larry Derfner, "A State of Corruption," *U.S. News and World Report,* July 1, 2002.

means all of it, and maybe not most of it, either—urged children to the front against the Israeli army. Khaled, Kevin Whitelaw, and I wrote:

> Arafat's Palestinian Authority is quite direct in its encouragement of child fighters. In its TV, radio, and newspapers, the youngsters are praised as the "generals of the intifada," the "brave stone throwers." The "martyrs" are eulogized as heroes and role models. After Israeli helicopters bombed another of his military headquarters last week, Arafat called for renewed resistance by young activists, "these children who throw the stones to defend Jerusalem, the Muslims, and the holy places."

But at the same time, as we wrote:

> There is a Palestinian silent majority, or at least a substantial minority, that's battling the PA for the hearts and minds of their children. A teacher at a refugee camp near Hebron says some of his students have been wounded in battle, but others stay clear of the fray for fear of their fathers' wrath. "A lot of fathers have been beating their sons to keep them home," says the teacher.
>
> Dissenters who do speak out tend to do so anonymously for fear of Arafat's tentacular security establishment. Intimidation is blatant. In the PA's leading official newspaper, *Al-Hayat Al-Jadeedah*, editor in chief Hafez Al-Barghouti wrote a signed editorial denouncing as "corrupt and disgusting" anyone who counsels self-preservation to Palestinian youths, including their own fathers. "Let us be wise and put them on trial when this is over," wrote Barghouti in his editorial titled "The Fifth Column."

But the most disturbing impression of the Palestinians that has stayed with me is—there is no other way to describe it—the streak of savagery that emerged. The lynching in Ramallah, and the crowd reaction to it, was savagery. One of the Palestinians reportedly in that crowd was Amneh Muna, who said later that she'd been "excited" by what she saw; a few months afterward, posing in an Internet chat room as a love-struck Moroccan Jewish immigrant named Sally, she lured a 16-year-old Israeli boy, Ofir Rahum, to Jerusalem for a rendezvous, then drove him to the outskirts of Ramallah, where three Palestinians got out of a car and shot him to death with 15 bullets.[5] Another time, two 14-year-old boys in the settlement of Tekoa went missing; they were found dead in a cave outside the settlement, their faces bashed literally to a pulp with rocks. And I remember watching a tape of Marwan Barghouti, the coolest Palestinian leader since Arafat gave up his Ray-Bans, exulting on a Palestinian talk show when someone called in to announce the latest "operation," which turned out to have been a suicide bomber going off in Jerusalem near a couple of mothers tending their baby carriages. Of the 11 people killed, two were toddlers and another three were seven years old or younger. Barghouti didn't know those details from the call, but why was he so triumphant over any of these "operations" that targeted buses, restaurants—crowds of ordinary Israelis? My view of Palestinian terror has changed, but not my revulsion at the displays of Palestinian excitement over those mass killings of people who did not deserve such a fate.

In the end, I was proven wrong, along with the rest of the left: There was a military solution to the second intifada. After we had been pointing out for four years that every Palestinian terrorist leader whom Israel assassinates just gets replaced, the Palestinians ran out of replacements. Between the Shin Bet's collaborator-fed intelligence and the IDF's might, it became impossible for the Palestinians to make a move; resistance eventually became futile. Also, the wall, the separation barrier that we ridiculed—as if walls could stop desperate people!—proved hugely effective in stopping Palestinian

5. "Murder of Ofir Rahum," *Wikipedia*, last modified October 16, 2016, https://en.wikipedia.org/wiki/Murder_of_Ofir_Rahum.

terrorists from reaching Israeli cities. There's a well-known Israeli saying: "What force won't fix, more force will," and after four years of Israeli force, the Palestinians gave in. I hadn't thought Israel could get away with holding Yasser Arafat prisoner, with assassinating Hamas leader Ahmed Yassin in Gaza and right afterward assassinating his successor, Abdel Aziz al-Rantisi, but we did. The Palestinians simply didn't have the wherewithal anymore to strike back. And nobody came to their aid, nor did anyone try to rein Israel in. For me, it was a great lesson in the efficacy of military power. Also a lesson in the resilience of the occupation, and, of course, in the difference between how I want the world to work and how it actually tends to work.

Like all other Israeli Jews, regardless of their politics, I was deeply relieved when the intifada ended, when the angel of death finally passed over. The ugly cloud blocking the future dissipated. For a while.

CHAPTER NINE

I HEART SHARON

Probably the most dramatic political scene I ever witnessed in Israel happened on the night of October 26, 2004, at the Knesset's do-or-die vote on the disengagement from Gaza. The whole thing was almost surrealistic; outside, Peace Now was chanting in support of Sharon, their old nemesis, while the settlers, his former admirers, were driving around the Knesset in wishful imitation of the Israelites who'd circled Jericho before conquering it. I wanted to be sure to get a seat up in the press box, so I went in an hour before the vote was scheduled. Aside from a few photographers setting up their tripods, I was the only journalist there. The big, imposing hall was silent. Below, the seats on the parliament floor were empty—except one. In it sat Sharon, writing, presumably working on his speech. After a while, he turned to look up at the press box, peering at us like George C. Scott in *Patton*. Haughty, disdainful, intimidating as God.

I loved him by that time. I most definitely didn't used to, but when, in his second term, he turned against the settlers and made the long march out of Gaza (an incomplete one, I would realize later), I loved and admired him like I had no other American or Israeli leader before. Partly, I admit, because he reminded me of my father, with his girth and white hair, his power, confidence, charisma, sharp intellect, and sly humor. But even without that resemblance, in strictly political terms—for Sharon to change so radically, to take on what had seemed to be Israel's invincible power, the settler movement, and beat it single-handedly in a fight that went on for nearly two years, to shlep the extraordinary pullout from Gaza on his back, alone, to its conclusion—this surpassed even the first President Bush's handling of the 1991 Gulf War. It was the greatest show of leadership I'd ever seen from a head of the state in which I was privileged to be living.

A little later that night, when the Knesset session began, Sharon got up heavily from his seat, lumbered to the podium with a slight limp from an old war injury, and, in a voice somewhat weakened with age, gave a most un-Sharon-like speech. Speaking of the occupation, he said, "Israel, which wishes to be an exemplary democracy, will not be able to bear such a reality over time." He reminded listeners that he had "repeatedly and publicly said that I support the establishment of a Palestinian state alongside the State of Israel." He even quoted Menachem Begin in chiding Gush Emunim, the spearhead of the religious settler movement, for its "messianic complex." There was a feeling in the hall of historic change. A moment of low comedy came when Finance Minister Netanyahu and a few other cabinet members who opposed the disengagement, and who were trying unsuccessfully to get Sharon to delay the vote, were reduced to scurrying down the aisle into their seats before their names were called so they could, despite it all, vote "yes"—to keep Sharon from firing them, as he promised to do to any minister who didn't vote in favor of the pullout. That was one of the collateral benefits of the Gazan disengagement: getting to watch Sharon beat Netanyahu like a drum in one political contest after another.

At the time, disengagement seemed like the beginning of the end for the occupation; it turned out, instead, to be only a bright interlude in the dimness of 21st-century Israel. It was our Camelot. It was better than Oslo because it succeeded; it actually removed thousands of settlers and soldiers from the Gaza Strip for good. It announced the policy of unilateral withdrawal combined with military deterrence—"Sharon's way"—as the new, golden path out of Israel's troubles, a revival of hope after the failure of Oslo, and Israelis flocked to it. The Likud and Netanyahu seemed finished.

The whole world, meanwhile, had fallen in love not only with Israel, but with its old war criminal of a prime minister. It seems hallucinatory today, but Thabo Mbeki, Nelson Mandela's successor as president of South Africa, not only wrote Sharon a letter of congratulations on disengagement, he conveyed his sympathy for the uprooted settlers. "We are acutely conscious of and sensitive to the pain that will have to be borne by the Israeli families to which Gaza had become home," Mbeki wrote him. Fumi Gqiba, then South Africa's ambassador to Israel and a former general in the ANC army Umkhonto We Sizwe, told me, "Sharon should be supported, because without his leadership Israel never would have gotten out of Gaza. . . . We support him and hope the international community will close ranks around him." These are like dispatches from a different world, a different dimension, but that was Israel in 2005.

And it was a fluke. As the South African ambassador said, only Sharon could have gotten Israel out of Gaza: Nobody else had the political power (owing to Sharon's huge popularity with voters), plus the cunning and will to see it through. Not to mention the ruthlessness. About a year and a half before the pullout, after Sharon had begun to make his plan public, he decided to put it to a referendum among Likud members, pledging to abide by the results. At the time, the polls showed Likudniks backing disengagement by a large margin, and Sharon was confident of winning the referendum. But the settlers and Likud rejectionists mounted a furious campaign, mau-mauing party members on the phone, on the street, accusing them of abandoning the Land of Israel to terrorists. On the day of the referendum, Gazan terrorists shot to death settler Tali Hatuel, who was eight months pregnant, and her four daughters sitting in the car with her. Some 100,000 Likud members cast their ballots in the referendum, and disengagement lost by a landslide, 60 percent to 40 percent.

So what did Sharon do? He disregarded the results. Without breaking stride, he went back on his word and just kept barreling ahead—no apologies, no explanations. Naturally, there was a rebellion in Likud, but it failed for lack of a leader to challenge Sharon for the party chairmanship; the only one in the rejectionists' ranks who might have done so was Netanyahu, and he decided it was a losing battle.

If I'd been a Likudnik, I would have cursed Sharon for pulling off the most deceitful, anti-democratic move imaginable. But since I was definitely not a Likudnik, I could only shake my head in wonder and thank God that the guy who'd decided to get us out of Gaza had such unbelievable balls.

The decision to leave Gaza was a complete turnaround for Sharon: unexpected, anything but inevitable. I put it down to luck. Why he decided to quit Gaza is a mystery. He said he wanted to pre-empt the world from imposing an Israeli withdrawal from both Gaza and the West Bank, but I find it hard to believe that this is what drove him; the world was never close to doing any such thing, then or now. The only explanation I have is that Sharon just had a genuine, if very belated, change of heart, and came to see Gaza as the albatross it was and decided to cut it loose. Something happened to him to change his calculations, as it has with some Israeli leaders (Begin, Rabin, and Olmert) and not with others (Shamir and Netanyahu). Whatever it was that happened to Sharon, it might just as easily not have happened. That it did was a blessed accident.

As huge a political affair as disengagement was, it didn't cause the slightest stir on the streets of mainstream Israel. The only people getting worked up over it were the settlers and their supporters—the right-wingers, the losers in the deal. They were screaming and protesting like crazy. Meanwhile, the left and center, who supported the pullout, didn't have to do anything; Sharon, the army, and the cops were taking care of business for us. My image of Modi'in in that momentous summer of 2005 was of people lying on lawn chairs under sun umbrellas around the pool at Holmes Place, the goings-on in the Gush Katif settlements of Gaza very, very far from their minds. At a local shopping center toward the end of the week-long evacuation, I ran into Anat, who'd been an art teacher at Gilad's nursery school, a very sensitive, expressive woman, and she started fulminating: "What's going on? Nobody's doing anything. Nobody's saying anything; it's like nothing's happening." I sympathized with her; except for the true-believing right-wingers, nobody gave a shit about "politics" anymore. The Israeli media turned the disengagement into a tear-jerker, as it does with every political issue (unless it's turning it into nationalistic red meat). The story coming out of Gaza was the sobbing and screaming settlers being dragged out of their homes and synagogues, and everybody was supposed to cry in solidarity with them. Israel Radio's promo for its disengagement coverage was: "All the news, all the feelings." (It rhymes in Hebrew.) I asked my son Alon's teacher if she was discussing the events with the kids in class, and she said she was, but explained, "We can't talk about the politics, so we talk about the feelings." For Modi'in and the rest of middle-class Israel, the historic pullout from Gaza was one more reality show.

For nearly all middle-class Israeli youth, it wasn't even that; politics in general was (and still is) a non-issue for them, beyond the mindless grousing they pick up from the atmosphere and repeat. Some months before the disengagement I'd gone to do a feature story about Holon, a Tel Aviv suburb that, like so many other Israeli towns, had risen from its shabby working-class origins and, beginning in the '90s, changed into a largely bourgeois, fairly sparkling place. I hung around outside one of the city's best high schools, near the recently built Kiryat Rabin highrise project, and talked to teenagers on their way home. I saw pretty soon that I had a story not on Holon, but on the new generation of mainstream Israeli youth, the first that had grown up amid Western-style prosperity. I talked to about 20 teenagers outside the high school, at a couple of malls, and at a downtown hangout, and, except for their Hebrew, I could have been talking to 20 middle-class teenagers in Tucson, Toronto, Perth, or any prosperous Western city.

"What's politics?" frowned one girl when I raised the subject. "We never talk about it, maybe once in a blue moon," said another. "Oh, all that news, I never pay any attention to it," said one of the boys. "Except if there's a terror attack, it's not something I ever think about," said another girl. And what were their thoughts on the upcoming disengagement from Gaza? "I don't understand anything about it," said Shlomi, an 18-year-old. And these were smart kids; they all planned to go to college. It was fair to say they were right-wing, they distrusted Arabs, but it was all in the vaguest, most superficial way. This was the generation that had grown up with the bus bombings of the second intifada—and it had left no discernible mark on them. They seemed very happy. All they cared about was hanging out at the malls, drinking and dancing all night in Tel Aviv on the weekends, hooking up, playing on their computers, driving around, going for food, running with the crowd. They didn't seem to want anything different out of life than what they had. "I'd be very satisfied to have the life my parents have," said Tomer, Shlomi's 17-year-old friend. "I only want more than what they've got. You know, kids always want more than their parents had." Tomer summed up his plans: Get good grades, go into the army, then college, then career, along the way get married, buy a nice home, raise a family, and give them even more of the abundance his parents had given him. Shlomi agreed: "We're normal. We want the stable life."

People who don't live in Israel think Israelis' personal identities are shaped by the national events that make the news: war, terror, elections. That may have been true of earlier generations—though probably much less so than people think—but it is definitely not true of the Israeli generation that's come of age in the 21st century. These kids have been shaped, instead, by consumerism, technology, and globalization.

For me, of course, disengagement was a very emotional issue. One of the things I felt that summer was pissed off—at all the anti-pullout posters and displays of orange that had shoved the pro-pullout posters and displays of blue off the street. When the battle for public opinion began the year before, there were two sides visible in the street. Little by little, the right-wingers tore off every, or virtually every, pro-disengagement poster and bumper sticker and blue antenna ribbon in sight. By summer 2005, the summer of disengagement, Israel was all orange. Meanwhile, the right was marching on Gaza, sneaking into and reinforcing the Gush Katif settlements, blocking highways, fighting soldiers, and leaving fake bombs at bus stations—while we leftists were sitting quietly in our usual impotence. I'd tied a blue ribbon to my car antenna and put a bumper sticker on my car ("When it's all shit, evacuate"), and they got torn off. I tried again, putting on a new bumper sticker ("Removing settlements, choosing life"), and that got ripped away, too. In middle-class, suburban Modi'in.

Having vowed to take 10 eyes for an eye, I went out and tore an orange ribbon off a car antenna outside the shopping center, but I decided that that was the last one—if I got caught orange-handed, as it were, by a right-wing car owner, I'd sound pretty childish trying to defend my behavior. Then, driving home one afternoon a few weeks before the pullout, I saw a three-foot-high Star of David made of orange ribbons tied to the "Modi'in" sign at the city's main entrance. Symbolically, it was as if the settlers had taken over the city. The message was that all of Modi'in was against disengagement. Who gave them the right? I pulled my car over on the highway, got out, and tore the orange Star of David off. Then I turned the corner and saw another one, twice as tall, tied between a couple of poles, and I tore that one off, too.

I wouldn't have done this if there had also been pro-disengagement signs on the highways, but there weren't because the right-wingers had ripped them down, so I felt totally justified—especially since I wasn't stopping anybody from expressing their views on their privately owned car (except for that one time), but rather stopping the defacement of public property. The next week, while driving out of the city, I pulled over on the highway and yanked down a few yards of "The nation is with Gush Katif" banners tied to a guardrail. Driving back that evening and seeing that they had been replaced with "A Jew doesn't expel a Jew" banners, I pulled over and tore them off, too. The following morning I ripped down about six yards of "A Jew doesn't expel a Jew" plastic banners taped between utility poles. Drivers passing by saw me at work. A few yelled unintelligible things at me, and I always yelled back, "This is public property!" A few other drivers smiled and gave me the thumbs-up. One called out, "*Kol hakavod*" ("Good for you"), and a motorcyclist congratulated me for doing "holy work."

I felt so good. I was standing up to the right-wing's intimidation campaign. I was breaking out of the liberal paralysis. What I did wasn't much—it meant nothing in the national scheme of things—but for the first and only time during the entire saga of disengagement, I was an engaged citizen. I took an active part, even if miniscule, in the history being made in my country. For an Israeli suburban liberal dad like me, it was a rare, invigorating experience.

After the settlers were evacuated from Gaza, I was elated. I was proud of my country, which was such an unusual sensation, and a welcome one. Israel had done its part, and now we were back on the right track. In the first months after the withdrawal, there were very few rockets coming from the Strip, and in January 2006, four months after the IDF locked the gates of Gaza behind them, Sharon had a brain hemorrhage and went into a terminal coma with his aura intact and the wisdom of his "way" unchallenged. Ehud Olmert, his successor as head of the new Kadima party, won the snap election easily, running on his "reconvergence" plan to follow up on the Gazan disengagement by withdrawing unilaterally from about 90 percent of the West Bank. Meanwhile, the Likud, reduced to its anti-disengagement rump and led again by Netanyahu, plummeted to 12 Knesset seats from the 38 it had won behind Sharon in the previous election.

But very soon everything changed. By the middle of the year the rockets from Gaza returned in torrents. Gilad Shalit, an Israeli soldier in a tank unit on the Gazan border, was captured. The West Bank flared up again. (That Israel was dealing out far worse punishment to the Palestinians naturally went unnoticed.) Olmert quietly mothballed the reconvergence plan. Bibi and Likud, loudly claiming vindication, were suddenly on their way back.

What had gone wrong? Why didn't disengagement work? When the IDF retaliated so harshly against Hamas for its rockets, why didn't Hamas take the hint and stop firing—especially when Israel's new prime minister had won a mandate to withdraw from 90 percent of the West Bank? And why was Hamas, which was getting Palestinians killed because it evidently couldn't take yes for an answer, enjoying such support from the Palestinians?

The consensus conclusion among Israelis was that they'd given the Palestinians two chances to choose peace over war—first by negotiations, then by unilateral withdrawal—and been rebuffed both times, so there would be no third chance. (Which indeed there hasn't been.) The Palestinians were incorrigible—that was the new Israeli view, and as much I wanted to say it was wrong, I no longer could. During that horrible hangover from disengagement, I was writing things in the *Jerusalem Post* like this:

> I still believe what I've always believed—that Israel has no right to rule the Palestinians, that ruling them is bad, not good, for Israeli security, so it's both immoral and impractical for Israel to gobble up the only territory the Palestinians have for their own.
>
> However, the belief I've lost is that the Palestinians are a basically rational, reasonable nation, that they can be talked into putting down their weapons and making peace with Israel—if not out of good will, then out of their own self-interest.[1]

1. Larry Derfner, "Giving Up on the Palestinians," *Jerusalem Post,* July 6, 2006.

And things like this:

> Now it's time for the IDF, especially the Air Force, to really go
> to work on the terrorists in Gaza. There will no doubt be more
> innocent Palestinian children killed accidentally—but such
> tragedies happen in the most justified of wars, and Israel's war
> against Gazan terror is absolutely justified.[2]

Like Israelis at large, I believed we had gotten out of Gaza and
left it an independent entity, or at any rate that was what I wanted
to believe, so I didn't examine this perception too closely. I knew,
somewhere in my mind, that Gaza wasn't independent—that Israel
still blockaded its coast and airspace, still allowed no ships or planes
to go in or out, and had set up and enforced, with sharpshooters, a
no-go zone on the Gazan side of the border. But I put all this down
to Israel's security needs; after all, it was Hamas in control over there.

What I didn't know was that the disengagement had not ended
the economic siege on Gaza in the slightest—that the people there
remained as destitute and trapped as ever. A couple of years after the
pullout, James Wolfensohn, the ex–World Bank president who was
the international community's representative in the Strip, gave an
interview to *Haaretz* in which he blamed the rise of Hamas and the
subsequent violence mainly on the dashing of the Gazans' economic
hopes, which he in turn blamed mainly on the Bush administration, especially its Likud-minded Middle East envoy Elliot Abrams.
Wolfensohn, an Australian-born Jew and longtime supporter of
Israel, cannot be accused of being biased in the Palestinians' favor;
he's the closest thing to an objective insider to be found from the
post-disengagement period. According to him, the key to Gaza's
development had been an agreement for Gazan imports and exports
to move through the Israeli-controlled border crossings, but Abrams
saw to it that "every aspect of that agreement was abrogated." Thus,
Wolfensohn said:

---

2. Larry Derfner, "'Sharon's Way' Is Still the Right Way," *Jerusalem Post*, June
29, 2006.

Instead of hope, the Palestinians saw that they were put back in prison. And with 50 percent unemployment, you would have conflict. This is not just a Palestinian issue. If you have 50 percent of your people with no work, chances are they will become annoyed. So it's not, in my opinion, that Palestinians are so terrible; it is that they were in a situation . . . [that] . . . became impossible. And you can blame the Palestinians because there were those among them who were firing rockets or you can blame the Israelis for overreacting.[3]

But none of this was going to penetrate my mind. Like I said, I was so pleased to be able to say, for once, that my country had done right by the Palestinians, and it also sat very well with me to lay all the blame on Hamas. Unlike the Israeli majority, though, I did not become a believer in war as the solution. Instead, with a deflated spirit, I accepted the "realistic" view that the best we could do was "manage the conflict."

I'm sure it was just a coincidence, but right around that time I was diagnosed with prostate cancer. From the beginning, the doctors told me my chances of beating it were excellent, so after the emotional shock of the news, I became very clear-eyed and practical, completely focused on making the decisions I had to make and doing the things I had to do to overcome the challenge. To be more precise, I became militaristic in my thinking: Cancer was the enemy and I intended to defeat it. My metaphor was that cancer had invaded my country (my body) and taken a beachhead (my prostate). It was a setback, but now I was sending in the Marines (my doctors) to rout the enemy and win the war. I was 100 percent confident of victory and so was Philippa, so I got through it fine (and remain fine). I went into the hospital for surgery on July 11, and the following day, while I

3. Shahar Smooha, "All the Dreams We Had Are Now Gone," *Haaretz*, www .haaretz.com, July 19, 2007.

was lying in a Herzliya hospital bed recovering, the Second Lebanon War broke out.

I went home from the hospital with a catheter in me and doctor's orders to lie in bed for a month, so I watched the war on TV from our bedroom. I lost a lot of money by not covering it for *U.S. News and World Report*, but I was glad not to be there. I hate being in a pack of journalists. What's more, I don't believe in risking my life to get just a little bit closer to the battle, especially when hundreds of other reporters are covering it, and I don't like the idea of being unarmed and vulnerable in the vicinity of people who would like to kill me because of my nationality. I never wanted to be a war correspondent, I've always been bored reading war reportage, and I was happy to have a doctor's note to miss the gig up north.

That war remains an exceptional one, in that Israel was genuinely fighting in self-defense. The Second Lebanon War truly was a "war of no choice." I thought so then and still do. Israel was not occupying Lebanon or limiting its sovereignty in any way when Hezbollah fighters snuck across the border and killed 10 Israeli soldiers. The only Lebanese prisoner Israel still held was Samir Kuntar, who in 1979 shot an Israeli man to death on the Nahariya beach in front of his four-year-old daughter, then killed the girl by smashing her head against the rocks with his rifle butt.[4] Thus I concluded that Hezbollah's killing of 10 Israeli soldiers that day was an act of aggression and agreed fully that Israel had to teach them a harsh lesson.

For the first week of the fighting, I didn't mind taking a break, either, from my weekly column in the *Post* because everybody was in favor of the war, so what did I have to add? But after that first week, I began writing again, catheter or no, because now I did have something to say that nobody, as far as I could gather, was saying or writing in the mainstream Israeli media: that Israel's retaliation had gone on long enough, and that we should accept Hezbollah's offer of a cease-fire. From the politicians to the media to the public,

---

4. "2006 Lebanon War," *Wikipedia*, last modified December 7, 2016, https://en.wikipedia.org/wiki/2006_Lebanon_War.

the near-unanimous view was that teaching Hezbollah a lesson wouldn't do—no, the official war goals were the permanent ousting of Hezbollah from south Lebanon, which Israel had failed to accomplish during 18 years of fighting *within* Lebanon, and Hezbollah's surrender of the two soldiers it had captured (and killed, it would be learned later), even though Israel had never in its entire history managed to gain the release of POWs except in prisoner exchanges following a cease-fire. But the whole country had suddenly been stricken with amnesia; until the very end of the 34-day war, polls showed that upward of 90 percent of the Jewish population supported it. Olmert was giving Churchillian speeches about "pain, tears, and blood." The popular new bumper sticker read, "We will win!" The defense minister, Labor's Amir Peretz, ostensibly a dove, was literally shouting that Hezbollah leader Hassan Nasrallah "will remember the name Amir Peretz!" Even liberal columnists were writing that Iran was watching us, and that if we did not vanquish Hezbollah, Israel's existence and even that of the free world would be imperiled by a soon-to-be nuclear Islamic republic.

Since I was in the house all the time, I didn't feel the mood on the street except through the TV screen and newspapers until, after a month on my back, I went to a festival one evening in a Modi'in park. A dad I knew in his early 40s was saying how he was trying to volunteer his way into the war. Another dad, a TV sports reporter of about the same age, was saying how he'd like to join, too, but his wife objected. "With me there's no wife, no nothing. I'm going," said the first dad, leaving the sports reporter sheepishly silent. A friend of mine who lived near the Lebanese border, a Meretz voter and opponent of the First Lebanon War, couldn't understand why I was in favor of a cease-fire. "We can't let Hezbollah stay there. They'll just attack again," he said. In my first column of the war, titled "There Is a Limit" and published two weeks into the fighting, I made, modesty aside, a prescient point:

[I]f Israel winds the war up now, it can still win. Once the fighting stops and the dust settles, Hezbollah will retain plenty of capability to hurt Israel, but I don't think it will be in a hurry to try. Lebanon does not want to go through this again. . . .

Israel has exacted a very high price for Hezbollah's aggression, and by doing so it just may have achieved the one realistic, legitimate goal of this war—the reestablishment of Israeli military deterrence.[5]

Basically, I wanted Israel to do exactly what it did in the war, but for a week rather than 34 days. And what Israel did in the war included what can only be called state terrorism: It deliberately punished the civilian population of Lebanon to achieve a political goal—turning the Lebanese people against Hezbollah attacks on Israel, thus creating a domestic political deterrent against future attacks. From the beginning, Israeli leaders telegraphed their intention to make the Lebanese homefront pay a heavy price for Hezbollah's aggression. IDF chief Dan Halutz said at the outset, "If the [two captured] soldiers are not returned, we will turn Lebanon's clock back 20 years."[6] Not Hezbollah's clock—Lebanon's. When Israel warned south Lebanon's hundreds of thousands of civilians to flee north because the Air Force was going to bomb the area to bits, Justice Minister Haim Ramon said anyone left there was a legitimate target—even though masses of people in south Lebanon were either too old, sick, or poor to leave, or else they were understandably scared of becoming "collateral damage" if they tried.

Israel Air Force bombers killed families trying to get out of southern Lebanon, they killed farm workers, they killed UN peacekeepers who'd warned them 10 times that they were getting too close. They knocked down one high-rise apartment building after another, and who knows if any Hezbollah men were inside. They blackened Lebanon's entire coast with oil after bombing a power plant. They hit medical aid convoys and Red Cross ambulances. They bombed the Beirut airport, highways, bridges, and other national infrastructure

---

5. Larry Derfner, "There Is a Limit," *Jerusalem Post*, July 27, 2006.
6. "2006 Lebanon War," *Wikipedia*.

on the easy rationale that while these facilities were used by the civilian population, they were also used by Hezbollah.[7]

I don't believe that Israeli pilots knowingly took aim at plainly civilian targets (for instance, at families on the run), certainly not as a matter of policy. They're not monsters. But they did very knowingly take aim at any number of civilian buildings and a vast store of other civilian infrastructure, and—what do you know—there were often civilians in and around the target zones. So the Air Force didn't have to aim at Lebanese civilians to kill or maim them, which was an unstated goal of the war; all it had to do was adopt an attitude of "when in doubt, bomb," and the rest would take care of itself. Israel would have "plausible deniability."

As I said, I supported this policy, only in a much smaller dose. I wrote this in the *Post* at the end of the war:

> How do you deter Hezbollah when its members are only too eager to die for the privilege of killing Israelis, and when their dead are so easily replaced, as Israel learned during its 18 years of fighting them? You can't deter Hezbollah. But what you can do, it would seem, is make life so miserable for Lebanese citizens, mainly the Shi'ites, that once the war is over, they will act as a constraint on Hezbollah from rocketing or raiding Israel again. . . . Which means I'm saying I favored the killing of innocent men, women and children. Which, of course, is why I love war so much.[8]

In that column, "Flirting with State Terrorism," I reiterated that "Israel should have ended the war after a week at the latest." But what should have been was one thing; what was, was another. I continued:

> [T]he condition that Lebanon and masses of its people are in shows that Israel wasn't nearly as morally pure in this war as we

---

7. Ibid.
8. Larry Derfner, "Flirting with State Terrorism," *Jerusalem Post*, August 17, 2006.

like to think. When you define enemy targets so permissively that you know that bombing them will result in massive "collateral damage" to civilians—and you also know that civilian suffering is vital to your purpose in the war—then you are flirting very dangerously with terrorism. Which is what Israel did in [its late offensive] Operation Change of Direction, and what I did in supporting the war at first.

Forget the bit about "flirting"; I was justifying Israeli terrorism in response to aggression, which I still do. It would be a few years before I acknowledged that in my view of the rights and wrongs of Palestinian responses to Israeli aggression, I had been going by a double standard.

The war, as far as the Israeli public was concerned, ended as a horrible failure. Hezbollah was still there, it still had our two soldiers, and Israel had paid a heavy price—mainly some 160 slain soldiers and civilians (compared to about 1,800 on Lebanon's side, along with incomparably worse destruction, all of which, as always, failed to register with the Israeli public).

The Second Lebanon War was a very good illustration that despite what sentimental liberals like to believe, it's not the big, bad Israeli leaders who drag the peace-loving public to battle; it's much closer to being the other way around. From the beginning, the public demanded victory. It insisted on a fairy-tale ending where Hassan Nasrallah agrees to march Hezbollah out of south Lebanon and hands over the two Israeli soldiers, maybe licking their boots in contrition. And the media fell in line, feeding the public a daily diet of blood-and-guts patriotism, with only the rare journalist challenging this mania. (*Yediot Ahronot*'s star columnist, Nahum Barnea, was such a rare journalist, writing a series of increasingly skeptical weekly dispatches while he was embedded with the army in Lebanon, ending with the call, "Take the cease-fire, Olmert. Take it with both hands.")

And sure enough, after the war ended there were several years of absolute quiet on Israel's northern border, without so much as a single Hezbollah rocket or bullet being fired, which proved the Second Lebanon War to have been a success—though very few Israelis are ready even now to admit it. Just a couple of weeks after the fighting ended, Nasrallah, in a startling admission on Lebanese TV, nearly an apology, made it clear he'd learned his lesson:

> We did not think, even one percent, that the capture [of the two soldiers] would lead to a war at this time and of this magnitude. You ask me, if I had known on July 11 . . . that the operation would lead to such a war, would I do it? I say no, absolutely not.[9]

The all-but-perfectly quiet years for Israelis in the north since the 2006 war have illustrated a principle that likewise goes right past just about everyone in this country: that if Israel 1) withdraws *fully* from occupied territory, and 2) convinces the other side it will strike back very hard against subsequent attacks, then 3) Israel's massive military superiority will deter the other side's aggression, no matter how fanatic its ideology. (There have been many Hezbollah attacks against Israeli soldiers on the border since the war, but these are weak, typically failed reprisals against Israel's severe assaults on Hezbollah in Lebanon and Syria; more about this later.)

The end of the fighting also marked the end of Olmert as anything but a lame duck prime minister; clearly, it was just a matter of time until Netanyahu regained control of the country. The year 2006 turned out to be a watershed one for Israel. The rockets from Gaza and Lebanon left people convinced that withdrawing from occupied territory only emboldened the enemy and got more Israelis killed. (The fact that Israelis had gotten killed at a much higher rate when the army was stuck inside Gaza [1967–2005] and south Lebanon

---

9. Rory McCarthy, "Hizbullah Leader: We Regret the Two Kidnappings that Led to War with Israel," *The Guardian*, www.guardian.co.uk, August 28, 2006.

[1982–2000] disappeared down the national memory hole.) The public shifted sharply back to the right. Israelis wanted a "strong" leader again.

And as 2007 began, the leading candidate for strong leader offered a glimpse of what he had in store for us. The world would be shocked on Election Day 2015 to hear Netanyahu scaring up votes with his announcement that "Arab voters are heading to the polling stations in droves." But on January 2, 2007, hardly anyone noticed when he publicly took credit for "dramatically" reducing the Israeli Arab birthrate. A nauseatingly racist statement, the kind that would cause a scandal for any Western politician who made it, but in Israel, even though Netanyahu's remark was reported in *Haaretz*[10] and *Yediot Ahronot*,[11] it got no further attention—except from me.

Netanyahu was at the time seeking to mend fences with the ultra-Orthodox, or haredim, who had given him blanket, crucial support in the 1996 election, but who became alienated from him when, as finance minister under Sharon, he slashed government child subsidies, which badly hurt large, poor families. In Israel, there are two demographic groups in which large, poor families predominate: haredim and Israeli Arabs. So when Netanyahu went to speak to a conference of haredi officials at the start of 2007, he tried to show the upside of those deep cuts he'd made to child subsidies. He explained:

> Two positive things happened: Members of the haredi public joined the workforce in earnest. And on the national level, the unexpected result was the demographic effect on the non-Jewish public, where there was a dramatic drop in the birth rate.

10. Yair Ettinger, "Netanyahu Defends Child Allowance Cuts at Haredi Meet," *Haaretz*, www.haaretz.com, January 3, 2007.
11. Neta Sela, "Netanyahu: Pensions Cut—Arabs' Birth Rate Declined," www.ynetnews.com, January 3, 2007.

There was a dramatic drop in the "non-Jewish" (i.e., Israeli Arab) birthrate—and Netanyahu, speaking to a Jewish audience, was not only citing this as a "positive thing," he was bragging that it was his decision to further impoverish large, poor families that did it. He didn't just say this once, either; I'd read in the news that he'd made the same boast to a group of ultra-Orthodox Knesset members.

Since evidently nobody in Israel or anywhere else considered his remark worthy of further notice, I devoted my next *Jerusalem Post* column to it. In "A Bigot Called Bibi," I wrote that Netanyahu had gone beyond the pale and put himself in the category of racist demagogues like Jean Marie Le Pen and Jorg Haider.

And who sprang to his defense? Ron Dermer, then minister of economic affairs at the Israeli Embassy in Washington, later Israel's ambassador to the United States and impresario of Netanyahu's outrageously insolent congressional speech against Obama's Iranian nuclear deal. In a sarcastic reply in the *Post,* which he titled "The Nerve of Bibi," Dermer wrote:

> Netanyahu was caught red-handed. Who would have thought that an Israeli leader circa 2007 could think, let alone say, something so shocking? And we thought the quaint notion that leaders of the Jewish state wanted more Jews than non-Jews in it was passe.[12]

Dermer's point was that since a Jewish state is legitimate, and since a Jewish state requires a Jewish majority, deterring non-Jewish citizens from having children by hurting them economically is legitimate, too. And there's nothing wrong with bragging about it in front of Jews either. He concluded:

> But while [Derfner] should be commended for bringing this story to our attention, he is mistaken in calling Bibi a bigot. He is only a Zionist, and apparently even a proud one.[13]

---

12. Ron Dermer, "Right of Reply: The Nerve of Bibi," *Jerusalem Post,* www .jpost.com, January 8, 2007.
13. Ibid.

By now everyone outside the American-Israeli right-wing axis has figured out that Dermer, like his boss, is an arrogant, warmongering, arch-conservative Republican. But already in January 2007, master and mentor both revealed themselves to be proud, even gloating anti-Arab bigots, too.

Olmert, for his part, was an interesting political figure, a man of contradictions, even of extremes. Before becoming prime minister, he'd shifted from the right to the left of the Zionist political spectrum in the space of a few years. In office, he went further toward the Palestinians in peace negotiations than any other Israeli prime minister before or since. Then he aborted those negotiations by launching a savage military onslaught against the Gaza Strip, one of the most one-sided "wars" ever fought, setting a precedent that Netanyahu would follow. A few months before "Operation Cast Lead" began, my political views would move suddenly and decisively to the left.

CHAPTER TEN

CAST LEAD

Ten thousand Israeli Arabs, along with a smattering of leftist Jews, were marching through the center of Tel Aviv with red flags, black flags, and Palestinian flags on the eighth night of Operation Cast Lead. The chanting was mainly in Arabic; the only word I could understand was "Falastin." In Rabin Square, the border policemen looked jumpy, ready to shoot; the Arabs standing near them looked scared. Groups of right-wingers stood on the sidewalks of Ibn Gvirol Street, the route of the march, behind the barricades, cursing the protesters ("Traitors, terrorists, fifth columnists, go die in Gaza!") and trying to get at them, but the police, I must say, did a standout job of holding them back. Toward the end of the demonstration, a guy in a denim jacket brushed past the cops and, from the curb, hollered in the marchers' faces, "It's all over! The Golani Brigade is eating them up! The mosque is destroyed!" The breaking news was that the army's ground invasion of Gaza had begun.

As the rally ended and the Arabs boarded buses back to the Galilee, the last protesters, mainly Jewish, gathered in front of the Tel Aviv Cinematheque, which was cordoned off by police, and they looked happy and satisfied that they'd made a strong statement. Then, as the police started to drift away, a crowd of rightists, including a few in Betar Jerusalem gear, surged toward the leftists, shouting "Anti-Semites" and shoving them out of their way. The police rushed back and blocked the marauders' advance as the leftists took cover inside the Cinematheque. The right-wingers, triumphant at last, unfurled a giant banner of Gilad Shalit and chanted, "Death to the Arabs." The leftists made their way home, the police called it a night, and the right-wingers wrapped in Israeli flags had the run of the street. In the eateries on Ibn Gvirol, the TVs were tuned to the infantry's invasion.

That happened on January 3, 2009. The IDF's offensive started over Chanukah, and there's a Chanukah poem that speaks of a dreidel "cast in solid lead"; the army considered this a strong Jewish image, so they named the war Operation Cast Lead, thinking it would put people in mind of a sturdy dreidel, which it didn't. The army also barred Israeli journalists from going into Gaza during the three-week campaign, which was fine with me, so I ran around Israel, writing stories about the home front.

On the third day of the war, a war that Israel started by bombing Gaza from the air in the middle of a clear Saturday afternoon, killing some 230 fighters and civilians, I went to Umm el-Fahm. The name alone strikes fear into Israeli Jews. It is the most politically and religiously radical of any Israeli Arab town, the home of the country's Islamic Movement. The Galilee riots in October 2000 started there. Like other Galilee towns, it is built on steep hills, and standing at the town's summit is the towering Abu Rubeida mosque, where Israel's single most feared Arab, Sheikh Ra'ed Salah, founder of the Islamic Movement, preaches. If I tell the average Israeli Jew that I went with a photographer to Umm el-Fahm on the third day of Operation Cast Lead, he'd think I was suicidal. Two out of three Israeli Jews won't even drive into an Israeli Arab town in normal times.[1]

It was a cold day, black flags and Palestinian flags hung from storefronts and homes on the narrow streets, and my photographer

---

1. Sammy Smooha, "Index of Arab-Jewish Relations in Israel, 2003–2009," Haifa University, www.soc.haifa.ac.il, December 2010.

partner, Jonathan Bloom, and I might well have been the only Jews in this city of 40,000-plus. The Abu Rubeida mosque was empty except for a couple of old men sitting on chairs, who welcomed us in and spoke with us as much as their limited Hebrew allowed. In the clinic downstairs, a devout Muslim nurse in robes and head scarf said the televised scenes from Gaza "were painful to watch," but she said it shyly, without a hint of accusation against us. Seeing a cut on Jon's hand, she taped a bandage on it.

Outside, a pickup truck flying a black flag moved slowly along an alley. I stepped in the pickup's way, motioned the driver to stop, and told him in Hebrew we were from the *Jerusalem Post* and asked if we could interview him. The driver, a salesman and father of six, pulled over, got out, and said he'd put up the black flag after watching "all the scenes of children being killed. I couldn't stand it. But it hurts me the same way when I see innocent Jews killed by Palestinians." Not what you would expect from an Arab flying a black flag in Umm el-Fahm on day three of Operation Cast Lead.

In the cafes and grocery stores, the TVs were tuned to Al Jazeera. Countermen and customers watched the scenes of Gazan corpses being carried away, of women screaming hysterically, of crowds running, of Israeli jets in the sky, of Nasrallah preaching interminably. Again, we told people in Hebrew we were from the *Jerusalem Post,* and would they mind being photographed, and would they mind sitting a little closer so we could get them in the frame, and everyone cooperated. It wasn't servility; it wasn't fear. We acted like respectful guests, and Arab graciousness just kicked in, war or no war.

But these people, of course, were hurt and enraged. "You go into every house in Umm el-Fahm, every Arab house in Israel, and you'll see people crying. Look what they're saying on the news: 330 dead, 1,450 injured," said a grocery store owner as Arabic text ran across the bottom of his TV screen.

There were a couple of people I spoke with at length, and after a while I heard an anguish rising in their voices that scared me a little—that made me end the interview, apologize for all the killing, thank them, and say goodbye. I heard it when the grocery store owner talked about "watching little children lying there in pieces, their faces burned. Oh God, if Israel were only killing fighters, but they're killing women and children, too!" I also heard it from the owner of a clothing store near the mosque. Standing outside his store, he told us at the outset, "I'm worried about you two wandering around here today. People are really in a horrible mood." As he continued talking about Gaza, a few people gathered around, and an agony seemed to enter his voice and grow, and it was starting to overtake him, and then someone called him into his clothing store, so I took that opportunity to go inside, thank him, and leave. Later I went into a candy store, heard a kid call out, "Yahoodie," and I turned and walked out.

Otherwise, the only precaution we took was to keep a reasonable distance from clusters of teenage boys. If Israel were being bombed by Arabs like we were bombing Gaza, I wouldn't advise a pair of Arab journalists to go into a religious, nationalistic Jewish town, and certainly not to get anywhere near gatherings of adolescent boys. Considering what Israel was doing to Gaza, Umm el-Fahm was amazingly safe and even remained hospitable to a pair of Israeli Jews. That day was a clear illustration of something I've learned from writing dozens of stories about Israeli Arabs and thousands about Israeli Jews: The former are more than ready to live in peace with the latter, and the latter don't know it.

On the day before the Air Force attacked Gaza to start the war, Amos Oz, the long-time "spiritual leader" of the Israeli peace camp, wrote a page-one opinion piece in *Yediot Ahronot*: "The State of Israel must defend its citizens. . . . The suffering of the residents living near Gaza cannot continue." Yet a few paragraphs down, he added: "The best course for Israel is to reach a compromise cease-fire in return for an easing of the siege on Gaza." This was also the view taken by David Grossman, the new-generation voice of Israeli doves, in his *New York*

Times[2] and *Haaretz*[3] op-eds. Meretz took the same position. Haim Oron, then head of the party, told me, "A few hours after the war began, I went on Channel 2 and said clearly, and I may have been the first to say so, that our goal now must be to reach a new cease-fire." I asked him why he endorsed going to war in the first place, and Oron said, "People think that since I'm on the left I'm supposed to say Israel should turn the other cheek, then the third, then the fourth— I'm sorry, that's not me." Peace Now, for its part, took no position on the war at all. The organization's leaders were "divided in their opinions and ill at ease about the situation," Tel Aviv professor Dan Jacobson, an influential voice in the movement, told me.

Operation Cast Lead marked another rung on the Zionist left's way down. The leadership of the mainstream peace camp supported the launching of a war in which Israel would kill 1,400 people, more than a third of them civilians, and lay waste to much of the Gaza Strip—while losing 13 people, including four soldiers to friendly fire, and taking scattered, negligible property damage from Hamas's aimless rockets. The Zionist left supported going to war because prior to Israel's massive attack, Hamas was rocketing the kibbutzim, moshavim, and towns near the Gazan border. But the country's liberals didn't take into account that prior to the Air Force's Saturday-afternoon opening assault, Israel had been killing far more Palestinians and doing immeasurably worse damage than it had been taking. (In the three years and four months between Sharon's disengagement and Operation Cast Lead, 28 Israelis were killed by Gazans[4]—and 1,250 Gazans were killed by Israel.[5]) Also,

2. David Grossman, "Fight Fire With a Cease-Fire," *New York Times,* www .nytimes.com, December 30, 2008.
3. David Grossman, "Gaza Success Proves Israel Is Strong, Not Right," *Haaretz,* www.haaretz.com, January 20, 2009.
4. "Victims of Palestinian Violence and Terrorism Since September 2000," Israel Ministry of Foreign Affairs, Palestinian Terror, www.mfa.gov.il.
5. "Protection of Civilians (Weekly)—Archive," United Nations Office for the Coordination of Humanitarian Affairs—Occupied Palestinian Territory, www.ochaopt.org.

the liberals of course failed to consider that Gaza was under Israeli siege—"the world's largest open-air prison," as it was often described.

Finally, the call by Oz, Grossman, Meretz, and the others for a cease-fire a few days into the war was disingenuous. Everybody in Israel had known that if the IDF went into Gaza this time, it would be for the long-awaited "big operation" that the politicians and generals had been talking about, not another two- or three-day incursion of the sort Israel undertook every few months. So the liberals' call for an early cease-fire was made in bad faith; they had backed the start of a horrible slaughter that they had to know would not end quickly.

The people in Sderot and other Israeli communities within rocket range of Gaza suffered, some of them traumatically, from the years of rushing into their bomb shelters and from knowing people nearby who'd been killed or injured. Over the years I did several stories from the area, and toward the end of Cast Lead, by which time the rocketing of the border towns had slowed to barely a trickle, I stopped in Sderot. I asked a counterman at a falafel stand, a grizzled-looking guy of about 50 with a gray mustache, how things were going. "We're okay now," he said. There was a spark in his eye and a controlled joy in his grin that implied what a dangerous, nerve-wracking ordeal he had just come through.

When the cease-fire went into effect, I called Antoine Grand, head of the Red Cross team in Gaza, as part of a morning-after story for the *Post*. "It's like waking up from a nightmare," he said, speaking from his residence, which he said had a shell crater and fallen white phosphorous (which burns like napalm) in the garden, and broken windows and shrapnel inside. Grand said that once, during their evacuations of people from bombed-out apartments, he and his

team came upon a group of children cowering next to their mothers, who'd been dead for days:

> We saw destroyed houses with traces of tanks having run over
> them. Houses that were completely black from fire. Ambulances
> that had been crushed down. Pieces of artillery shells in houses
> and apartments. Roads destroyed, gardens with olive trees
> destroyed.
>
> Some of the houses that had been occupied by Israeli sol-
> diers had graffiti on the walls. Some of it was in English. "Don't
> fuck with us." "Where is Hamas?" There were obscene draw-
> ings, such as a penis pissing on a Palestinian flag.

In his eight years with the Red Cross, Grand, a Frenchman,
had worked in war zones such as Congo, Ethiopia, Ivory Coast, and
Afghanistan:

> I'm not saying that what happened in Gaza was worse than what
> happened in those countries, but I personally have never wit-
> nessed such destruction as I have here in the last three weeks.

Dr. Harald Veen, a Red Cross doctor from Gibraltar who'd come
to work in Gaza's Shifa Hospital, talked to me from Jerusalem on his
way to catch a plane home:

> Many children were brought in dead. That was the hardest part
> of it. Since I left Gaza a day and a half ago, I've been walking
> around and those pictures come back—corpses of children,
> with big holes in the back, spinal cord damage, paraplegic,
> traumatic amputations, shrapnel in the brain.
>
> There were always a lot of family around. The mothers were
> holding the leftovers of the bodies of their children, and you
> cannot do anything.

As the cease-fire began and Gazans were pulling scores of corpses out of the rubble, Israeli authorities held a news conference in the empty terminal at the border crossing on the Israeli-Gazan border. They were there to announce the opening of Israel's Regional Medical Clinic for the People of Gaza. They had 30 medical staffers and lots of great equipment on hand to treat Gazan war casualties. Isaac Herzog, then the government's minister of social services, denied it was a public relations stunt. "Israel knows how to fight terror, but it also knows how to be humane," he said. The head of Israel's Magen David Adom ambulance service, Eli Bin, gave a pep talk to the staff:

> This is not going to be an easy mission. The eyes of the world are going to be on us. We're going to give these people the best care we possibly can, and they're going to go back to Gaza and be ambassadors for MDA, and show that Israel has nothing whatsoever against the people of Gaza.[6]

Right before I filed the story, three days after the clinic opened, the MDA spokesman told me that a total of seven Gazans had come in for treatment, all of them patients already getting special care at Israeli hospitals. I asked him if anybody came in who was hurt in the war. "No," he said.

By the time of Operation Cast Lead, I'd been writing weekly op-eds, which would turn into a column titled "Rattling the Cage," for a total of eight years at the *Post*. It was a great intellectual adventure. I was continuously challenging my own ideas and often changing them. In fits and starts, it was a journey leftward, toward a more and more critical view of the "Israeli narrative."

---

6. Larry Derfner, "Picking Up the Pieces," *Jerusalem Post Upfront*, January 23, 2009.

The most discomforting but also vital experience in writing op-eds, at least for me, comes from facing my fears. So often I'll be writing a piece, or thinking about writing one, and I'll become aware that there's something I'm afraid to say, something I'm even afraid to think. Then I'll dare to think that thought (because once you realize there's something you're afraid to think, you either have to think it or admit that you're a coward). Then, after thinking the thought, I ask myself if it's right, if it's true. And if it seems true, I ask myself other questions, like is it a decent thing to say publicly; is it hurtful to innocent people; is any purpose served by writing it? Naturally, the thoughts I'm hesitant to write are the unpopular ones, the ones that may make a lot of people think bad things about me, the ones that, in those first glimmerings of their appearance, may have me thinking bad things about myself.

For instance, it took me a long time to admit that there was no good reason why Israel had to hold onto Arab East Jerusalem. When I finally wrote that op-ed, in 1997, anyone challenging Jerusalem's standing as the "united, indivisible, eternal capital of Israel and the Jewish people" was breaking about the most forbidding taboo in Israeli political discourse. Talk of giving up any part of the nation's capital was like sticking a knife in Israel's heart—which is the sort of metaphor that was being employed to discourage such talk. Over the years, I'd given myself plenty of reasons why we couldn't relinquish any part of Jerusalem, but finally it was just fear that had guided my thinking; breaking taboos is scary, especially one as imposing as that. When I finally looked at the issue squarely and logically, I couldn't see what was so sacred to Israel and the Jewish people about the all-Arab neighborhoods that only became part of "eternal Jerusalem" when Israel conquered them in 1967—the places with Arab names that few Israeli Jews had ever heard of, let alone wanted to visit. Why insist on keeping them, every inch of them, when having a capital in East Jerusalem was so vital to the Palestinians? Why not divide Jerusalem between us—out of spite? For the sake of a nationalistic religious myth? So I changed my opinion, first privately, and then in the *Post*. That, for me, is the intellectual adventure of writing op-eds.

It's impossible for me to trace precisely what triggers the new thoughts that come into my mind and cause me to change my views. It's not that I think one way, then see something and suddenly start thinking another way. It's a gradual, cumulative process that I suppose climaxes in one clarifying moment, though I can't say for sure about that moment because I can only recall two of them. One was the sight of that crowd of Palestinian celebrants on TV in Ramallah after the lynching of those two soldiers, which suddenly washed away my confusion about the second intifada. The second came in late October 2008, two months before Operation Cast Lead, when Israel refused to allow a delegation of Western doctors, nurses, and psychiatrists to cross into Gaza for a mental health conference, and also refused, before relenting under pressure, to allow a protest boat carrying medical supplies to dock at the Gaza Strip.

Until then, for two and a half years, I'd accepted the rationale of the government that it had to blockade Gaza for security purposes— to keep weapons from reaching Hamas and Islamic Jihad's hands. (It was only after Cast Lead that everyone learned about Israel's casually sadistic prohibitions on imports to Gaza during those years, on toys, musical instruments, chocolate, spices, newspapers, fishing rods, and scores of other basic items.[7]) But these weren't weapons that Israel was stopping in late October 2008: It was doctors and psychiatrists, protesters and medical equipment. Until then I'd pushed away all the things I'd read about the "world's largest open-air prison," about the humanitarian crisis being caused by the electricity shortages, about the deaths and destruction from Israeli "retaliations," and justified them all as being necessary for Israel's security. In this particular view, though, I hadn't been sustained by fear of breaking a taboo, but rather by the need to believe. I'd believed in disengagement, and it felt so good to be sure that Israel was in the right—that it had taken the high road—and I just didn't want to give up that belief. But barring the doctors' delegation and the peace flotilla from entering Gaza was so indefensible, so wanton, that it threw

---

7. "Partial List of Items Prohibited/Permitted Into the Gaza Strip," Gisha—Legal Center for Freedom of Movement, www.gisha.org, June 2010.

Israel's whole policy toward the Strip into doubt, and had the effect of beginning to dislodge the blockade in my mind and opening it up to the idea that Gaza was indeed the world's largest open-air prison, with Israel as its warden.

That was the turning point in my political thinking. That was the moment when I began to stop seeing the Israeli-Palestinian conflict since 1967 as one in which both sides shared the guilt, and started seeing it more and more as one of oppressor and oppressed, of Israel being guilty and the Palestinians innocent. (Not that Israel was bad and the Palestinians good, but that Israel was the strong side in the conflict and was using its strength to subjugate the Palestinians, which the Palestinians were not doing to Israel.) In what was for me the pivotal column, "Doctors Aren't Terrorists," I wrote in reference to the medical delegation and protest boat:

> Keeping them out of Gaza has nothing to do with security and everything to do with punishment—punishment of Gazan society as a whole. Not just the terrorists, not just Hamas and Islamic Jihad, but every man, woman and child.[8]

Next I began to wonder about the blocking of weapons from getting to Gaza: Did Israel expect Hamas, of all regimes, to agree to live without arms when Israel, its enemy next door, had the biggest arsenal in the Middle East? Would any government in any country agree to such an arrangement? Is this what Israeli leaders call "disengagement"? The Strip was still under Israeli occupation, I concluded, only now by remote control—which put a whole different spin on the rockets Hamas and Islamic Jihad were firing at us, especially when the other side of Palestine, the West Bank, was under full Israeli control, inside and out.

By this time, a little more than a month before Cast Lead, while the rockets were pouring down on Sderot and its environs, I wrote about the invisible side of the story, the hell we were raining down

---

8. Larry Derfner, "Doctors Aren't Terrorists," *Jerusalem Post*, October 30, 2008.

on the Strip, and maintained that already "Israel's war with Gaza has to be the most one-sided war on earth. . . ." I also noted that it was Israel, not Hamas, that had broken the five-month cease-fire by attacking what it called a "ticking tunnel" deep inside Gaza and killing a half-dozen Hamasniks, setting off the exchanges that would devolve into Israel's air attack that started Operation Cast Lead. That fateful assault on the Gazan tunnel was carried out, according to the IDF, to prevent an imminent abduction like the one of Gilad Shalit. I quoted *Yediot Ahronot*'s Nahum Barnea about it, and because that Israeli incursion set Operation Cast Lead in motion, the Barnea quote bears repeating:

> In front of the microphones, Israeli officials placed all the blame on Hamas. Privately, some of them took a different view. They talked about the excessive zeal of IDF commanders and an excessively deep incursion into Gazan territory by our forces, in violation of the unspoken rules of the cease-fire. According to this view, Hamas didn't initiate the renewal of the fighting—it was responding to Israeli actions.

A few days before the Air Force's initial assault, with the violence escalating on both sides, Hamas spokesman Mahmoud al-Zahar went on the Channel 10 news and offered Israel a complete cease-fire, in both Gaza and the West Bank.[9] I titled my last column before the war "Accept Hamas' Offer." Don Quixote rides again.

Israel's offensive turned out to be very much like the one it waged against Lebanon in 2006; this time it was the Gaza Strip's clock that got turned back 20 years. The all-important difference, though, was that in Operation Cast Lead, Israel, being the occupier of Gaza and the West Bank, was the aggressor. Also, Hamas wasn't nearly as strong as Hezbollah, so the disparity in casualties and destruction between Israel and Gaza was much greater than it had been between Israel and Lebanon.

---

9. Roee Nahmias, "Hamas: Willing to Renew Truce," www.ynetnews.com, December 23, 2008.

Other things, though, didn't change: Except for *Haaretz,* the Israeli news media gave minimal, token coverage to what was happening on the other side. The polls showed as much as 94 percent of the Jewish public supporting the war.[10] I didn't need to wait for the postmortems from Amnesty International, B'Tselem, and the UN to tell me we had bombed civilian facilities: The IDF announced in its wartime press releases that it was doing so, only it categorized these facilities as legitimate targets. After the war ended, I wrote:

> We deliberately bombed Gaza's parliament and other government buildings because they were "symbols of Hamas power." We bombed Islamic University because it employs scientists who develop Hamas' military arsenal. (Qassams? How much of a scientist do you have to be?) We say that we fight cleaner than they do. If the kill ratio were 100-to-1 in their favor instead of ours, would we still say that? If our cities looked like Gaza does today, would we call that a clean war?
>
> If Hamas or any other enemy bombed the Knesset, the government ministries, the police stations and other "symbols of Israeli power"—if it bombed the Technion because it employs scientists who develop the IDF's military arsenal—would we say these are "legitimate targets"? The truth is that this time, the Palestinians fought much cleaner than we did. . . . We bashed their brains in. We were like a 280-pound wrestler beating up a kid. All in all, we're better than Hamas, but this time we, not they, were the bad guys.[11]

After the war, some Israeli soldiers with guilty consciences began talking about what they'd seen or done. In a discussion among

---

10. "Israeli Public Opinion Polls: Opinions on Fighting with Hamas," www.jewishvirtuallibrary.org, January 4–6, 2009.
11. Larry Derfner, "The Moral Superiority of an F-16," *Jerusalem Post,* February 5, 2009.

graduates of the Yitzhak Rabin military academy (the transcript of which was published by *Haaretz*), a couple of them described the "cold-blooded murder" of two unarmed women walking in no-go zones. The army interrogated them and announced that they'd admitted seeing nothing with their own eyes, so it was all hearsay and rumors. Then 26 other soldiers who'd served in Operation Cast Lead gave testimony to Breaking the Silence, the anti-occupation soldiers' organization, and recounted the same sorts of incidents and atmosphere that the Rabin academy graduates had described.

I interviewed one of the 26, a young reserve combat medic and Orthodox Jewish father who was studying Jewish philosophy in college, and whose living room wall was lined with holy books. He said his unit spent a week in an abandoned rural village where about 50 houses had stood, and that by the time they left most of the houses were rubble. "I saw every kind of destruction I could think of. Houses were blown up by airplanes, helicopters, artillery, D-9 bulldozers, machine guns, mortars." He said the battalion commander explained to them they were leveling an abandoned village "to make sure the ground was flat so that after we left, Hamas would have no place to hide." The Orthodox Jewish medic also said an IDF rabbi told him and a few of his comrades that "this was a war between the children of light and the children of darkness," and that "we would not have to account for our sins." The last thing the rabbi told them, the medic recalled, was this: "Remember, guys, aim for the torso."

The IDF doesn't like Breaking the Silence. But I really thought that when faced with 100-odd pages of testimony from 26 soldiers who'd fought in Operation Cast Lead—testimony that only reinforced what the Rabin academy soldiers had said, not to mention human rights groups, foreign journalists, and Palestinian survivors— the army would at least say they were disturbed by these accounts, that they would look into them. That's the minimum any army genuinely concerned about "purity of arms" would do. I called the army spokesman's office and asked for their reaction to the Breaking the Silence report.

"How do you know it's true?" a deputy spokesman demanded, pointing up the army's supposed trump card against these whistle-blowers: The soldiers didn't identify themselves. Breaking the Silence was "hiding behind their anonymity," the deputy maintained. He also noted triumphantly that the accounts from the Rabin academy soldiers had been "proven" false. Breaking the Silence, he continued, had an "agenda." I asked him if the IDF considered these fighters' accounts of the war to have any meaning, any value at all. The deputy spokesman couldn't think of any and just recited the army's talking points again.

The IDF was acting in the worst of bad faith regarding Breaking the Silence. They knew very well why these soldiers didn't want to identify themselves publicly—most of them still served in the army, either as conscripts or reservists, and they didn't want to be ostracized in the ranks, nor did they want their extended families and everyone they knew to find out that they'd "ratted" on the army's conduct in war against the Palestinians, something that's already beyond taboo in this country. Since then, Breaking the Silence, seeking to flush the IDF out of its denial, has published reports in which soldiers do give their names and show their faces on camera. The IDF, forced to change tack, has dismissed the credibility of these reports, too, because Breaking the Silence refused to show them to the army prior to publication.

I used to think that this organization, founded in 2004 by a handful of IDF veterans who'd done occupation duty in Hebron (and which now has published testimonies from over 1,000 Israeli soldiers), would make a difference. I thought they wouldn't be so easy to dismiss as left-wing traitors. But that's exactly how Breaking the Silence has been branded by the Israeli political establishment and the right-wing chickenhawks of organized American Jewry—as another European-funded group of Israeli subversives out to tear this country down.

I had the same hopes for the Goldstone report on Operation Cast Lead, but the same thing that happened to Breaking the Silence happened to Richard Goldstone, only in a much, much more vicious way. The South African was not only one of the most respected jurists in the world, he was a lifelong Zionist, recipient of a Hebrew University honorary doctorate, and former chairman of a major Israeli charity. His daughter had lived here. It would be hard, I figured, for Israel to smear him as a liar and traitor. Yet after the release of the UN-appointed Goldstone Commission's report, a 575-page chronicle of Israel's war crimes—and those of Hamas—the judge came under an Israeli-Diaspora establishment attack of a ferocity that has never been visited on any other Jew I can think of. Alan Dershowitz called him "an evil, evil man"[12] and "an absolute traitor" to the Jewish people. Peres, the president, called him "a small man, devoid of any sense of justice."[13] He was cast in the media as a monster; it would not have been safe for him to be spotted on the streets of Jerusalem. In South Africa, the Jewish community's machers and rabbis threatened to protest outside the synagogue during the bar mitzvah of his grandson until he agreed to stay away. *Yediot Ahronot* ran an "exposé" about Goldstone's "dark past" as an apartheid-era judge[14]; the fact that he'd repeatedly stretched the law to its limits on behalf of non-whites, enough for Mandela to appoint him to the country's highest court, didn't impress "the newspaper of the nation," the nation that had supported and benefited from apartheid-era South Africa like no other. I've never seen such a character assassination of such a great man as Israel and Diaspora Jewish leaders carried out on Goldstone. It was like a lynching, only it went on for about a year.

---

12. "Dershowitz: Goldstone Is a Traitor to the Jewish People," *Haaretz*, www.haaretz.com, January 31, 2010.

13. Shuki Sadeh, "Peres: Goldstone Is a Small Man Out to Hurt Israel," *Haaretz*, www.haaretz.com, January 1, 2009.

14. Tehiya Barak, "Judge Goldstone's Dark Past," www.ynetnews.com, May 6, 2010.

The Goldstone report made major waves worldwide, but the Obama administration, protecting Israel as always, made sure it didn't go anywhere in the UN. Thus, Israel got away with Operation Cast Lead. Like many other liberals, I'd believed Obama might be serious enough and commanding enough to force Israel, now in the second age of Netanyahu, to end the occupation. And Obama did get off to a promising start by insisting on a settlement freeze, but it wasn't long before he wilted under Netanyahu and the Israel lobby's fury and dropped the demand, calling afterward only for "restraint" in settlement expansion. Obama blinked, and from then on the Netanyahu government treated him and his lieutenants, especially Secretary of State John Kerry, with undisguised contempt and did as they pleased with the Palestinians.

They did as they pleased with the Turks, too. In mid-2010 Israeli naval commandos boarded the Turkish ship Mavi Marmara, which was heading for Gaza with a cargo of humanitarian supplies, and killed 10 activists aboard after the first, unarmed commandos were beaten with clubs and rods. On the news, Israeli reporters, commentators, and interviewees were all repeating the official line: that Israel had acted in self-defense, that the guilty ones were the terrorists on the ship. No one questioned whether we had the right to blockade Gaza. No one stopped to take in the lopsided casualty toll. No, once again we were the persecuted, they were the persecutors. On the radio I heard a reporter interviewing one of a handful of leftists demonstrating against the raid, and afterward, to provide "context" for his listeners, the reporter said of the interviewee, "He failed to mention that he wouldn't be able to say such things in an Arab country."

I watched the Channel 2 news that afternoon with Israelis in a hospital waiting room, and it was like sitting with the home team fans at a game. "Some humanitarian act, some peace activists," said one fellow aloud. When one of the TV reporters said Jordan had condemned Israel for the raid, one of the guys in the hospital lobby responded for all to hear, "Jordan! They kill Palestinians by the dozens." The only criticism leveled at Israel's action by the Channel 2 news panel had to do with the narrow military aspect of the raid; otherwise, their focus was on how Israel should spin the violence and bloodshed to the world.

Spontaneous demonstrations in praise of the commandos broke out across Israel, including at the entrance to Modi'in. Everybody was on board, excuse the pun: government, media, and public, in a chain reaction of nationalist fury, a surefire cycle of brainwashing.

The situation was now pretty bleak. Israel had become ossified. There was no opposition at home and none abroad either; Obama had caved in, so had the rest of the "international community." Meanwhile, I was shifting further and further left. The more immovable Israeli tyranny became, the harder I was finding it to condemn the radical actions by its Palestinian victims. I was growing a little desperate. In my writing I kept moving closer to the edge. Soon, inevitably, I suppose, I went too far.

CHAPTER ELEVEN

TERROR

In my long, bumpy trek leftward on the Israeli-Arab political front, the two questions that have continually pushed me ahead are these: 1) Why should we have certain rights, but the Arabs not? 2) If we were in their place, what would we do?

I'd never condoned terrorism, neither that of the Palestinians nor of Menachem Begin's Irgun and Yitzhak Shamir's Lehi before independence. But in the weeks prior to Operation Cast Lead, when I realized that Israel had never freed Gaza and my thinking began to shift, I started to see what this blanket prohibition on Palestinian use of violence against Israeli targets meant: It meant Israel could keep the Palestinians down indefinitely, by force—absurdly superior force—and it was the Palestinians' moral duty to accept this peacefully. Otherwise they were terrorists, and terrorists were always evil. In Cast Lead, this meant that Israel's devastation of Gaza and 100-to-1 kill ratio was self-defense against terrorism, while the Palestinians' meager resistance was terrorist aggression. This did not sit well with me, but it's extremely hard to entertain the thought that the people trying to kill you, your family, and your countrymen are within their rights. (Not that I ever doubted I would stop Palestinian terrorists in the act if I could; blood is thicker than ideology.) It's even a harder thought to hold when your country is Israel and the people trying to kill you are Hamasniks and others who don't think Israel has a right to exist in the first place. But by this time, I couldn't really stop that thought—that the Palestinians had the right to fight back—from invading my mind. And little by little, it shook my view of terrorism.

Eight months after Cast Lead, I wrote a column titled "Our Exclusive Right to Self-Defense":

> How dare anyone deny us the right to self-defense! How dare anyone deny us the right to fight back against terrorism! . . . But I'd like to ask: Do the Palestinians also have the right to self-defense? We probably wouldn't admit it out loud, but in our heads we would say—again, in one voice—"No!" . . .
>
> Here is our idea of the "laws of war": When Israeli bulldozers rolled across the border into Gazan villages and flattened house after house so Hamas wouldn't have them for cover after the IDF pulled out, that was self-defense. But if a Palestinian boy who'd lived in one of those houses threw a stone at one of the bulldozers, that was terrorism.[1]

At the end of that year, 2009, I wrote a column, "A Taboo Question for Israelis," that attracted by far the most attention of anything I'd ever written at the *Jerusalem Post*:

> The question we have to ask ourselves is this: If anybody treated us like we're treating the people in Gaza, what would we do?

I used to get a lot of letters to the editor and a great many more online comments to my *Post* columns—about 95 percent of them

---

1. Larry Derfner, "Our Exclusive Right to Self-Defense," *Jerusalem Post*, October 8, 2009.

anti, most of them hostile, on rare occasions threatening. My colleagues at the *Post* were for the most part right wing, my family and friends were largely center-left—with a few rightists in the mix—so as an Israeli-American Jew who could no longer even blame the Palestinians for terrorism, I was pretty much in a minority of one in my circles. Also, I'd always been a very dutiful polemicist, reading the American and Israeli right-wing pundits, testing my ideas against theirs. So between that and hearing from the readers of my columns and from a lot of people I knew, and also from following the Israeli media and imbibing the general atmosphere, I decided I'd given the right wing a long, rigorously fair hearing, and it was time to test my ideas against those of the people to my left.

The first, obvious thing to do was join Facebook. My other idea was to start a blog that would be a running debate between me, a liberal Zionist who opposes the occupation but wants Israel to remain a Jewish state, and an anti-Zionist who opposes both the occupation and Jewish statehood. I got Richard Silverstein, who writes the Tikun Olam blog out of his home in Seattle, and we called our effort "Israel Reconsidered." It didn't work out, though, mainly for political reasons, so I kept it going by myself and debated with the commenters.

One morning, in my capacity as Israel Reconsidered's chief correspondent, I went to Ben-Gurion Airport to see what would come of the organized "fly-in" by activists from various countries, who planned to ride from the airport to the West Bank for solidarity visits with the Palestinians. The government was treating the protest as another threat to Israel's existence, and the security people pledged to send them right back home from Ben-Gurion. A few minutes after I got to the arrivals hall, a couple of Israelis planted themselves in front of the hive of reporters and cameramen, held up their little signs, and started chanting "Israel apartheid!" and "Free Palestine!" The cops tore the signs from their hands and started pushing them toward the exit. After a minute of watching in shocked silence, people in the terminal started to boo. Men were cursing loudly—"sons of bitches," "garbage," and things in Arabic (presumably spoken by Mizrahi Jews) that I didn't understand.

A couple dozen people, mainly men but also a few women, followed very close behind the tightly bunched demonstrators, cops, and journalists to the police van. "Throw them in the garbage," shouted one woman. An old man tried to get at one of the activists, but the police stopped him.

I was there ostensibly as a journalist, and I was scribbling notes, but I felt cowardly not saying anything to these fascists, so I started asking them rhetorically in Hebrew, "What are these people doing?" The woman who wanted them thrown in the garbage said, "They're hurting us!" I told her, "They're talking," and the little mob turned on me. A couple of the men raised their fists. The woman told me, "Go back home. Get out of here." I told her, "I live here." The cops mistook me for a demonstrator, put me in the police van with one of the protesters—a Tel Aviv teenager I'd interviewed for the *Post* after he'd gotten shot in the eye with a rubber-coated bullet by a border policeman at a West Bank protest—but when I showed them my press card, they let me go.

Thank God the cops arrested those demonstrators and protected them on the way to the vans. Otherwise that mini-mob would have beaten the shit out of them. Watching my enraged countrymen at the airport, I imagined the daily headlines about Israel versus the world having been distilled into a kind of political methedrine and mainlined into their veins.

The next month I went with my family on a week-long vacation to Stockholm. During that time there was a terror attack near Eilat in which eight Israelis were killed, six of them civilians. The Israeli reports said the killers were Palestinians from Gaza. When you're overseas and a major act of terrorism like this occurs, it affects you. You read everything you can about it, and if you have close friends or family in the area of the attack you'll probably call. That, at least, is how Philippa and I react. However, when you're overseas, you're not exposed to the heavy, thick, solemn gloom that comes through the Israeli media nonstop on the day of a big attack, subduing the country's mood. I'd missed that in Sweden, and when I returned to Israel a couple of days after the killings, it had dissipated. Had

I been in Israel during the terror attack, I might not have dared to write what I was about to write. But I'd been overseas, and when we returned home I wanted to get back to my blog right away, and with a strong post. For a while I'd thought about publicly "updating" my views of terrorism, because not only did I now reject the holy of holies of Israeli dogma—that Palestinian terrorism is simple murder, lacking any shred of justification—I also recognized that this credo was the linchpin to the argument for the occupation. But I'd always hesitated to write that update because I was afraid I wouldn't be able to lay out all my caveats and all the complexities of the issue in the space of a newspaper column or blog post. This time, though, with the Eilat attack making the issue so timely, I put aside my hesitations. On Sunday, August 21, 2011, the day after we returned from our Stockholm vacation, I sat down and wrote a post on Israel Reconsidered titled "The Awful, Necessary Truth about Palestinian Terror."[2] I would very soon come to regret the timing and some of the phrasing of the post, but this is what I wrote at the time:

> I think a lot of people who realize that the occupation is wrong also realize that the Palestinians have the right to resist it—to use violence against Israelis, even to kill Israelis, especially when Israel is showing zero willingness to end the occupation, which has been the case since the Netanyahu government took over (among other times in the past).
>
> But people don't want to say this, especially right after a terror attack like this last one that killed eight Israelis near Eilat. And there are lots of good reasons for this reticence, such as: You don't want to further upset your own countrymen when they are grieving, you don't want to say or write anything that could be picked up by Israel's enemies and used as justification

2. Philip Weiss, "Read the Post for Which Derfner Was Fired: 'The Awful, Necessary Truth About Palestinian Terror'," August 29, 2011, *Mondoweiss*, www.mondoweiss.net, August 29, 2011.

for killing more of us. (These are good reasons; fear of being called a traitor, for instance, is a bad reason.)

But I think it's time to overcome this reticence, even at the cost of enflaming the already enflamed sensitivities of the Israeli public, because this unwillingness to say outright that Palestinians have the right to fight the occupation, especially now, inadvertently helps keep the occupation going.

When we say that the occupation is a terrible injustice to the Palestinians, but then say that Palestinian terror/resistance is a terrible injustice to Israel, we're saying something that's patently illogical to anyone but a pacifist, and there aren't many pacifists left, certainly not in Israel. The logical, non-pacifist mind concludes that both of those statements can't be true—that if A is hurting B and won't stop, then B damn sure has the right to hurt A to try to make him stop. But if everybody, not only the Right but the Left, too, is saying that B, the Palestinians, don't have the right to hurt A, the Israelis, then the logical mind concludes that Israel must not be hurting the Palestinians after all, the occupation must not be so bad, the occupation must not be hurting the Palestinians at all—because if it was, they would have the right to hurt us back, and everybody agrees that they don't. So when they shoot at us or fire rockets at us, it's completely unprovoked, which gives us the right, the duty, to bash them and bash them until they stop—and anybody who tries to deny us that right doesn't have a leg to stand on, so we're just going to keep right on bashing them. And when the Palestinians complain about the occupation, we Israelis can honestly say we don't know what they're talking about.

This, I'm convinced, is how the Left's ritual condemnations of terror are translated in the Israeli public's mind—as justification for the occupation and an iron-fist military policy.

But if, on the other hand, we were to say very forthrightly what many of us believe and the rest of us suspect—that the Palestinians, like every nation living under hostile rule, have the right to fight back, that their terrorism, especially in the face of a rejectionist Israeli government, is justified—what effect would that have? A powerful one, I think, because the truth is powerful. If those who oppose the occupation acknowledged publicly that it justifies Palestinian terrorism, then those who support the occupation would have to explain why it doesn't. And that's not easy for a nation that sanctifies the right to self-defense; a nation that elected Irgun leader Menachem Begin and Lehi leader Yitzhak Shamir as prime minister.

But while I think the Palestinians have the right to use terrorism against us, I don't want them to use it, I don't want to see Israelis killed, and as an Israeli, I would do whatever was necessary to stop a Palestinian, oppressed or not, from killing one of my countrymen. (I also think Palestinian terrorism backfires, it turns people away from them and generates sympathy for Israel and the occupation, so I'm against terrorism on a practical level, too, but that's beside the point.) The possibility that Israel's enemies could use my or anybody else's justification of terror for their campaign is a daunting one; I wouldn't like to see this column quoted on a pro-Hamas website, and I realize it could happen.

Still, I don't think Hamas and their allies need any more encouragement, so whatever encouragement they might take from me or any other liberal Zionist is coals to Newcastle. What's needed very badly, however, is for Israelis to realize that the occupation is hurting the Palestinians terribly, that it's driving them to try to kill us, that we are compelling them to engage in terrorism, that the blood of Israeli victims is ultimately on our hands, and that it's up to us to stop provoking our own people's murder by ending the occupation. And so long as we who oppose the occupation keep pretending that the Palestinians don't have the right to resist it, we tacitly encourage Israelis to go on blindly killing and dying in defense of an unholy cause.

And by tacitly encouraging Israelis in their blindness, I think we endanger their lives and ours, their country and ours, much more than if we told the truth and got quoted on Hamas websites.

There's no time for equivocation anymore, if there ever was. The mental and moral paralysis in this country must be broken. Whoever the Palestinians were who killed the eight Israelis near Eilat last week, however vile their ideology was, they were justified to attack. They had the same right to fight for their freedom as any other unfree nation in history ever had. And just like every harsh, unjust government in history bears the blame for the deaths of its own people at the hands of rebels, so Israel, which rules the Palestinians harshly and unjustly, is to blame for those eight Israeli deaths—as well as for every other Israeli death that occurred when this country was offering the Palestinians no other way to freedom.

Writing this is not treason. It is an attempt at patriotism.

My post got mixed reviews from liberal commenters on my blog and on Facebook. The negative ones were quite negative. "Simply disgusting. I've always admired your work—but you crossed the line. Revolting," read one. A right-winger, but a moderate one and a very warm-hearted guy, wrote, *"Refuah shlema"*—"Get well." I defended myself online against all my critics, but after a couple of days, doubts started entering the back of my mind. I had an uncomfortable image of visiting my family in Kfar Hasidim, who tell me they heard I was in favor of Palestinians killing Israelis, and I tell them, "I didn't say I was in favor of it, I said it was justified." Pretty weak.

A couple of days after I put the post on my blog and Facebook, an American immigrant reporter for right-wing US Jewish publications saw it and published a news story about how I, a *Jerusalem Post* columnist and feature writer, had justified terror. I wouldn't find out until later, but that news story was picked up immediately by an American immigrant professor who propagandizes American Jewish philanthropists to cut off their contributions to "left-wing" Israeli universities. On his blog, this guy initiated an email campaign to get me fired from the *Post,* along with one to get me indicted for racism and incitement to murder.[3] His effort was joined by other right-wing Jewish websites, as well as by a group called "The Legal Fund for the Land of Israel."

Over the coming days, the *Post* got hundreds of emails from readers threatening to cancel their subscriptions if I wasn't canned. In the past, the editors had gotten plenty of emails, letters, and phone calls to that effect, and they'd always backed me up. But there had never been an avalanche like this, and for the first time I was worried about my job. Another novel part of the backlash, for me, was that hostile reactions from readers had never bothered me before because they'd never convinced me I was wrong—but this time I was beginning to wonder.

An antagonistic right-wing critic wrote that my blog post had been "obscene," and as personally and politically malevolent as his critique was, the word "obscene" helped clarify the problem for me: In my insistence on not pulling punches—on not shying away from the full implications of what I was saying—I had written very directly and plainly not just about the Palestinians' right to use terror against the occupation, but specifically to kill those eight Israelis whose deaths a few days before were still fresh in people's minds. I'd intended to shock people into awareness of what we were doing to the Palestinians, but maybe I had indeed only revolted them.

I decided to ask a couple of people who were very close to me, whose political opinions I respected a lot, to read the blog post and tell me what they thought. The first one said, without rancor, that it sounded like I was saying it was okay for Palestinians to kill his children. The second one said, "I don't know—to say that they have the right to kill Israelis, a sentence like that, it's too much." "You think it's obscene?" I asked. "Yeah," she said.

---

3. "A Call to Arms—Please Help Put Larry Derfner in Prison!" Zionist Conspiracy, www.zioncon.blogspot.co.il, August 24, 2011.

That was Thursday night, five days after I wrote the blog post. I called the first person whose reaction I'd sought, a very good friend of mine, to tell him that I now thought I'd done something wrong, something bad, and I just broke. I'd ripped at the wound Israelis carry for their dead. I'd meant to jar their thinking, but instead I'd hurt them where they don't deserve to be hurt. I'd betrayed them. On the phone, I sobbed like a baby. And I decided that the next morning I would apologize publicly.

In a blog post titled "Apology,"[4] I wrote about the insufficient distance between justifying terror and supporting it, about meaning to shock people awake but revolting them with an unwittingly obscene image. I also took back my justification of Palestinian terrorism. I still believe I was right to apologize for the revulsion and obscenity, and I've tried since then to be more careful about the images I evoke in my writing—especially in times of Israeli tragedy. However, I had my doubts from the beginning about retracting the claim that the occupation gives Palestinians the "right" and "justification" to use terror. I'd thought those words were at the heart of the problem, and if those were the wrong terms, I felt compelled that Friday morning at the computer, writing my apology, to come up with the right ones.

I wrote, "What I mean is this: The occupation does not justify Palestinian terror. It does, however, provoke it. Palestinians do not have the right to attack or kill Israelis. They do, however, have the incentive to, and part, though not all, of that incentive is provided them by the occupation."

Later I realized that those, too, were the wrong words.

After the apology, I felt a weight lifted from me. Many of the right-wingers I knew or corresponded with online forgave me; several of those I worked with at the *Post*, though not all, didn't. The Friday–Saturday weekend in Israel was beginning, and for me it was a good one. I sent my apology to the *Post* to be printed on Sunday, but because of what was explained to me as a logistical mix-up—and later presented publicly as a principled refusal—it wasn't. What did

---

4. "Read the Post," op. cit.

get published that Sunday was a column by one of the *Post*'s right-wing regulars, who devoted his space to an attack on me and my blog post, saying I was one of a long line of Jewish traitors and that I might be liable for prosecution for incitement to murder. It infuriated me, of course, and I wanted the right of reply. I called the editor, Steve Linde, and we agreed I would come in to talk the following day about where things stood in general.

When I came into his office, he told me that the *Jerusalem Post*'s owner, Eli Azur, had ordered him to fire me. I wasn't surprised. This problem wasn't going away; the subscribers' threats of cancellation had not stopped. Plenty of right-wingers had wanted to get me fired for years, and this time I'd given them the opening. The *Jerusalem Post* was basically a right-wing newspaper that appealed mainly to right-wing readers. With that blog post and the fury it was stirring up, I had become poison to the owner's business. In Linde's office I had to sign some papers, in which I did not contest my firing, but did contest the paper's stated reason: that I had expressed support for Palestinian terrorist groups. I was told I would not get a chance to reply in the *Post* to that right-winger's defamatory column. I understood that this was all the doing of the business side of the paper, and I left the meeting on good terms with the editor.

Getting fired from a job in the narrow field of English-language journalism in Israel when you're a month shy of your 60th birthday, and going through it in the accusatory glare of the English-speaking Jewish world, and, the worst part, knowing that this time your infamy is to some extent deserved, is bound to take a certain psychological toll on a person. I went home, called Philippa at work and gave her the wonderful news, put it on Facebook and my blog, sat down in the living room, and soon began to fear I was having a heart attack. I realized it was probably anxiety, but who knew, so I took myself to the clinic and they hooked me up to an EKG, which showed normal. Philippa came to the clinic from work; she was flying that evening to Toronto for a family wedding, and we decided I would buck up and she would give me moral support over the phone and be back in a week. Late that night I got an email from an editor

I'd once written a few stories for, and whose son, an Israeli soldier, had been killed many years before in a guerrilla attack, and she as much as accused me of justifying his killing. By that point I was in a fairly searing depression.

My firing was written up at length in the *New York Times'* online news blog,[5] Agence France-Presse,[6] and throughout the Jewish media (though not, I was happy to see, in the mainstream Hebrew press: I did not want my Israeli relatives and neighbors to know about this, and definitely not the way the Hebrew press would have played it). My favorite headline in all the coverage ran above an opinion piece by Gal Beckerman in the *Forward*:[7] "Is Derfner the Problem, or Are the Israeli People?" The *Forward* and Britain's *Jewish Chronicle* asked me to write my side of the story for them, and I did, very eagerly. I was spending all day, every day online defending myself, explaining myself. I felt I was at war, fighting for my reputation, and, really, fighting for my honor as a Jew and an Israeli. My fear was that this blog post was going to fatally discredit the most important part of my journalistic and political work—the 20 years I'd spent criticizing Israel in print—because it had now been "proven" that I'd never been a loyal oppositionist among Jews or Israelis; I'd been an internal enemy. Meanwhile, part of my online activity in those days was in defending my apology to the leftists who were saying it had been unnecessary or even a cave-in. There had been no pressure on me from the *Post* to apologize, otherwise they would have had a hard time firing me after I did. As for caving in, I pointed out that this wasn't exactly the first time I'd been hammered and cursed by loads of right-wing readers calling for my head, and if that hadn't gotten me to apologize before, why would it now?

---

5. Robert Mackey, "Israeli Columnist Is Fired for Writing that Palestinian Terror Is 'Justified,'" *New York Times,* The Lede, www.thelede.blogs.nytimes.com, August 30, 2011.

6. "Jerusalem Post Fires Writer over Right to Terror,'" AFP, Ma'an News Agency, www.maannews.com, August 30, 2011.

7. Gal Beckerman, "Is Derfner the Problem, or Are the Israeli People?" *Forward,* www.forward.com, September 6, 2011.

I was swamped by this affair—totally engulfed by it, to the point that mentally I'd gone slightly off-center. I had the sense that my mind was somewhat out of sync with my surroundings. People tried to make me laugh, but it was no use. You need a sense of perspective to have a sense of humor, and I had no perspective. I was at war and nothing else was going on in the world. However, as the days passed, I began to get better. I was receiving tremendous support from Philippa, my sister Suzie and brother Armand, and my friends and family abroad—including the right-wingers—and from several people I'd worked with at the *Post* and elsewhere. I was also getting a lot of support from Facebook friends and blog commenters, and in the media. Among those writing against my firing were two fellow columnists in the *Post*, Jeff Barak and David Newman. The *Post*'s print edition ran a half-page of letters to the editor on my dismissal, which ran eight-to-seven against it. Also, *+972 Magazine*, a spirited, intelligent left-wing Israeli-Palestinian group blog based in Tel Aviv, with an incomparably larger readership and impact than Israel Reconsidered, asked me to join them, and I immediately, gratefully accepted. At home, meanwhile, with Philippa gone, I was also trying to play single father to Alon and Gilad, and not doing the greatest job. After a few days, I asked Alon if he could see I was getting better, that I was pulling out of my depression. "You seem worse," he said, which I thought was pretty funny, which, in turn, I took as a good sign.

I was still on reasonably good terms with the *Post*. I resented the management's official reason for my firing, and I didn't like them denying me the right to reply to that right-winger's column—but they had printed two columns in my defense and had definitely given me fair treatment on the letters page. What's more, I didn't hold it against the owner for firing me. Journalistically, of course, it was wrong. But Eli Azur, as far as I could gather, wasn't too interested in journalism: He was much more interested in making money, and most of his customers were right-wing, and if I'd stayed on I would have driven a whole lot of them away, I would have damaged his business's standing in the community it served, and I didn't expect him to lose money on my account, to pay a substantial price for defending my right to express opinions he no doubt hated. If he'd been a more conscientious publisher and the *Post* had not been so strongly identified with the right, I would have expected to keep my job. But it was what it was, and under those circumstances I was not, on balance, angry at the paper. I watched the news story on my firing, broadcast on Israel's English-language TV news program, in the office of one of the *Post*'s editors. We agreed that the report had been very fair.

I was coming out of the tunnel. Then, on Friday, when Israeli newspapers publish their big, end-of-the-week edition, I opened up the *Post* and saw Linde's column. It was titled "Caging the Tiger," in reference to my column "Rattling the Cage." It even carried a photo of a forlorn-looking tiger lying in his cage. He wrote that my blog post had served to "endorse and encourage, if not incite and inflame, terrorism against Israel," dismissing my apology for its "obscene sentiments," and concurring fully with the *Post*'s decision to fire me. He wrote: "The move, I stress, had nothing to do with threats to cancel subscriptions or advertisements; it was an editorial decision taken on moral grounds."[8]

I'll just say this: My blog post was published August 21, and I was fired August 29. If the intervening threats to cancel subscriptions and advertisements (the latter I hadn't even known about) had nothing to do with my firing, why did it take the *Post* eight days to decide that I'd written something that violated their sense of morality?

That Friday column came as a complete shock, and it threw me for a loop, sending me back into a depression. Then that night, Alon, Gilad, and I went over to the house of one of my best friends, somebody who doesn't give a rat's ass about politics. My friend, however, has strong principles, and he didn't think I should have apologized for stating my opinion on my own blog. His wife and I had to convince him that in this case I'd done the right thing by apologizing. After that, we began to talk as usual, about any old thing—people we knew, movies we'd seen, routine stuff. I got into the conversation—and it was such a soothing relief, such a deep and

---

8. Steve Linde, "Caging the Tiger," *Jerusalem Post*, September 2, 2011.

thorough pleasure, to get my mind off myself and my troubles after a solid, harrowing week of focusing on nothing but them. From that night on, I was fine.

But I was still an infamous character among Israel's right-wing "Anglo" crowd. So when I got a call from *+972* writer Dimi Reider to meet him in Jerusalem to talk about writing for the group blog, I was worried. I had been basically locked up in my apartment since I'd gotten fired, and Jerusalem is filled with crazy settler types from America, many of whom had to know about the "scandal" surrounding me and might recognize my face from the photo that had run with my column and that was seen occasionally on right-wing Jewish websites, or from the video clip of me that had just been broadcast on the English-language TV news. I didn't want to be recognized on a crowded street or in a café by one or more of these yahoos; I imagined them cursing me and me cursing back and a fight breaking out, with me being badly outnumbered. But I told myself this was paranoia, and Dimi suggested a café in Rehavia, the most liberal Jewish neighborhood in the capital, so I drove in to meet him. We sat down in the café, and before we could even order, a guy came over from another table and asked me in American-accented English, "Excuse me, are you Larry Derfner?" I looked him in the eye and said, "Yeah." And he put out his hand and said, "I just want to tell you I really respect you, and I've been reading your work for a long time."

And I was thinking: *Thank you, Jesus.*

Like I said, I realize that I shouldn't have tried to convey my potentially incendiary view of terrorism in the narrow confines of an op-ed or blog post—but right here in this book might be a good place. By now I think I've made it clear enough why I believe Palestinians under occupation have the right to attack at least Israeli military targets. But I also believe they have the right to target civilians—within limits. Nobody, for any reason, has the right to deliberately kill children, who are by definition utterly innocent, even of collective responsibility, which adults are not. Furthermore, there should be no attacks on defenseless people in a house of prayer; such a thing can only be understood as religiously inspired killing, holy war. And obviously there is the question of proportion, of limits to the magnitude of terror: Palestinians don't have the right, after all, to poison the Sea of Galilee.

But if we say that Palestinians, or any people being subjugated by a much stronger power, are only entitled to attack military targets, then we are telling them they must play into their oppressor's strength. They must fight with one hand tied behind their back against the side that is sitting on top of them, that enjoys huge military superiority, and that kills many more civilians as "collateral damage" (and as ill-defined "legitimate" targets) than Palestinian terrorists manage to do deliberately. This is the Israeli line on terrorism. It's also the American line, and the line of every powerful country that ever occupied or colonized or otherwise oppressed a weaker nation. Forgive me for suspecting that it is spoken not out of principle or morality, but out of self-interest. Would Israelis prefer that the Palestinians fought like the IDF, with state-of-the-art precision weaponry, so that instead of attacking Israeli civilians on the street with knives, guns, pipe bombs, or suicide vests—or with rockets having the crudest aim and that hit nothing 99 percent of the time—the Palestinians attacked military targets and "symbols of Israeli power" only? Would Israelis have a higher opinion of Palestinians if they, God forbid, sent F-16s to destroy the Defense Ministry compound in the middle of one of the most densely populated residential areas of Tel Aviv, so that the masses of Israeli civilian casualties were collateral damage and not the deliberate targeting of civilians—in other words, not terrorism? I don't think they would. (In such a horrible case, I don't think Israeli leaders would accept blame for placing their military headquarters "behind human shields" in the middle of Tel Aviv, either.)

But I'm not saying there's no difference at all between targeting civilians and soldiers. If the Palestinians had the kind of weaponry Israel has, you could put the same prohibition on them aiming at civilians that's put on Israel (or America, or any other country with advanced weaponry). But the Palestinians don't have anything close to that kind of weaponry, and they are the ones fighting in self-defense, so the same prohibitions that are applied to Israel cannot be applied to them.

Besides, Palestinians *do* target Israeli soldiers, no less than they do civilians, a fact Israeli spokesmen deliberately overlook. What's more, in the world of terrorism (or guerrilla warfare, or asymmetrical warfare, or whatever you want to call it), fighters naturally get more "points" for killing a soldier than a civilian, and the higher the soldier's rank, the more points they get. In fact, countries at war with guerrillas play by the same rules: Israel retaliates much more harshly for the killing of a high military officer than it does for the killing of a private, not to mention that of a schoolteacher or bus driver. And while Israel may say for propaganda purposes that it sees terrorists, those who deliberately kill civilians, as the worst kind of fiends, in truth Israel and Israelis make no distinction between those who kill their soldiers and those who kill their civilians. In the language of the government, media, and Israelis at large, they're all "terrorists." The sorrow and rage over the killing of a soldier is no less and no different than the sorrow and rage when a civilian is the victim. There are very, very few Israelis who, after denouncing Palestinian killings of civilians, will turn around and say it's legitimate for them to target Israeli soldiers, or that it's a lesser crime. Finally, in the eyes of Israeli law, there is no distinction whatsoever between the deliberate slaying of an Israeli soldier and that of a civilian: They're both acts of murder and both carry a life sentence.

Yet this hypocritical attitude toward intentional attacks against civilians is taken not just by the cynical colonial powers, but also by Amnesty International, Human Rights Watch, Judge Goldstone, the whole global human rights community. Like Goldstone once said, the distinction between targeting soldiers and civilians has become almost a "religious" principle for them. And that's exactly the problem: It's a dogma; it doesn't differentiate between the weak and strong, or, even worse, between the side that's right and the one that's wrong. Human rights investigators not only refuse to apply different rules to the forces fighting in aggression and those fighting in self-defense, they even refuse to try to determine which side is which. To choose sides would take away the investigation's "objectivity." And they'll only fault an attack on a military target if it's accompanied by civilian casualties. Otherwise, in the eyes of Amnesty International et al., such attacks are legitimate; they do not violate human rights.

I agree that an army marching through an enemy countryside should not slaughter villagers along the way, and that fighter bombers flying through enemy skies should not pick out residential neighborhoods for targets. I'm not saying there's no problem ever with killing civilians. But the prohibition on targeting civilians, which grows out of a healthy moral impulse, has been hardened, even by well-meaning people, to the point that it inherently favors the strong over the weak and the aggressors over the defenders. Further, it serves to cheapen the lives of soldiers: In the eyes of both the human rights community and the community of "enlightened" oppressor nations, intentionally killing 1,000 soldiers or guerrillas in a bad cause is morally superior to intentionally killing one civilian in a good cause. I'm sorry, that's wrong. Soldiers are humans, too.

And they tend to be very young humans. In 1944, when the Axis and Allies were bombing each other's cities, George Orwell wrote in the *Tribune* that it was hypocritical to cheer for victories over enemy armies but deplore attacks on enemy civilians, when the former were no less a human tragedy than the latter, and often more of one:

["N]ormal" or "legitimate" warfare picks out and slaughters all the healthiest and bravest of the young male population. Every time a German submarine goes to the bottom about fifty young men of fine physique and good nerves are suffocated. Yet people who would hold up their hands at the very words "civilian bombing" will repeat with satisfaction such phrases as "We are winning the Battle of the Atlantic." Heaven knows how many people our blitz on Germany and the occupied countries has killed and will kill, but you can be quite certain it will never come anywhere near the slaughter that has happened on the Russian front.

War is not avoidable at this stage of history, and since it has to happen it does not seem to me a bad thing that others should be killed besides young men.[9]

The hypocrisy over "legitimate" targets is compounded when you remember that in Israel—and not just Israel—people are bred literally from kindergarten to become soldiers. They may be drafted when they're 18—as adults, supposedly—but in a sense, they were conscripted as children. Is it right to say they're fair game in war, but old men who've lived out their lives aren't? And is every soldier a part of his side's war machine in a way that no civilian is; can it be fair to target an army installation in which the victims will likely include cooks, clerks, and drivers, but not the building of a high-tech company whose product line includes arms components? And are attacks on civilians really so "wanton" and "senseless"—do they never advance a political goal, sometimes a legitimate one, the same as an act of war by the army of a state?

Society purports to place terrorism beyond the pale, but it doesn't. If Americans really loathed the deliberate killing of civilians so completely, they would have erased Harry Truman's name after Hiroshima and Nagasaki. The British would have done the same to Churchill after Dresden. What's more, people would consider the 9/11 attack on the World Trade Center terrorism, but not the 9/11 attack on the Pentagon. But of course Americans love Truman, everyone loves Churchill, and nobody sees any difference between crashing planes into the World Trade Center and slamming one into the Pentagon.

And if we're talking about Israeli condemnation of terrorism, it's just absurd. The single greatest terror attack in the history of

---

9. George Orwell, *As I Please: 1943–45 (The Collected Essays, Journalism and Letters of George Orwell)*, vol. 3 (New York: Harcourt, 1978; London: Penguin Books, 1984), 180.

the Israeli-Palestinian conflict—the 1946 bombing of Jerusalem's King David Hotel, which housed British colonial headquarters in Palestine, an explosion that killed 91 people, the great majority of them civilians—was ordered by Menachem Begin. At the 60th anniversary conference on the bombing, organized by veterans of Begin's Irgun militia, the headliner was then-opposition leader Benjamin Netanyahu.[10] He defended the slaughter because the bombers, after all, had called in a warning (issued over the phone by a 17-year-old girl) to the hotel switchboard (25 minutes before the explosives went off in the middle of a weekday). Yitzhak Shamir, another future Israeli prime minister, engineered the 1948 assassination of the UN envoy to the Middle East, Count Folke Bernadotte, who'd saved thousands of lives during the Holocaust. Begin, Shamir, and their underground organizations killed scores of British soldiers and policemen, as well as hundreds of Arab civilians in bombings of hotels, buses, and open markets. Israel names streets and schools after these "patriots"; it's the last country, or certainly one of the last, with the right to complain about terrorism committed by people living under its military rule.

I have come to judge terrorism the same way I judge conventional war: The most important issue is whether it is waged for a just cause or not. Today I no longer condemn Begin and Shamir for those bombings; the Jews of Palestine were under foreign rule, they were entitled to independence, and they were no more terroristic toward the Arabs than the Arabs were to the Jews. And while I don't know enough about Hiroshima and Nagasaki to say if there was a less lethal way at hand to end the war and prevent the deaths of many more Allied soldiers, if there was no such apparent alternative, and seeing as how Japan forced the war on the United States at Pearl Harbor, I don't condemn Truman for his decision.

I do, however, most definitely condemn Al-Qaeda for 9/11; America was not ruling any Muslim country against its will or fighting

---

10. Tom Segev, "The Spirit of the King David Hotel," *Haaretz*, www.haaretz .com, July 23, 2006.

an unjust war against any of them. But Palestinian terrorism against the Israeli occupation is no less justified than Zionist terrorism was against British rule. And as I wrote in my notorious blog post, in saying this I'm much less concerned about inciting Palestinians to terror—after all, they don't take their cues from me—and much more concerned about shaking Israelis awake so they will end this occupation, which is the proximate cause of Palestinian terror.

At the end of my piece for the *Forward* about my blog post, I wrote, "I don't think my opinions have changed, but I have to find new ways to articulate them. . . ." I'd thought the problem in the phrase "justified in killing Israelis" was the word "justified" because it was a laudative: It implied that I was lauding the killing of Israelis, when that was the last thing I wanted to do. Yet if "justified" was the wrong word, what was the right one? I couldn't come up with it.

Later on, I understood that the problem was not the word "justified," but rather joining it to the words "killing Israelis." It's too vivid; it's obscene. At some point I also put into words something I knew at the time I wrote that blog post, but hadn't been aware I knew, and that I wish now I had been: that the Israeli victims of terror attacks do not deserve to be killed. The adults among them—like all Israeli adults—bear collective responsibility for the tyranny to which this country subjects the Palestinians. But no Israeli bystander or minor cog in that tyranny bears such responsibility that he or she deserves to be killed for it. The first time I expressed this in pretty much the way I wanted was at the end of a post I wrote for *+972* in November 2012, in the midst of Israel's second "mini-war" of aggression in Gaza, Operation Pillar of Defense. I went to Kiryat Malachi, where a rocket had hit a residential building, leaving a giant hole in place of what had been the balcony and living room of a fifth-floor apartment. A giant, squarish hole surrounded by raw concrete blasted into a mess of jagged angles. Three Israeli adults inside were killed. I quoted from *Haaretz* some personal details about them, then wrote:

I don't want those Gazan rockets to hurt anybody. But I'm not "rooting" for Israel in this war, either, because I don't want to go on hurting the Palestinians. The three people who got killed in that building in Kiryat Malachi were innocent—but the State of Israel is not. Finally, it's the hurt that the State of Israel inflicts on the Palestinians which provided most of the fuel for that monstrous rocket.[11]

Today, instead of calling the victims "innocent," I might say that they, like any other Israelis at random, certainly did not deserve to be killed. Other than that, I wouldn't change or apologize for a word of it.

---

11. Larry Derfner, "Tragedy, Farce and Denial in Kiryat Malachi," November 16, 2012, www.972mag.com.

CHAPTER TWELVE

BIBI'S ISRAEL AND BDS

I f there's one image from Israeli life that illustrates the national mentality in this decade, it's the sight of cars backed up in front of you on the highway, and as far and wide as you search, you probably won't find a single political bumper sticker. No slogans, no parties, no movements. You see quite a few true-believing Orthodox Jewish stickers—"We have no one to depend on except the Blessed Holy One" is a favorite—but aside from them, virtually the only stickers on Israeli bumpers in the 2010s are commercial advertisements, with "How am I driving?" easily being number one.

This marks a radical change from decades past, when it seemed every newly arrived foreign correspondent from a major newspaper wrote about the vehement political debate going on between Israeli cars on the road, which was seen as a perfect illustration of the passion Israelis brought to political life. In 2004, novelist David

Grossman wrote the lyrics of a famous song—"The Sticker Song," which strung together 54 Israeli bumper-sticker slogans, most of them political—"A whole generation demands peace," "Let the IDF win," "The nation is with the Golan," "Yes to peace, no to violence," "Shalom, *haver*," "It's all because of you, *haver*," "Hebron, always and forever," and so on. That was in 2004. Except for the few old leftover stickers that haven't been peeled off, they're all gone and no new ones have taken their place.

I can't think of the last political sticker that caught on with Israelis, not on the right or the left. I always used to have a left-wing sticker on my car; it was a matter of principle. But that was in decades past. The last one I can remember putting on my car was "When it's all shit, evacuate" for disengagement in 2005. Which one would I put on today? Peace Now? Is Peace Now doing something; are there any demonstrations? (This is another conspicuous absence that tells so much about contemporary Israel.) Should I put up another Meretz sticker? Meretz still says all the right things; it's still a brave, honorable party, but it has no impact anymore. Yet there's another reason why leftists like me haven't put political stickers on our cars in recent years: We're afraid. Afraid they'll just be torn off, one after another, which is kind of humiliating, as I described earlier—but also that our cars could get vandalized if we parked in the wrong place, such as Jerusalem (never mind a West Bank settlement). In the late 1990s, I was stopped at a light in Jerusalem with a Peace Now sticker on my rear bumper, and the car sitting in back bumped me—not hard enough to cause a dent, but enough to show the driver's mind was somewhere else. I turned around and glared at him, then turned back around. A few seconds later, he bumped me again. I looked in the rear-view mirror and saw a young man in the driver's seat staring at me grimly. The light turned green and I drove off. The only explanation I have is my Peace Now sticker that was staring at him.

Nowadays, I think displaying left-wing sentiments would be more dangerous than in decades past. Right-wing marauders in Jerusalem and other cities used to be accustomed to the sight of peacenik bumper stickers—they were all over the place—but the new generation grew up without them, and if they suddenly started seeing cars sporting left-wing or antiwar stickers, or, God forbid, ones for the despised New Israel Fund, B'Tselem, or Breaking the Silence, I think they'd go wild.

And just as the left's hopelessness and timidity explain the absence of left-wing bumper stickers, the right's awareness of the left's lack of spirit explains the absence of right-wing bumper stickers: They don't need them anymore. They've won. They don't need to get in the left's face any longer—the left has backed down. Is the "national camp" in danger of being overthrown by the "peace camp"? Is there any threat to the settlements? Is there a Palestinian state looming on the horizon? In this second age of Netanyahu, and starting even a couple of years before, an Israeli putting a right-wing bumper sticker on his car would just be bursting through an open door.

We are in a post-political era in this country. The central, overriding political fact of national life, the occupation, is no longer a subject for discussion. As far as the public and the major parties are concerned, it's settled (in more ways than one). The January 2013 campaign, the first of the decade, was also the first in which the question of the occupied territories, and of war and peace in general, was not disputed between the large parties. The Likud's prescription—more of the same—went unchallenged as the Labor Party, for the first time, dropped the whole matter and concentrated strictly on economic issues. Meanwhile, the star of that election, media personality Yair Lapid, head of the new Yesh Atid (There Is a Future) party, turned indifference to the occupation into an art. Campaigning against corruption, the high cost of living, and the economic, military, and religious burden of the ultra-Orthodox, Yesh Atid won enough votes to become the second-largest party in the country behind Likud.

This indifference carried on later in the year when John Kerry started up a new peace process. Everybody but Kerry knew it was going nowhere. After nine months, the Netanyahu government, which had shown its attitude to the negotiations by announcing one new settlement project after another, reneged on its commitment to release the last set of long-serving Palestinian prisoners,[1] and that was that—"poof," as Kerry would haplessly put it.

Neither would there be any questioning of the status quo during Israel's third mini-war of aggression in Gaza, this one in summer 2014 and named Operation Protective Edge. It was basically a rerun of Operation Cast Lead from the turn of 2009: There had been a lengthy cease-fire, then Israel badly overreacted to what it saw as Hamas aggression (in this case the kidnap-murders of three Israeli teenagers by a renegade Hamas-aligned clan in Hebron, evidently without the authorization or even knowledge of Hamas leadership[2]), then Hamas started the rockets flying again, and then Israel went to war. This time the devastation in Gaza was even worse than in Cast Lead, and the death toll in the Strip went from 1,400 to over 2,100, while the number of Israelis killed rose from 13 to 70, mainly due to the new tunnels Hamas used for attacking IDF soldiers. At the beginning, Israel racked up a kill ratio of about 200 to 1, so the gung ho spirit in the country was relatively subdued. But when Hamas guerrillas began coming out of the ground on the Israeli side of the border and killing soldiers, the mood changed. Channel 2's All-Israeli news anchorman Danny Kushmaro anointed Protective Edge as a *"milchama al ha-bayit,"* a war for our home. With the notable exception this time of Meretz, which was under new leadership, the Zionist left supported this onslaught, too. Yuval Diskin, who'd been the most woeful of all seven former Shin Bet chiefs lamenting the occupation in the documentary *The Gatekeepers*, wrote in *Yediot Aharonot*, "We need to expand the ground operation because it must not end with the status quo." During the 50-day war, Israeli Jewish support for it reached as high as 97 percent.[3]

---

1. Barak Ravid, Nir Hasson, and Jonathan Lis, "LIVE BLOG—Cabinet Approves Release of 104 Palestinian Prisoners," *Haaretz*, www.haaretz.com, July 28, 2013.

2. Isabel Kershner, "New Light on Hamas Role in Killings of Teenagers that Fueled Gaza War," *New York Times*, www.nytimes.com, September 4, 2014.

3. "July 2014 Peace Index," The Israel Democracy Institute, www.en.idi.org.il, July 29, 2014.

The 2015 election campaign matched the pattern of contemporary Israeli political life. The only change is in the hardening of the status quo: The country gets more paranoid, more racist, more aggressive. Netanyahu's Election Day appeal to right-wing voters that "the Arabs are heading to the polls in droves, the left-wing NGOs are bussing them in" has become notorious, but it was only the culmination of an already vicious campaign, the worst he'd ever run, which is saying a lot.

For decades he had been accusing his centrist rivals of being "leftists," but this time he charged Isaac Herzog, Tzipi Livni, and their Zionist Union list with being "anti-Zionists," which, in the Israeli political vocabulary, is worse than being leftists. A leftist may be merely naïve, a bleeding heart, someone who speaks up for the Arabs out of that old, unkillable Jewish guilt—but an anti-Zionist is a declared hater and enemy of the State of Israel, an anti-Semite. Netanyahu accused Israel's friendliest Arab, sportscaster and intercommunal peacemaker Zohair Bahloul, the only Arab high enough on Zionist Union's ticket to be electable, of "giving character testimony in praise of Hezbollah"—which, as Bahloul's testimony from the trial in question showed, was the exact opposite of the truth.[4] Netanyahu's single deadliest campaign video, set to a sound track of Arabic rap music, showed a truck full of ISIS men asking an Israeli, "How do we get to Jerusalem, bro?" The Israeli replies, "Take a left," and the ISIS team drives on with shouts of jubilation. Punctuated by the sound of gunshots, the words, "The left will surrender to terror," appear on the screen in red letters with bullet holes.

And it worked. I spoke to voters in different mainstream right-wing strongholds, and while they all talked like civilized, friendly people, which you wouldn't have guessed from the campaigns of the parties they supported, the sentiment I heard over and over, in one phrasing or another, was fear of the so-called left taking over. (And this when the "left-wing" opposition, for the second straight election, had airbrushed the occupation and the Palestinians out

---

4. "Netanyahu Hits New Low in His Campaign of Fear," The Third Way, www.mitchellplitnick.com, January 22, 2015.

of their campaign, lined up behind Bibi on security, and focused strictly on domestic, chiefly economic, issues.) The remark that stood out for me came from a 24-year-old biotechnology student at Bar-Ilan University named Reuven Gersovitch. "God forbid Zionist Union wins," he said, sitting at an outdoor campus café. "They live in a different world. They're nice people, they're good people, but their way of looking at things is just not suitable to where we live."

Israelis were growing more and more complacent. The economy was good enough for most and great for many, we'd won the war in Gaza, there were no rockets flying our way, no terror to speak of from the West Bank, and the riots in East Jerusalem, which had been sparked by the burning alive of a 16-year-old Palestinian boy by local Jews, had pretty much faded. Between the wars, now falling every couple of years or so, Bibi was keeping us pretty safe and prosperous. For a Jewish state in the Middle East looking out for number one, this was the best of all possible worlds.

In October 2015, the knifings began, and the car-rammings. First in East Jerusalem, then in the West Bank and Israeli cities. It seemed the Palestinians had not thrown in the towel after all. The suicidal attacks continued into 2016, more or less every day, without leadership, without mass mobilization, a privatized, low-boil intifada that neither boiled over nor simmered down. In Modi'in we stayed off Route 443 at night and out of East Jerusalem and the Old City at all times. I warned Gilad once about going on a walk to the forest at the edge of town because Beit Sira, a Palestinian village, was 200 yards away. Life got more dangerous, and people got used to it—same shit, different "wave of terror." Polls consistently showed that the politician whom the public trusted most to put down the violence was the neo-fascist ex–foreign minister, soon to be defense minister, Avigdor Lieberman.

If I were a bookie, I would lay very long odds against the situation ever changing, or at least any time before global warming settles the issue. And if I were not living in this place with my family and did not feel so attached to it, I would simply write off Israel's future as a decent, respectable country and urge the Palestinians to leave and consign this land to their dreams, like the Jews had done 2,000 years before—better that than go on with this. But I do live here with my family, and I am attached to this place, and what's more I'm not a fortune teller: Who am I to write Israel off? And though the odds are long, they're not impossible. And so, even while recognizing that this may well be wishful thinking, I have found a reason for hope, albeit a slim one. It's called the boycott, divestment, and sanctions movement, better known as BDS. With lots of reservations, I see it as an adjunct to another development that holds out at least a small hope: the Palestinian Authority's "UN strategy" or "internationalization of the conflict." Together, these two tactics are based on the "South African model"—of ending the occupation through international pressure on Israel, just as international pressure on South Africa ended, or certainly helped end, apartheid.

I'd never supported BDS before and considered it a fringe movement of anti-Zionists driven mainly by people who saw Israel as being rotten to the core, rotten from birth. My opinion—not of the tenor of the movement, but of BDS as a tactic—changed in 2013 when Stephen Hawking announced he would boycott Shimon Peres's star-studded "President's Conference" in Jerusalem. I realized after hearing the news that I was thrilled. Hawking's gesture shook up the establishment, something that hadn't happened since Obama had caved in to Netanyahu years before. Hawking was no fringe leftist and no Israel-basher; he'd visited the country four times. He didn't accuse Israel of genocide or even apartheid; the harshest thing he said in his announcement was that "the policy of the present Israeli government is likely to lead to disaster." Hawking's no-show in Jerusalem had brought the boycott into the mainstream. This was BDS with a human face, and I was all for it—and in principle I still am. Not that I like the idea of advocating the boycott of my country, but since it is now clear that Israel will not change of its own accord and that America is unwilling to force it to change, there's no way left but the South African model to end the occupation, and so BDS seems the lesser of two evils, the greater one being occupation forever. That the boycott movement doesn't seem to be out to fix Israel but rather, as maverick leftist Norman Finkelstein has said, to make it "disappear," is something I can live with. As I wrote in +972:

> I have no problem supporting BDS because I know that if Israel ever gets to the point where it's ready to concede to international pressure, it will be responding not to the small left-wing groups calling for it to give up Jewish statehood, but to the powerful forces in the democratic world calling for it to give up the occupation alone.[5]

The justice and necessity of BDS are self-evident among the international left, with whom I've come in pretty close contact, at least online, as a result of getting fired the way I did, blogging on Israel Reconsidered, moving to +972, and getting onto Facebook and other social media. I'm sort of an ultra-liberal-Zionist annex to the Israel/Palestine section of this ideological community, which has gotten me into some pretty spirited debates. I've learned a tremendous amount from the left. The exposure has moved me further in their direction, mainly in recognizing the justice of the Palestinians' insistence on the right of return for refugees who were run out of the country in 1948.

But my recognition of that justice has not led me to accept the left-wing view that Zionism is racism or that the Jewish state must be dismantled and replaced with a non-sectarian, Western-style democracy. Given the political geography and history of the Middle East, I don't see how Arabs and Jews will all serve together in the

---

5. Larry Derfner, "After Kerry, Only BDS May Save the Two-State Solution," www.972mag.com, May 19, 2014.

military and intelligence agencies of a country whose potential enemies are all Arab and Muslim states and militias—and if Jews and Arabs in Israel, the West Bank, and Gaza can't defend a state together, they can't maintain one together. As far as I'm concerned, the one-state idea for Israel-Palestine is the local equivalent of the idea of a one-world-government: It sounds sublime, and if it were workable it would obviously be preferable to nationalism, Jewish or otherwise, but that's not how people live. If the left's idea for Israel and Palestine were actually implemented, I believe it would lead to a civil war whose end would only come once most of the Jews or most of the Arabs were gone. So while I think the Palestinian refugees have the right of return, I also think the Jews of Israel have the right to live in a stable, secure country, and the only possible country of that kind, at least in the Holy Land, is one with a solid, lasting Jewish majority. So the Palestinian right of return and the Jewish right to security have to be balanced. As for feasibility, as unlikely as Israeli Jews are to ever give up the occupation, they'll come around to that a long time before they'll give up the Jewish state.

These are not popular ideas on what I call the international left—they are considered ethnocentric, colonialist, racist ideas. And this makes it difficult for me to debate with many of those who think along the lines of the international left, who include many (though by no means all) Israeli "one-staters." In these precincts, the title "liberal," and certainly "liberal Zionist," is viewed with condescension at best, more commonly with contempt.

And while in general left-wing dogmatism isn't much more than a harmless irritation—it has no power in the world outside Western academe, the arts, and leftist NGOs and media—for the the BDS movement it's fatal. The only way BDS can succeed is by spreading through the Western mainstream, like the anti-apartheid movement did—and international leftists not only cannot appeal to the mainstream, they really don't want to, whether they admit it or not. Finkelstein described BDS as a "cult," which I thought was an exaggeration, but he was definitely on to something. While BDS is not a cult, it does operate rather like a clique: It has the most rigid standards for determining who's in and who's out, and anybody who's out is anathematized. The BDS movement demands absolute fealty, and if you don't uphold that standard, you're the enemy; you're on the side of Netanyahu and the settlers.

I don't mean all branches of the movement. Jewish Voice for Peace isn't a closed-minded operation, nor are many if not most of the institutions, such as the Presbyterian Church USA, that have divested from companies profiting from the occupation. But the hardcore BDS movement, the one that seems to show only a hostile, intimidating face on college campuses, that screams at people working or shopping in a Max Brenner chocolate shop or a supermarket carrying SodaStream drink mixers, that cannot bear to hear a word about anything having to do with Israel that isn't caustic—that movement will always remain a marginal left-wing phenomenon. While it may spook Israel from time to time, its main practical effect will be to provide the right wing with a useful boogeyman and fundraising angle. It will never be able to do what BDS must do to succeed: gradually get the Western-aligned world—governments, major industries, people of influence—to start turning its back on Israel, while making it clear that everything for Israel will go back to normal, and even improve, once it ends the occupation.

Doing that requires a "big tent" strategy, and BDS is not interested. The clearest, and for me most agonizing example of this, the greatest missed opportunity imaginable, came in October 2015 with J.K. Rowling, author of the *Harry Potter* series. After signing a letter by British artists in opposition to the cultural boycott of Israel, Rowling answered her pro-Palestinian critics by tweeting that while it was indeed her position that the cultural and academic boycott wrongly "silenced" much of the Israeli left, it was also her position that:

> The Palestinian community has suffered untold injustice and brutality. I want to see the Israeli government held to account for that injustice and brutality. Boycotting Israel on every

possible front has its allure. It satisfies the human urge to do something, anything, in the face of human suffering.[6]

Wow. J.K. Rowling said that. The writer of our time, the cultural goddess of our age, one of the most admired and beloved human beings on earth, wrote publicly that Israel inflicts "untold injustice and brutality" on the Palestinians, that Israel must be "held to account" for it, and that a total boycott of Israel "has its allure." This, I felt instantly, was another Stephen Hawking moment. I continue to believe that if Hawking's no-show in Jerusalem had inspired other globally respected figures to at least speak out unequivocally against Israeli policies, it would have had a ripple effect that might have actually spelled the beginning of the end of the occupation. It didn't happen—but Rowling had provided another chance. A statement like that from her was worth more to the anti-occupation cause than an actual boycott by any number of academics and pop musicians. I assumed that other people on the left realized this, too, and I alerted my social media contacts, scores of whom promote the BDS movement, to Rowling's statement with the note "THIS MUST BE PUBLICIZED FAR AND WIDE."

The reaction? Silence. The international left's response to Rowling's publicized views on Israel-Palestine stopped after she came out against the cultural boycott; her follow-up, ringing condemnation of Israeli policies made no difference. She wouldn't take the oath, so the clique blackballed her. The loss wasn't Rowling's, or the international left's, or mine; we'll be all right. The loss was the Palestinians'.

---

6. "J.K. Rowling Criticizes Israel, but Says Harry Potter Would Understand Her Opposition to Boycott," www.haaretz.com, October 28, 2015.

CHAPTER THIRTEEN

RULES FOR LIBERALS

I've concentrated in this book on Israel's mania regarding the Palestinians and the occupation that grows out of it because that is the defining fact of Israeli life, as well as the worst one, the one that deserves the most attention. But it's not the only moral high crime that Israel has been committing in recent years; there are two others that could each be the subject of any number of books, and I want to at least mention them here.

One is the treatment of some 60,000 refugees from Eritrea and Sudan who've crossed the Sinai and climbed over the Egyptian border fence into Israel since 2004. The government and popular media refer to them as "infiltrators," deliberately calling up the image of terrorist invaders, when not one of them, in all this time, has been found to be involved in anti-Israeli activity. When the Sudanese refugees—black survivors of Sudanese Arab genocide either in Darfur or what would become South Sudan—first started trickling in, Israel put them in jail for a year or more as illegal aliens from an enemy country. The Supreme Court released them in 2007, kibbutzim and hotels in Eilat gave them work and lodging, and I went down to Eilat to interview some of them. Their stories were no less horrible than those of the most traumatized Holocaust survivors. The person who affected me the most was a tall, mahogany-colored 21-year-old I referred to in the story as "George." I'd heard, whether it's true or not, that African males do not show their emotions; George was the only guy I interviewed who cried. He came from the south of Sudan, where he'd lived in a village with his parents and eight brothers and sisters, and which had been ravaged by government-backed troops. Sitting in an office in the hotel, dressed in his janitor's uniform of a white polo shirt and khaki slacks, George described what happened in his village one morning before dawn, when he was 13.

> They came on horseback, large numbers of them. They killed all the adults and the young children. I saw them come into our house and rape my sister. My mother heard her crying and she came into the room, and they killed my mother and my sister in front of me. I don't know what happened to the rest of my family. They kidnapped the older children in the village to work for Arab farmers. They beat me and blindfolded me and made us walk. I don't know how many days; I had no sense of time.
>
> We were put on a train and when it stopped, a man told me to get into his car and he drove me to a big house with a farm. The owner's name was Muhammad Suleiman. Later I learned that he was a very powerful man in the government. The first thing he told me was: "You are a black boy and you are now my slave." I was there for two years.

At the end of the interview, George said he was going to stay in touch with me, and after he moved to the area around Tel Aviv's central bus station, the "capital" of Israel's refugee and foreign worker community, he called me. We became friends and worked together on several stories for the *Jerusalem Post,* he acting as translator, introducing me to people and giving me tons of information. A very ambitious young man, his goal was to get to the West and go to college. I tried to help him but got nowhere. We lost touch for about a year, and then one evening I got another call from him: He was leaving Israel on a plane the next day for Norway, which had granted him asylum. We spoke again when he was living and studying at a Norwegian school; since then he's gone to Juba, the capital of South Sudan, which slid into civil war soon after gaining independence. I've tried to contact him in Juba but without success.

George's determination, smarts, and likeability got him to a school in Norway, at least for a while, but he was the rarest of exceptions among African refugees in Israel. The others are either on the run from the immigration police—they are not allowed to work, and do so illegally—or stuck in the minimum-security prison built for them in the Negev desert. Nearly a third of the original arrivals have either been deported to South Sudan or have agreed, under the threat of indefinite imprisonment and harassment, to accept a bribe and a free one-way ticket to Uganda or Rwanda, which Israel has paid to take some of the refugees off its hands.

In its treatment of the Eritreans and Sudanese, Israel comes off very badly—but not anywhere remotely close to as badly as Sudan and Eritrea; or Egypt, where the Sudanese stayed for years before crossing the Sinai to Israel; or the Sinai Bedouin, who ran something like Nazi concentration camps for their unsuspecting Eritrean charges desperate to reach the Israeli border. In the countries they'd lived in or passed through en route to Israel, the refugees' saga was marked by violent racism, harsh imprisonment, extortion, torture, rape, and murder. They escaped those places to come to Israel, sometimes dying along the way. So Israel is not by any means the bad guy in this tale, in comparison to the other powers that be that these refugees have had to deal with. And within Israel, there are many genuine good guys in the story: The Tel Aviv municipality has given the refugee children free health care and public school education, while many NGOs and many more individual volunteers have given them food, medical treatment, and legal aid.

But if the comparison is made not to the governments of Third World countries, but of other democratic countries, then the Israeli government has been startlingly callous to these people. Other countries have an annual quota of refugees to whom it grants asylum; Israel's quota is effectively zero. In February 2015, the Interior Ministry's statistics showed that out of 5,573 Sudanese and Eritrean requests for asylum over the years, the number granted was four.[1]

These people have been thrown to the dogs, a community of pariahs living four to a room among Israel's often-racist Mizrahi and Russian Jewish poor, who call them *kushim*, niggers—if they're not getting hauled off to a desert "detention facility." The overwhelming majority are young men, and as their masses have grown, some have gotten into alcohol-fueled crime and violence, including a few incidents of rape and murder. Given their circumstances, this should not surprise anyone. Meanwhile, the sole objective of Israeli policy has been to make their lives so miserable that they'll agree to go anywhere.

Yet there is a limit to how many refugees Israel can take, and by mid-2012 the number crossing in from Egypt grew to 3,000 in a month. Proportionately, that's like 120,000 refugees entering the United States in a month, or nearly a million and a half in a year. I agreed that Israel had to build a security fence along the Egyptian border to stem the tide. That fence was indeed built, and in the three years since its completion, the number of refugees typically entering Israel through Egypt per month has dropped to below 10.

I'd assumed that once the fence was built and the flood of refugees halted, Israel might take a more lenient view of those already here. Sixty thousand African refugees could be absorbed into this country and be allowed to live freely as citizens, or at the very least given asylum. As William Tall, the UN refugee agency's then-representative in Israel, told me, "If you look at the cumulative total over time, refugees make up less than one percent of Israel's population. European countries have taken in much larger proportions than that." Yet Israel's policy toward the Africans kept getting harsher: more immigration raids, longer detention, greater pressure

---

1. Ilan Lior, "Israel Has Granted Refugee Status to Only Four Sudanese and Etritrean Asylum Seekers," *Haaretz*, www.haaretz.com, February 19, 2015.

to leave the country. At one point, when thousands of them protested in Tel Aviv, Netanyahu told the Knesset that the demonstrations "won't help them, we are determined to deport them and all of those who succeeded in infiltrating."[2]

The future of the African refugees in Israel, like the future of the occupation, like the future of our wars with the neighbors, used to be a contentious issue here, but no longer. Again, the right has won. Everyone can see that the Eritrean and Sudanese refugees will continue to be forced out of the country little by little and that the ones who remain will remain pariahs. It's a done deal—another done deal—so why pay attention to it anymore?

The other moral high crime being committed in recent years by Israel that needs mentioning is the habitual acts of military aggression against our neighbors. I'm not talking now about our ongoing aggression against Gaza, but the periodic attacks on Lebanon, Syria, and previously Iran.

Since the mid-2000s, Israel has bombed an embryonic Syrian nuclear reactor; assassinated five Iranian nuclear scientists on Iranian soil;[3] interdicted at least one arms ship headed for Hezbollah; and assassinated Hezbollah and Iranian Revolutionary Guard field commanders in Lebanon and Syria.

Every few months since the Syrian civil war began in 2011, Israel has bombed convoys carrying sophisticated arms from Syria to Hezbollah, causing death and injury.[4] It also bombed a shipment

2. "Netanyahu Says Illegal Infiltrators' Protests Won't Help Them," *The Jewish Press,* www.jewishpress.com, January 6, 2014.
3. Dan Raviv, "U.S. Pushing Israel to Stop Assassinating Iranian Nuclear Scientists," CBS News, www.cbsnews.com, March 1, 2014.
4. Anshel Pfeffer, "Is Russia's Hand Somewhere in the Samir Kuntar Assassination?" *Haaretz,* www.haaretz.com, December 22, 2015.

of Russian anti-aircraft systems in a Syrian port.[5] And even after withdrawing its troops from Lebanon in 2000, it has been flying spy planes over that country on an almost daily basis.[6]

Can anyone imagine an enemy state or militia doing any of these kinds of things to Israel? Say, bombing the Dimona nuclear reactor? Assassinating Israeli nuclear scientists? Commandeering an arms ship due at Haifa? Blowing up arms deliveries to Israel and killing Israelis in the process? Assassinating Israeli army commanders? Flying spy planes over Jerusalem every day or so? No, none of this can be imagined because none of Israel's enemies have the wherewithal to do any of it. Israel would blow them up in the attempt and pay them back with high interest, so even though Hezbollah, Syria, and Iran would certainly like to do all those things and more, they don't try.

Yet it's not just that they don't attack Israel, they hardly hit back, if at all, when Israel attacks them. Syria did nothing after the 2007 bombing of its acorn of a reactor—just as Iraq did nothing after Israel destroyed its nuclear reactor-in-the-making in 1981. In return for the serial assassinations of five of its nuclear scientists and a few of its Revolutionary Guards officers, Iran once planted a pair of car bombs outside a couple of Israeli foreign embassies and managed to injure the wife of a diplomat in New Delhi. Hezbollah once killed five Israeli tourists on a bus in Burgas, Bulgaria, another time killed two Israeli soldiers on the northern border, and has injured a few more with explosive devices, which are ordinarily discovered and dismantled.

Compared to the dozens of deadly cross-border attacks perpetrated by Israel in the last decade—to which can be added the bombing of Gazan-bound arms convoys in Sudan and the bloody takeover of Turkey's Mavi Marmara, none of which met with any military response—the blowback from Israel's targets has been minor. And

---

5. Harriet Sherwood, "US Claims Israel Attacked Russian Missile Shipment in Syria," *The Guardian*, www.theguardian.com, November 1, 2013.
6. Jean Aziz, "Israeli Fly-Over Coincides with Attack on Lebanese Army," *Al Monitor*, December 8, 2014.

during the wars in which Israel was killing Gazans by the thousands, when the entire Muslim world was screaming bloody murder, not one of the region's proud Arab armies fired so much as a bullet at this country.

All this seems to indicate that Israel's enemies are afraid of it, because they know they are no match for its power. The question, then, is why Israel keeps up with these so-called "preemptive" attacks—why it keeps the tit-for-tat going when its enemies would seemingly be eager for an indefinite cease-fire, formal or not, so they could fight Israel strictly on the rhetorical battlefield, where they do so much better than they do on the military one. Considering all the missiles Israel's enemies do *not* fire at it—even after some of their top people and best weaponry get taken out by Israeli missiles and bombs—why doesn't Israel just cool it, just sit on its military superiority, and let it deter Hezbollah, Syria, Iran, and the rest? Why keep provoking the other side, why keep endangering Israelis and occasionally getting them killed—and why run the risk that one of these days it will rub its enemies' nose in their weakness once too often, the tit-for-tat will get out of hand and the Third Lebanon War will begin?

The answer, I think, can be found in one of the most cherished nuggets of Zionist wisdom ever uttered: "Peace will come," said Golda Meir, "when the Arabs will love their children more than they hate us."[7] This is what we believe: that the Arabs hate us so much, more than they love their own lives, more than they love their own children, that they don't care if we destroy them so long as they can destroy us, and that once they get the chance, once they get the right weapons, they will go for the kill—even if it means their own annihilation. And so we have to keep denying them those weapons, no matter the risk, no matter how much bad blood it creates.

This conviction about the goal driving the Arabs is, first of all, an expression of Jewish egomania, which is the other side of Jewish paranoia. It asks: What could the Arabs possibly have on their minds

---

7. "Golda Meir," *Wikiquote*, last modified July 25, 2016, https://en.wikiquote .org/wiki/Golda_Meir.

that's more important to them than hating the Jews? What could they possibly have in their lives that they wouldn't sacrifice for the privilege of dying en masse while killing us?

But beyond expressing Jewish egomania, this Israeli/Jewish view of the Arab/Muslim mentality is a dehumanizing one. When you say that Arabs hate Jews more than they love their children, you're saying they lack the most basic human instinct; you're saying they're just crazed killing machines. And if that's who you think you're up against, then you cannot trust in deterrence, because these people, in your view, are undeterrable. The only thing to do is destroy their ability to destroy you, and do it over and over again, until they learn—which you believe they never will, anyway, because they're "not like us": They don't care about their children. They're not just indifferent to death, they *want* to die. Ours is a "culture of life"; theirs a "culture of death."

It is this dehumanizing Israeli belief about Arabs that explains why even though this country has built a military arsenal to the sky and bombs its much weaker enemies with near impunity, it won't stop bombing them. Fear and aggression, one feeding the other—that's the Israeli mentality. And it doesn't stop with the Palestinians. Ending the occupation is the first historic change of policy that Israel needs to make, but not the last. What's needed is a transformation in the way Israeli Jews see themselves in relation to others. What's needed is for the State of Israel to stop being the neighborhood bully and start respecting its neighbors.

So—don't I have anything good to say about this place? In terms of political morality, meaning how Israel treats other nations, including those within its borders, then no, I can't think of anything particularly good to say about it, not anymore, and Israeli political morality is mainly what this book has been about. But as for Israelis as people, I can say a lot of good things, and I did in the introduction and chapter two, such as: They have good hearts, they're close with one another, they're ready to help people in trouble, they're smart, and, in the last generation, they've lost much of their hard edge and become pretty nice people. I also wrote about some of the great things Israel has given me, the things I was looking for when I immigrated—the subject that would enable me to find myself as a writer, and the opportunity to become part of a close-knit society where I feel attached, instead of being another face in the American crowd.

I'll say a few more good things about Israel: There's freedom of speech; it's a First World country economically and technologically; there's affordable, good-to-great health care for all citizens; there's a distinctive Israeli culture, especially literary, musical, culinary, and comedic; Ashkenazi discrimination against Mizrahim is no longer a severe problem; for all the street-level racism against Ethiopian Jews, the state has done more for them than any state may have ever done for an immigrant population; and there are hundreds of thousands of people here doing great humanitarian work. This is a partial list.

And I'll mention one more very important thing that Israel has given me, and for which I'm most grateful: a way to remain Jewish and pass it on to my children. This struck me most powerfully at Alon's and Gilad's bar mitzvahs—two of the greatest days I'll ever have, and I doubt I would have had them in the States. If I'd stayed there, I would have kept my Jewish friends, still listened to Lenny Bruce and read Philip Roth, still gone to eat at the delis, but that would have been it. Having no feeling at all for religion and hardly any for Israel, my Jewishness would have continued being a sentimental thing that lived off a glorious past but had no future. It's very unlikely I would have married a Jew; in America there are a few circles with high concentrations of marriageable Jews—the wealthy, the academic, the elite professions, and, of course, the Orthodox— and I moved in none of them. Plus, I didn't care about marrying a Jew. I still don't, but moving to Israel made it extremely likely that that's who I would marry. (My wedding was also a glorious day, but, unlike my kids' bar mitzvahs, it did not fill me with gratitude to Israel: Philippa and I got married in South Africa after I repeatedly failed to meet the medieval Israeli rabbinical establishment's standard of proof of being Jewish.) And thanks to Philippa—*eshet hayil*, a woman of valor—we do the whole Jewish thing here, we celebrate the religious holidays with friends and relatives, we live as Jews in a Jewish society—too Jewish, in fact. In Israel, I am all the Jew I ever wanted to be, and then some.

Another good thing about Israel: It's extremely important to so many Jews abroad. In South Africa once, I met an elderly lawyer, a liberal and no supporter of the occupation, who told me about the obstacles he'd faced starting out as a young Jewish lawyer in the Afrikaner heartland after World War II. He said, "I've been a Jew in the Diaspora when there wasn't an Israel, and I've been one when there was an Israel, and let me tell you, there's a difference." That remark has stayed with me. So has a conversation I had some years ago with a couple of Jews in Sweden, also liberals. One told me that neither she nor any Swedish Jew she knew wore a Star of David in public for fear of reaction from hostile Muslims or neo-fascists. "I'll wear a *chai* because they don't know what it is," she said. We started talking about Israel, and I said that when the Zionist movement began at the turn of the 20th century, the Jews needed a state of their own because of anti-Semitism, but that if there were no Israel today, nobody would need to invent it because anti-Semitism, while still around, is no longer so oppressive that Jews need to get away to their own country. With us was another Jewish liberal friend who disagreed with me. He said that without Israel, Jewish nationalism would still arise, naturally, out of a Jewish need for self-defense, a need that Israel has filled. "Israel gives Jews an image of strength," he said. "Now the anti-Semites know they can't mess around with Jews so easy—that Jews can hit back." My other Swedish Jewish friend agreed. Growing up around Jews in New York and L.A., I never for one moment felt insecure about being Jewish, so hearing these remarks in South Africa and Sweden gave me a new appreciation for Israel's importance to masses of Jews overseas.

A couple of days before writing this section, a time when I was thinking of things I liked about Israel, I was standing on the shoulder of the freeway near Tel Aviv, waiting for a tow truck to come get my broken-down car. A motorcycle rider pulled onto the shoulder and came to a stop in front of me. He wasn't a policeman, and I guess my old L.A. instincts kicked in: *Who is this guy? What does he want?* As he was removing his helmet, I squared off and asked him, "Did you stop to help me?" He said, "Yeah, you need some help?" I started to laugh, explained to him that where I come from a stranger approaching you on the shoulder of a freeway is assumed to be a thief or mugger, thanked him profusely, and went back to waiting for the tow truck. This was a completely typical Israeli scene—a stranger going out of his way to help another stranger in a bind. It's a beautiful Israeli trait.

Soon I would learn that on that same day, in Athens, Israeli Jewish passengers who'd boarded an Aegean Air flight to Tel Aviv decided that two Israeli Arab passengers flying with them were potential terrorists, and refused to let the plane take off with them aboard.[8] "It started with three or four people and by the end there were 60 to 70 people standing up, demanding that the pair disembark," a spokesman for Aegean Airlines was reported saying. None of the news stories mentioned any of the other passengers saying a word in defense of the two Arabs. The crew finally got them to "agree to disembark" (to the shame of Aegean Air). The Israeli Jews on board, however, still weren't satisfied, and demanded further security checks—after all, two known Arabs had been sitting next to them—at which point the pilot told the Israeli Jews to sit down or they'd be thrown off the plane, so they took their seats and returned home, no doubt clapping and happily singing *"Heveinu shalom aleichem"* when they landed at Ben-Gurion.

I said to myself, *Yeah, Israel's a great country to live in—if you're a Jew.* If you're an Arab living here as a citizen, you are insulted regularly by the country's right-wing leaders (and followers), you are discriminated against in any number of ways, and going to the airport means risking humiliation—not only from Israeli Jewish security inspectors, it turns out, but from Israeli Jewish passengers, too. The truth is that

---

8. Nick Squires and Agencies, "Anger After Arabs Forced off Plane by Jewish Israeli Passengers," *The Telegraph,* January 6, 2016.

no Jew in his right mind would willingly live in a country that treated its Jewish citizens like Israel treats its Arab ones. And compared to African refugees in this country and, certainly, to Palestinians in the West Bank and Gaza, Israel's Arab citizens have it good.

So how do I live with this—being a liberal, a believer in equality, in a country that is not only far less liberal and equitable than the one I left, but that is decisively illiberal and inequitable, that's running the world's last colonial military dictatorship, and, worst of all, that offers slim hope of ever changing? I live with this by keeping hope alive; by reminding myself that the West ended slavery and colonialism, South Africa ended apartheid, and Europe ended its addiction to war and conquest; and that a slim chance is still a chance. But at the same time I know that this is not exactly a disinterested view—I *have* to believe this or I, as a true-believing liberal, would find it extremely hard to go on living here in any sort of good spirits. And I want to go on living here because of all the good things Israel has got and all that it gives me and my family. So finally, I stay here for personal reasons—but one of the most important of them is my personal need to write in opposition to Israeli illiberalism, inequity, colonialism, and military dictatorship. In all, I don't feel guilty about choosing to make my life in this country, even though I know that as a Jew I'm in a position similar to that of whites in apartheid South Africa or the Jim Crow South. For many reasons—because I do raise my voice against the injustice, because I'm too old to leave and start over again elsewhere, because my wife and kids also have good lives here, and, maybe, because I just lack the necessary conscience, or I like my comforts too much, or I accept my limitations—I sleep well at night.

However, I have been not so subtly indoctrinating my sons to leave the country sometime after they finish the army. They have American passports, and I mean to see if I can get them European ones, too. And this is strictly because of the political situation here: It's one thing to say there's still a slim chance that Israel will end the occupation, the wars of aggression and the steady slide rightward—in which case I would be happy for my descendants to live here in perpetuity—but it's another thing to see your sons investing their futures on that chance. When they were younger, Alon and Gilad both would say they wanted to move to Europe when they got older, which was no wonder; we'd had a few great vacations there, and I was telling them Europe was the place to go. But the older they get, the longer they live in Israel, the deeper their roots grow, the more connected they get, and the more natural it becomes for them to eventually make their lives here, to raise families here.

Can I say I feel guilty for raising my children in Israel instead of back in the States? At this point, at least—and certainly now with Trump, *yemach shmo*, in the White House—no. Touch wood, Alon's army experience has done him only good, and it has nothing to do with any occupation; we'll see where Gilad's service takes him. They both have great lives. How can I feel guilty about raising them here?

But I've had my misgivings. Before I had kids, maybe even before I got married, I had a vivid, disturbing dream about my future as an Israeli parent. My kid, who was about five in the dream, was on an overnight hike with his class in the desert, the sort of thing Israeli school kids do year after year and which I've always seen, warily, as informal training for the army. They were lined up with backpacks on, shouting with excitement to go charging into the hills in the distance, shouting to give themselves courage for the "mission" that would take them into the wilderness and away from their parents. I was standing with the other parents behind the kids, and the teachers leading the hike were urging us to get into the spirit, to cheer our boys and girls on. I felt under extreme, close-in peer pressure to do this, to exhort my kid—I'm not sure if it was a son or daughter—to be a gung ho little soldier and go bombing across the desert with his classmates. I didn't want to do this—but I felt compelled to because I didn't want to go against everyone else, especially not with my kid there. I was standing amid the parents, feeling I had no choice but to go along, feeling I was about to succumb, to start shouting at my kid to charge because I was afraid to stand up to everybody. Then I woke up.

I have always felt it my responsibility as a parent to counteract the influences this society naturally brings to bear on my kids. Philippa and I both explicitly, repeatedly taught Alon and Gilad not to be racists, not to hate Arabs, not to be war-lovers, and it seems to have taken. But this is something that has to be taught; otherwise the anti-Arab, pro-war atmosphere here is liable to have its way with them, as it has with most young Israelis of this last generation. My kids grew up in a segregated city—a segregated society; they had no contact with Arabs. The only way they could have would have been for us to find them a Jewish-Arab youth "co-existence" group, which I always associated, probably unfairly, with some circa-1964 US campaign to "take a Negro to lunch." But maybe we should have found such a group because the atmosphere here is dangerous. My journalist friend in Modi'in, Leora Eren Frucht, wrote about an incident from the late 2000s:

> When my son was in fifth grade, his class went on a school trip to Jaffa, a mixed city of Jews and Arabs. There, his Jewish classmates had run down the street yelling hysterically when they saw an Arab woman, with her head covered, walking in their direction. "Terrorist!" some had shouted.[9]

You grow up seeing soldiers in olive-green uniforms with rifles all over; you're taught to report any unattended bag to someone in authority because it might contain a bomb. The issues of army and war and terrorism are in the news every hour—and who is the source of this ongoing alert? Arabs. When Gilad was born in 1999, the hospital sent us home with a bag of diapers and baby's first gas mask: wherever, whenever, we are ready. For the 10th anniversary of our neighborhood elementary school, all the kids and parents went on a Saturday afternoon walk through the forest that took us through the edge of the West Bank, and I've never seen so many guns sticking out of the waists of so many men wearing jeans. There was even a mom carrying a rifle. The Education Ministry's guidelines called for some

---

9. Leora Eren Frucht, "Israeli Life: Mothers," *Hadassah Magazine*, www.kintera.org.

small proportion of adults to be armed, but this was like a suburban militia. We had cops and cop cars with us; I seem to recall a helicopter maneuvering in the sky over our heads. A couple of hundred elementary school kids and parents on a weekend walk in the forest, and it looked like we were on our way to invade Jordan.

But I don't want to give the idea that all the parents and kids are nationalists, or even that the exceptions are rare. In fact, the school system is loaded with leftists, and a lot of the older kids, especially the smarter ones, are leftists too. Before giving a talk last year to Gilad's 11th-grade homeroom about journalism, I happened to mention to the teacher that my father had been a communist. "Mine too," smiled the teacher. My talk was about how the mainstream Israeli media brainwash the public for war because that's what the public unconsciously demands—and the students seemed very receptive. With the exception of one girl who said the Israeli media portrayed the situation the only way they could, and a boy who said my argument was pissing him off, the students' questions and comments sounded pretty sympathetic. One girl likened the mentality here to that of *Animal Farm*. And even the boy who said I was pissing him off told Gilad afterward, "I don't agree with your dad, but he's some dude." I have a lot of affection for Israeli kids. There's an open, unguarded quality about them that gets to me. They are not to blame for the shit they get fed.

On November 17, 2013, the day I'd long been dreading, Philippa, Gilad, Alon's girlfriend, Neta, and I drove Alon to Jerusalem to be inducted into the army. It was an emotional morning. I was so proud of him—but not because he was going to be a soldier, or a soldier in the Israeli army. I was proud of who he was, of the way he was. And I was worried, of course. Some of Alon's friends came to see him off; they would be going into the army very soon. I felt such warmth and concern for all the 18-year-olds at the induction center, and such a sense of shared fate with the parents. Serving in the army is at the core of being Israeli, and setting aside the immorality of so much of what the Israeli army does, there's a lot to be said for the experience. It teaches young people to look out for each other—to sacrifice for each other. It challenges them and gives them discipline and responsibility. If you could only take away the politics that the IDF serves, the excessive length of duty and of course the danger, sending Alon—and, soon, Gilad—to the army would almost be a cause for celebration.

This book has not been mainly about my life or my family's life, but about how I came to believe what I believe about Israel, so I want to close it not on a personal note but a political one. I don't expect to change right-wingers' minds, and as far as the overriding importance of ending the occupation goes, I don't need to change the minds of left-wingers. Instead, I want to address this last bit of polemic to liberals, Jewish and gentile both—those who know the occupation is immoral; who have not, or maybe cannot, give up on the goal of ending it; but who are confused about what to do or even say to further that goal. So here are some suggestions aimed at clearing away that liberal confusion.

1. This is not a popularity contest. It doesn't matter that Israel, for instance, treats gay people better than Palestinian society does. That doesn't give it the right to rob the Palestinians of their freedom and land. Nothing the Palestinians do or ever did justifies that. Black South Africans used terror against whites and against each other, often in gruesome ways; that did not justify apartheid. The Israeli-Palestinian conflict since 1967 is not about a more tolerant society versus a less tolerant one; it's about the right to be the master versus the right to be free.

2. Israel's problem is not what it may become, but what it already is. Liberals warn Israel that if it does not end the occupation, it will one day no longer be a Jewish democratic state. But what is supposed to happen in another 5, 10, or however many years that hasn't already happened after 50? Is it that the Arabs will one day outnumber the Jews? They're almost there already. Will Israel become an apartheid state only when the population reaches 50-percent-plus-one Arab, and remain a democracy when it's 50-percent-plus-one Jewish? No, I'm afraid Israel lost its democracy on the day after the Six-Day War, when it decided not to vacate the conquered territories and instead left its guns pointed at the conquered people. Liberals who for years on end warn Israel about the future are just afraid to admit that the future has long since arrived.

3. *The purpose of the occupation isn't security; it's conquest.* If Israel had only been interested in the West Bank and Gaza for security reasons, it wouldn't have built civilian settlements—colonies—for 600,000 people and counting. Instead it would have built only military installations. Residential neighborhoods, schools, shopping centers, and parking lots don't give you security. And you don't build colonies for 600,000 of your citizens as a "bargaining chip" to trade for peace. You build them because you mean to keep them. Israel doesn't occupy the West Bank for the sake of security, or at any rate not for security alone; it occupies the West Bank also for land, for water, for size, for power, for God, for glory, for all the reasons strong countries have overrun weaker ones throughout history. For conquest, and the many wonderful things that come with it.

4. *Stop blaming both sides equally.* I can't count the number of times I've read liberal newspaper columnists, politicians, and diplomats moan all the way down the page about Netanyahu, and then at the end declare that he and Abbas *both* have to change their ways. They're afraid to say that it's Israel, or certainly Israel in the main, that has to change—and if these liberals are Jewish, they may even be afraid to say it to themselves. By holding both sides equally responsible, they let Israel off the hook, they let Israel shrug and say, *Let the Palestinians change first.* I believe that if all the influential liberal politicians, diplomats, and writers were to suddenly tell the truth about who they think is mainly, if not fully, to blame for the conflict, the pressure on Israel would skyrocket. And anybody who honestly thinks both sides are equally to blame, or who thinks it's mainly the Palestinians at fault, is not someone whom I, at least, would call a liberal, not on this issue. Again, in a fight between the conqueror and the conquered, justice is on the side of the conquered.

5. *It is not Israel's democratic right to decide whether the Palestinians should or should not be free.* The Palestinians are not an Israeli domestic issue. They are a foreign people on a foreign land, and since Israel

refuses to get off their backs, it is the world's right, if not responsibility, to try to force Israel off. Appealing to the world to do so is not an "end-run around Israeli democracy"; it's an end-run around Israeli military dictatorship.

   6. *US diplomacy is not the solution; it's a central part of the problem.* Until America is ready to punish Israel for its intransigence, it's doing more harm than good with these "peace processes." Negotiations that go nowhere take international pressure off Israel, which is why Netanyahu almost always wants to negotiate.

   7. *If you're not ready to be a bleeding heart, you might as well be a Likudnik.* I've heard so many liberals argue for an end to the occupation "not for the Palestinians' sake, but for Israel's." They're eager to show that they're not guilt-ridden, naive lefties; they're tough, practical, self-interested realists. To those "liberals" who care only about Israel's practical self-interest, I suggest that they support Netanyahu. I would, if that's all I was looking out for. He's managing the conflict, so far at a very, very low price to Israeli Jews; why mess with success? Ending the occupation will be sheer hell for this country. It will mean relocating 100,000 to 200,000 enraged, very possibly violent settlers from the "Biblical heartland"; giving up Hebron; redividing Jerusalem; and losing military control of the West Bank and Gaza. It'll be some party. If you're concerned strictly for Israel's practical self-interest, you don't want that. You want Netanyahu.

   No, for an Israeli Jew or friend of the Jewish state, the only good reason to seek an end to the occupation is the moral one: because you know that what Israel does to the Palestinians is wrong, indefensible, and cruel and that Israel has lost its morality in the process. It's only if you think of a country's morality—the way it treats others, especially those who are weaker—as one of its vital assets, one it cannot do without, that you can reasonably make a "pro-Israel" case for dismantling the occupation. If Israel is to regain its morality, which it began losing 50 years ago, the Palestinians must gain their freedom. And if that's not a liberal cause, what is?

ACKNOWLEDGMENTS

I'd like to express my appreciation to the outstanding people at Just World Books—former associate publisher Kimberly MacVaugh, production project manager Marissa Wold Uhrina, marketing/outreach director Steve Fake, copy editor Jodi Brandon, former director of production Diana Ghazzawi, and cover designer Alan Dino Hebel. This has been a pleasure for me from start to finish; I think you did a brilliant job. I also want to say a special thank you to William Quandt, whose extraordinary knowledge and experience in regard to the Middle East, along with his sharp judgment, made his editing of the book invaluable. And I want to express my deepest gratitude to Helena Cobban, publisher and friend, for making this book possible—for making me a published author. Being naturally paranoid and never having written a book before, I had all sorts of trepidations going into this—and you made them all go away. If I ever have another book to write, you're the person I would want to publish it.

I'd also like to thank my very close friends Ed Goldstein and Leora Eren Frucht, whose lively intellects and understanding led me to ask them to read parts of the manuscript and tell me what they thought; their encouragement and criticism were both crucially important to me.

Finally, I want to thank my dear brother Armand Derfner and my dear sister Suzanne Zaharoni, authors both, for evangelizing me over the decades to do this—and for a lot more.

ABOUT THE AUTHOR

 Larry Derfner began his journalistic career in 1981 at City News Service of Los Angeles, and continued it in Israel as a columnist and feature writer with the *Jerusalem Post*, as a correspondent in Israel for *U.S. News and World Report*, and as a contributor to the *Sunday Times* of London, *Salon*, *The Nation*, *Tablet*, *Forward*, *+972 Magazine*, and other publications. He currently contributes op-eds to *Haaretz*, where he works as a copy editor. He lives in Modi'in, Israel with his wife Philippa and sons Alon and Gilad.